KEANU **REEVES** MATT **KINDT** RON **GARNEY** BILL **CRABTREE**

BRZRKR ™

VOLUME TWO

Published by

BOOM!
STUDIOS

Collection Designer
MARIE KRUPINA

Series Designer
MICHELLE ANKLEY

Assistant Editor
RAMIRO PORTNOY

Editors
ERIC HARBURN + MATT GAGNON

Special Thanks
ADAM YOELIN + STEPHEN CHRISTY + ROSS RICHIE

ROSS RICHIE Chairman & Founder
JEN HARNED CFO
MATT GAGNON Editor-in-Chief
FILIP SABLIK President, Publishing & Marketing
STEPHEN CHRISTY President, Development
LANCE KREITER Vice President, Licensing & Merchandising
BRYCE CARLSON Vice President, Editorial & Creative Strategy
HUNTER GORINSON Vice President, Business Development
JOSH HAYES Vice President, Sales
SIERRA HAHN Executive Editor
ERIC HARBURN Executive Editor
RYAN MATSUNAGA Director, Marketing
STEPHANIE LAZARSKI Director, Operations
ELYSE STRANDBERG Manager, Finance
MICHELLE ANKLEY Manager, Production Design
CHERYL PARKER Manager, Human Resources

DAFNA PLEBAN Senior Editor
ELIZABETH BREI Editor
KATHLEEN WISNESKI Editor
SOPHIE PHILIPS-ROBERTS Editor
ALLYSON GRONOWITZ Associate Editor
GAVIN GRONENTHAL Assistant Editor
GWEN WALLER Assistant Editor
RAMIRO PORTNOY Assistant Editor
KENZIE RZONCA Assistant Editor
REY NETSCHKE Editorial Assistant
MARIE KRUPINA Design Lead
CRYSTAL WHITE Design Lead
GRACE PARK Design Coordinator
MADISON GOYETTE Production Designer
VERONICA GUTIERREZ Production Designer
JESSY GOULD Production Designer

NANCY MOJICA Production Designer
SAMANTHA KNAPP Production Design Assistant
ESTHER KIM Marketing Lead
BREANNA SARPY Marketing Lead, Digital
AMANDA LAWSON Marketing Coordinator
ALEX LORENZEN Marketing Coordinator, Copywriter
GRECIA MARTINEZ Marketing Assistant, Digital
JOSÉ MEZA Consumer Sales Lead
ASHLEY TROUB Consumer Sales Coordinator
HARLEY SALBACKA Sales Coordinator
MEGAN CHRISTOPHER Operations Lead
RODRIGO HERNANDEZ Operations Coordinator
JASON LEE Senior Accountant
FAIZAH BASHIR Business Analyst
AMBER PETERS Staff Accountant
SABRINA LESIN Accounting Assistant

BOOM! STUDIOS

BRZRKR Volume Two, September 2022. Published by BOOM! Studios, a division of Boom Entertainment, Inc. BRZRKR is ™ & © 2022 74850, Inc. Originally published in single magazine form as BRZRKR No. 5-8. ™ & © 2021, 2022 74850, Inc. All rights reserved. BOOM! Studios™ and the BOOM! Studios logo are trademarks of Boom Entertainment, Inc., registered in various countries and categories. All characters, events, and institutions depicted herein are fictional. Any similarity between any of the names, characters, persons, events, and/or institutions in this publication to actual names, characters, and persons, whether living or dead, events, and/or institutions is unintended and purely coincidental. BOOM! Studios does not read or accept unsolicited submissions of ideas, stories, or artwork.

BOOM! Studios, 5670 Wilshire Boulevard, Suite 400, Los Angeles, CA 90036-5679. Printed in Canada. First Printing.

ISBN: 978-1-68415-815-7, eISBN: 978-1-64668-448-9 [Softcover]
ISBN: 978-1-68415-717-4 [Hardcover]
ISBN: 978-1-68415-714-3 [Kickstarter Exclusive Softcover]
ISBN: 978-1-68415-720-4 [Kickstarter Exclusive Hardcover]
ISBN: 978-1-68415-723-5 [Blood Red Limited Edition Hardcover]
ISBN: 978-1-68415-726-6 [Bronze Age Limited Edition Hardcover]
ISBN: 978-1-68415-729-7 [Gunmetal Limited Edition Hardcover]
ISBN: 978-1-68415-732-7 [Platinum Immortal Limited Edition Hardcover]

Cover by
RAFAEL GRAMPÁ
Character Designs by
RAFAEL GRAMPÁ + RON GARNEY

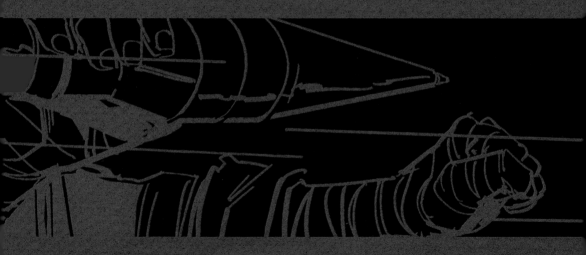

Kickstarter Exclusive Cover by
TYLER KIRKHAM
with colors by **ARIF PRIANTO**

Blood Red Kickstarter Exclusive Variant Cover by
LEE GARBETT

Bronze Age Kickstarter Exclusive Variant Cover by
JONBOY MEYERS

Gunmetal Kickstarter Exclusive Variant Cover by
RON GARNEY
with colors by **BILL CRABTREE**

Platinum Immortal Kickstarter Exclusive Variant Cover by
INHYUK LEE

Created by **KEANU REEVES**

BRZ

RKR

Written by
KEANU REEVES + MATT KINDT

Illustrated by
RON GARNEY

Colored by
BILL CRABTREE

Lettered by
CLEM ROBINS

CHAPTER
FIVE

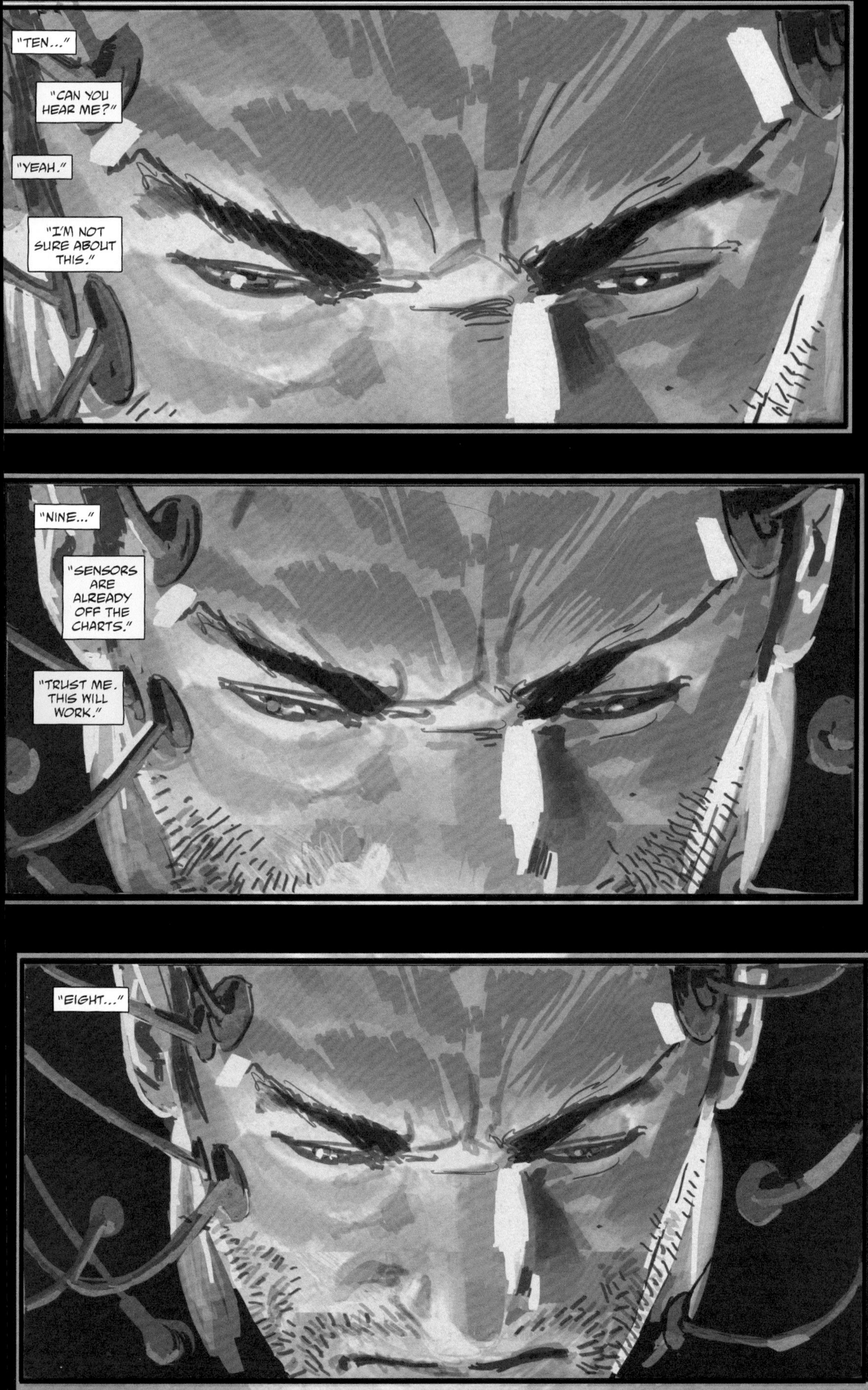
"TEN..."
"CAN YOU HEAR ME?"
"YEAH."
"I'M NOT SURE ABOUT THIS."
"NINE..."
"SENSORS ARE ALREADY OFF THE CHARTS."
"TRUST ME. THIS WILL WORK."
"EIGHT..."

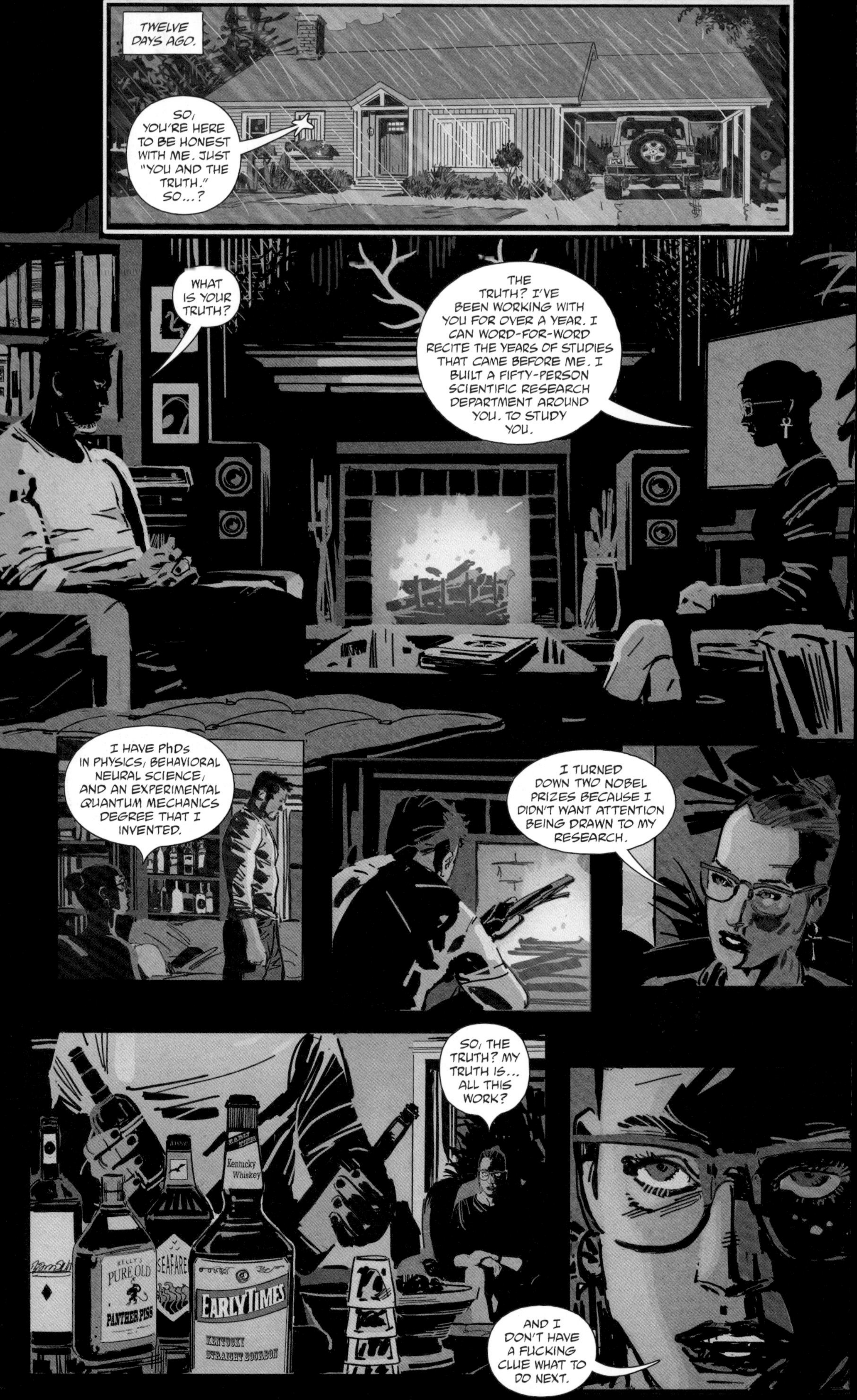
TWELVE DAYS AGO.
SO, YOU'RE HERE TO BE HONEST WITH ME. JUST "YOU AND THE TRUTH." SO...?
WHAT IS YOUR TRUTH?
THE TRUTH? I'VE BEEN WORKING WITH YOU FOR OVER A YEAR. I CAN WORD-FOR-WORD RECITE THE YEARS OF STUDIES THAT CAME BEFORE ME. I BUILT A FIFTY-PERSON SCIENTIFIC RESEARCH DEPARTMENT AROUND YOU. TO STUDY YOU.
I HAVE PhDs IN PHYSICS, BEHAVIORAL NEURAL SCIENCE, AND AN EXPERIMENTAL QUANTUM MECHANICS DEGREE THAT I INVENTED.
I TURNED DOWN TWO NOBEL PRIZES BECAUSE I DIDN'T WANT ATTENTION BEING DRAWN TO MY RESEARCH.
SO, THE TRUTH? MY TRUTH IS... ALL THIS WORK?
KELLY'S PURE OLD PANTHER PISS
SEAFARE
Kentucky Whiskey
EARLY TIMES
KENTUCKY STRAIGHT BOURBON
AND I DON'T HAVE A FUCKING CLUE WHAT TO DO NEXT.

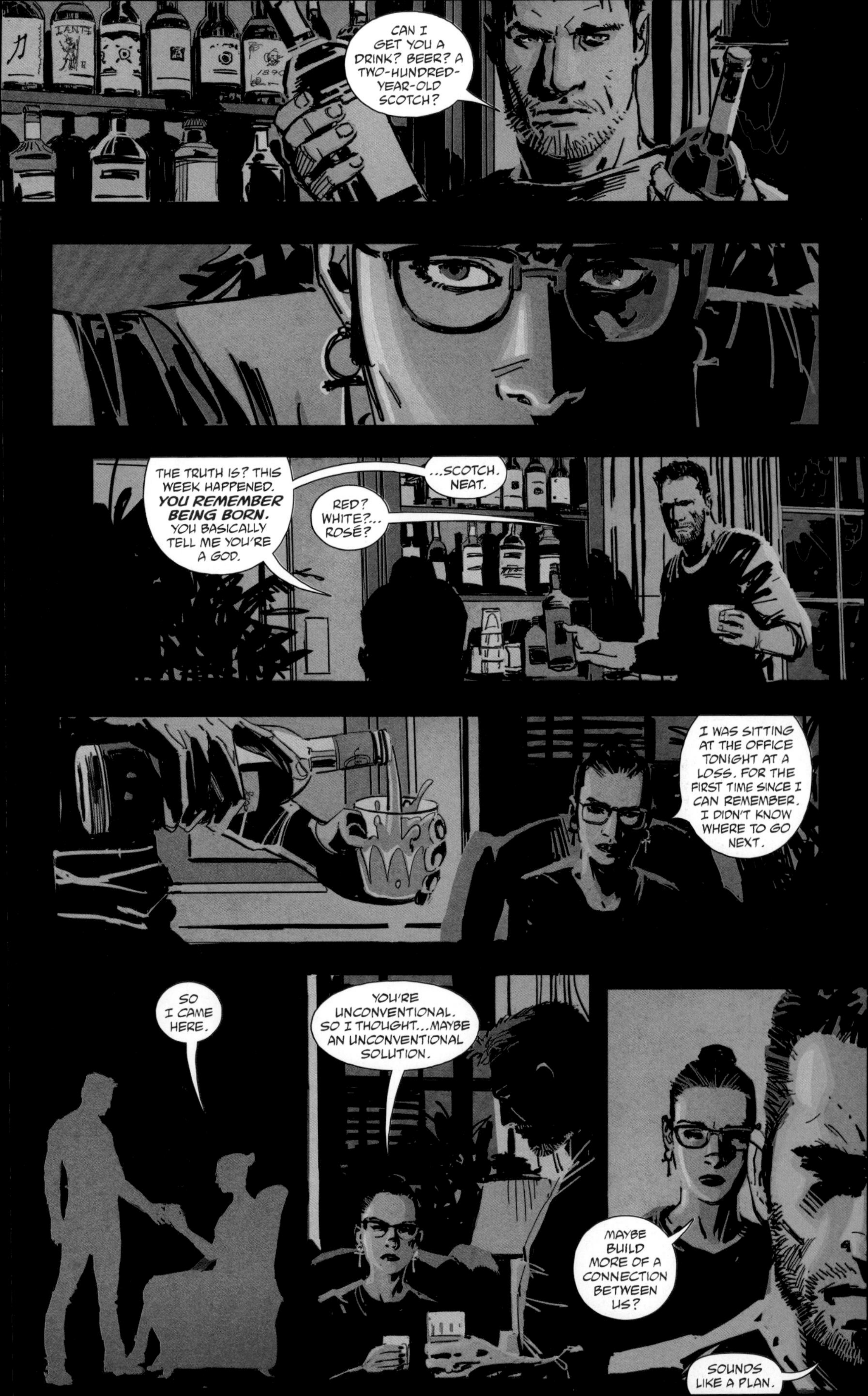
CAN I GET YOU A DRINK? BEER? A TWO-HUNDRED-YEAR-OLD SCOTCH?
THE TRUTH IS? THIS WEEK HAPPENED. YOU REMEMBER BEING BORN. YOU BASICALLY TELL ME YOU'RE A GOD.
...SCOTCH. NEAT.
RED? WHITE?... ROSÉ?
I WAS SITTING AT THE OFFICE TONIGHT AT A LOSS. FOR THE FIRST TIME SINCE I CAN REMEMBER. I DIDN'T KNOW WHERE TO GO NEXT.
SO I CAME HERE.
YOU'RE UNCONVENTIONAL. SO I THOUGHT... MAYBE AN UNCONVENTIONAL SOLUTION.
MAYBE BUILD MORE OF A CONNECTION BETWEEN US?
SOUNDS LIKE A PLAN.

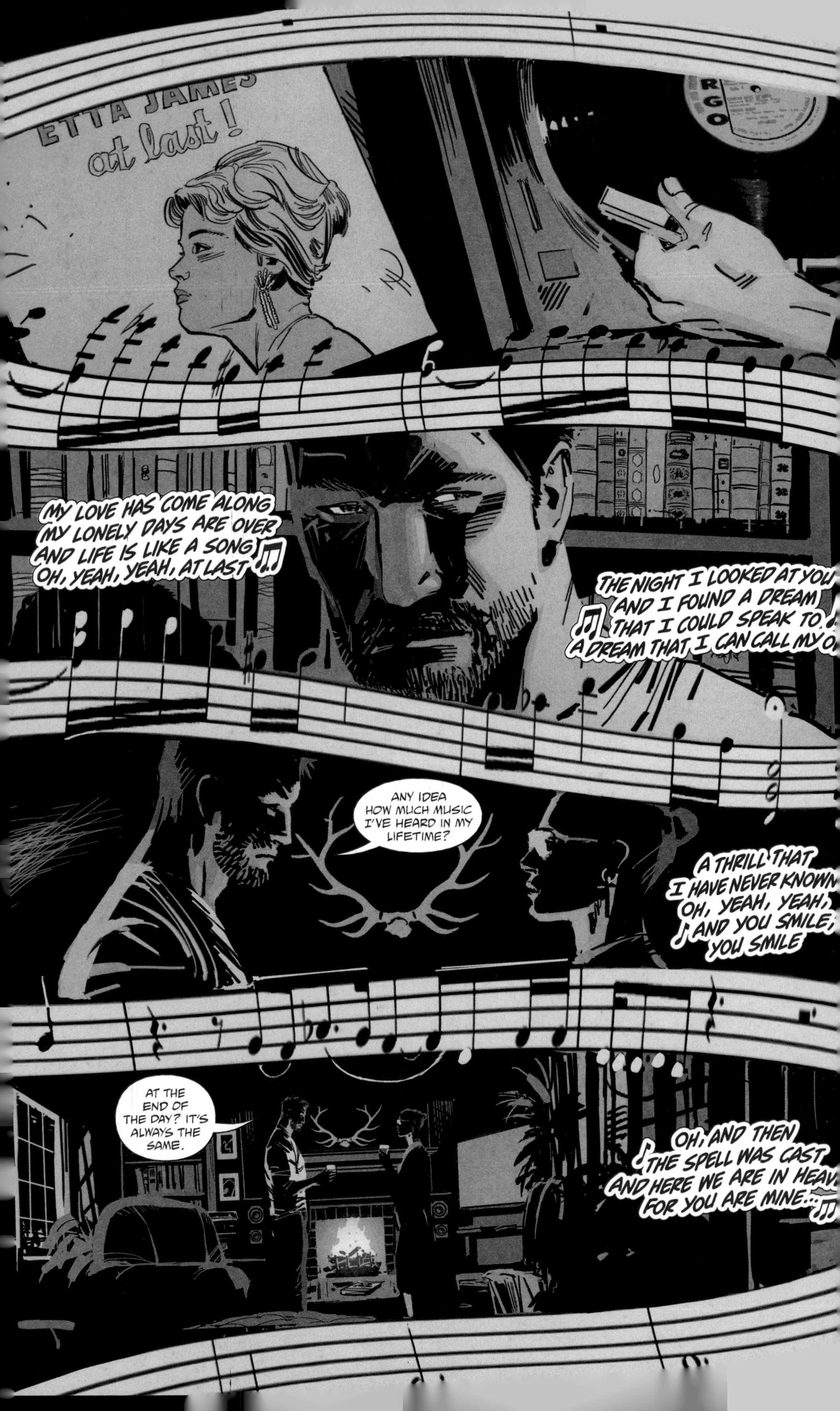
ETTA JAMES
at last!
RGO
MY LOVE HAS COME ALONG
MY LONELY DAYS ARE OVER
AND LIFE IS LIKE A SONG
OH, YEAH, YEAH, AT LAST
THE NIGHT I LOOKED AT YOU
AND I FOUND A DREAM
THAT I COULD SPEAK TO
A DREAM THAT I CAN CALL MY O
ANY IDEA HOW MUCH MUSIC I'VE HEARD IN MY LIFETIME?
A THRILL THAT
I HAVE NEVER KNOWN
OH, YEAH, YEAH,
AND YOU SMILE,
YOU SMILE
AT THE END OF THE DAY? IT'S ALWAYS THE SAME.
OH, AND THEN
THE SPELL WAS CAST
AND HERE WE ARE IN HEAV
FOR YOU ARE MINE...

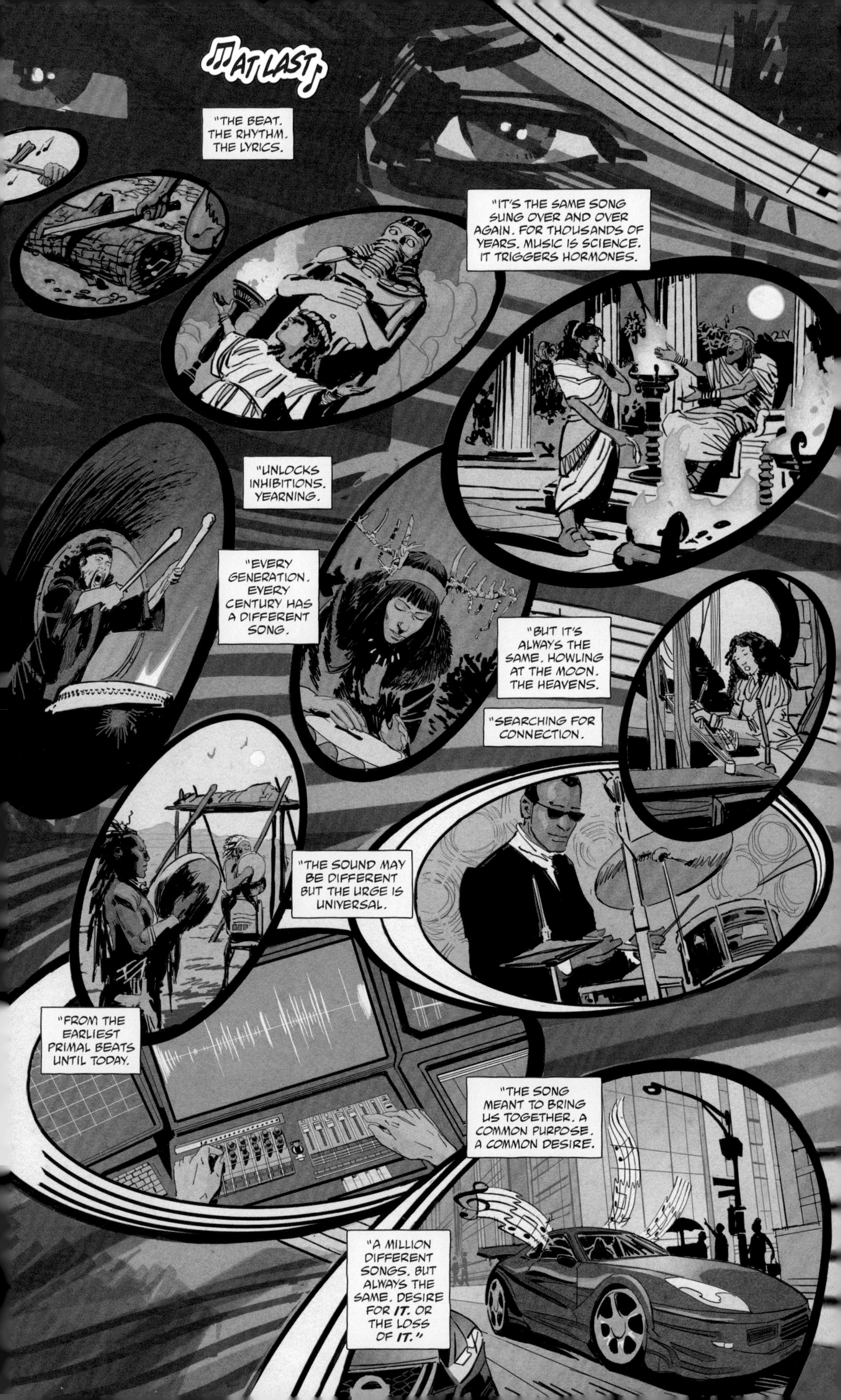
AT LAST
"THE BEAT. THE RHYTHM. THE LYRICS.
"IT'S THE SAME SONG SUNG OVER AND OVER AGAIN. FOR THOUSANDS OF YEARS. MUSIC IS SCIENCE. IT TRIGGERS HORMONES.
"UNLOCKS INHIBITIONS. YEARNING.
"EVERY GENERATION. EVERY CENTURY HAS A DIFFERENT SONG.
"BUT IT'S ALWAYS THE SAME. HOWLING AT THE MOON. THE HEAVENS.
"SEARCHING FOR CONNECTION.
"THE SOUND MAY BE DIFFERENT BUT THE URGE IS UNIVERSAL.
"FROM THE EARLIEST PRIMAL BEATS UNTIL TODAY.
"THE SONG MEANT TO BRING US TOGETHER. A COMMON PURPOSE. A COMMON DESIRE.
"A MILLION DIFFERENT SONGS. BUT ALWAYS THE SAME. DESIRE FOR IT. OR THE LOSS OF IT."

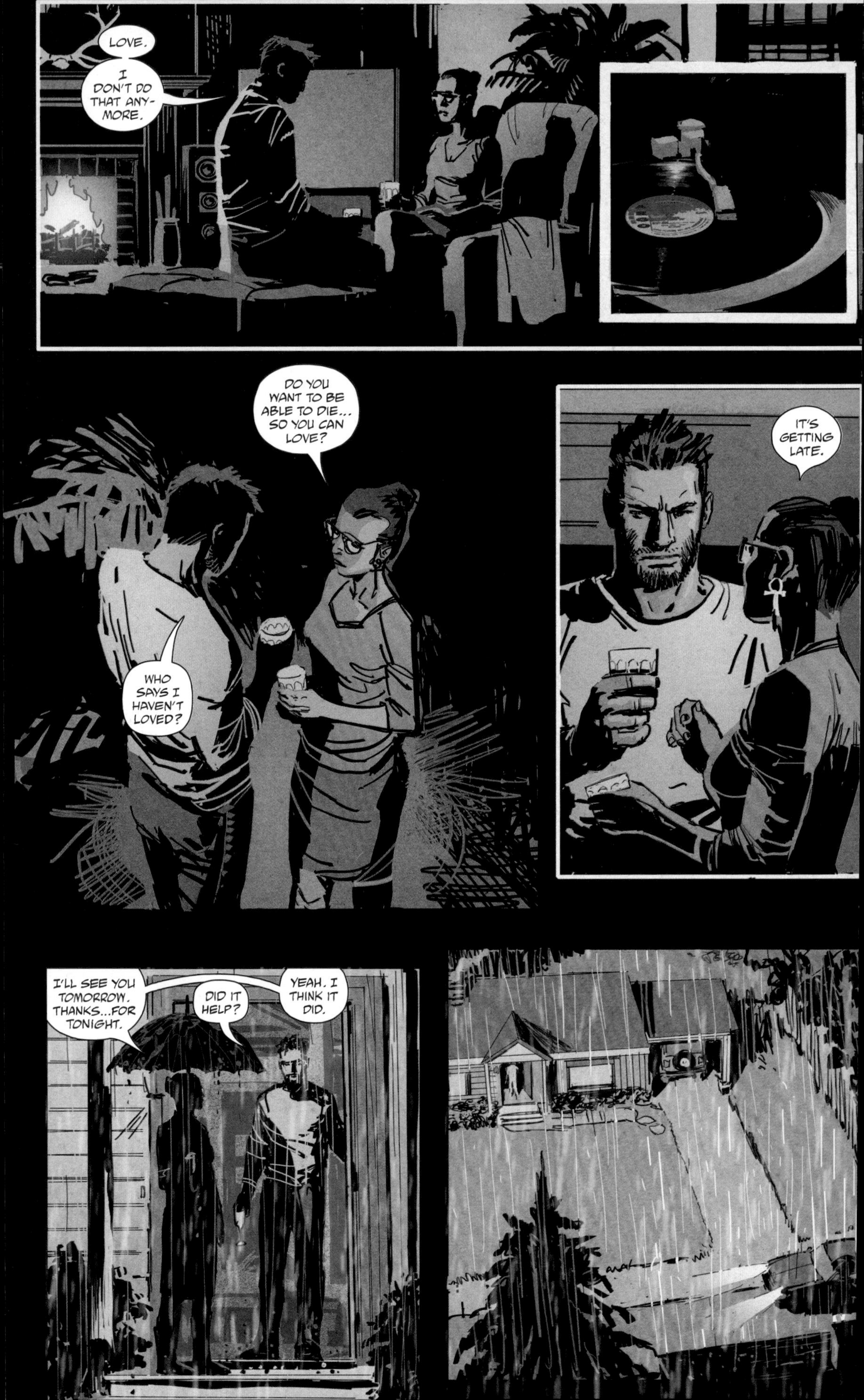
LOVE.
I DON'T DO THAT ANY-MORE.
DO YOU WANT TO BE ABLE TO DIE... SO YOU CAN LOVE?
WHO SAYS I HAVEN'T LOVED?
IT'S GETTING LATE.
I'LL SEE YOU TOMORROW. THANKS...FOR TONIGHT.
DID IT HELP?
YEAH. I THINK IT DID.

SORRY ABOUT LAST NIGHT.

WHY? I LIVE FOR INFORMATION. SOME THINGS YOU CAN'T DISCOVER IN A LAB.

TELL ME. WHEN WAS THE LAST TIME YOU TALKED ABOUT... YEARNING. LOVE...?

SO YOU DIDN'T WANT TO...?

I WANTED TO CONNECT. WHATEVER THAT MEANS FOR YOU. THE MORE YOU REVEAL, THE MORE I CAN UNDERSTAND.

I HYPOTHESIZED THAT YOUR BASE LEVEL EMOTIONS. YOUR TRAUMA. THAT'S THE KEY. YOU HAVE A PERFECT MEMORY. WE JUST NEED TO NAVIGATE IT. WE NEED TO GO TO THE PLACES YOU CUT OFF.

HERE. DRINK THIS.

WHAT IS IT?

IT'S BETTER THAN A TWO-HUNDRED-YEAR-OLD SCOTCH. SOMETHING TO HELP YOU RELAX.

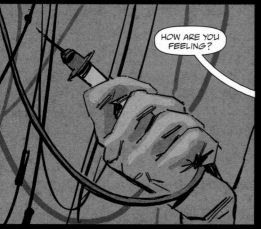

HOW ARE YOU FEELING?

...GOOD.

SO, WHAT...IS THIS?

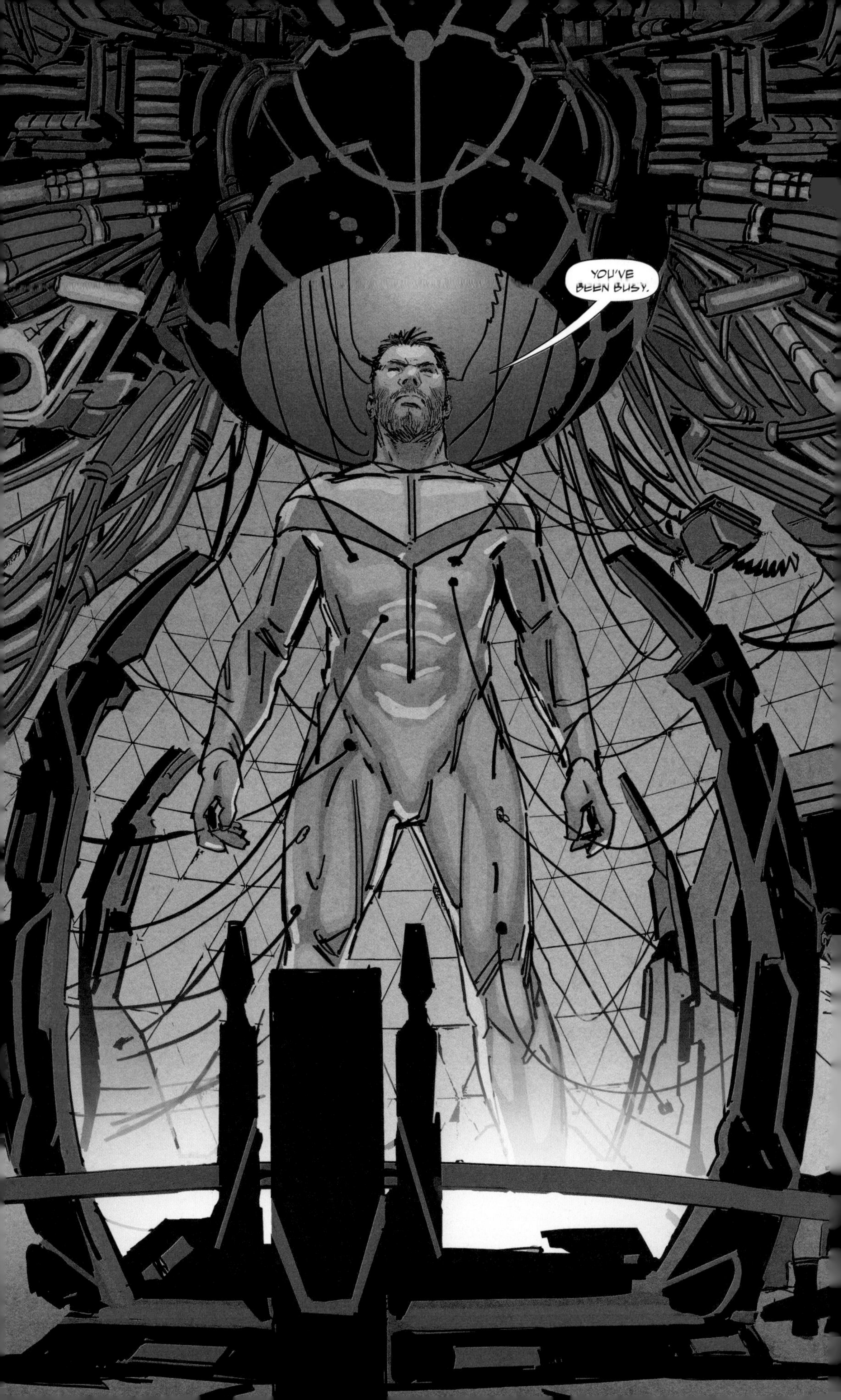
YOU'VE BEEN BUSY.

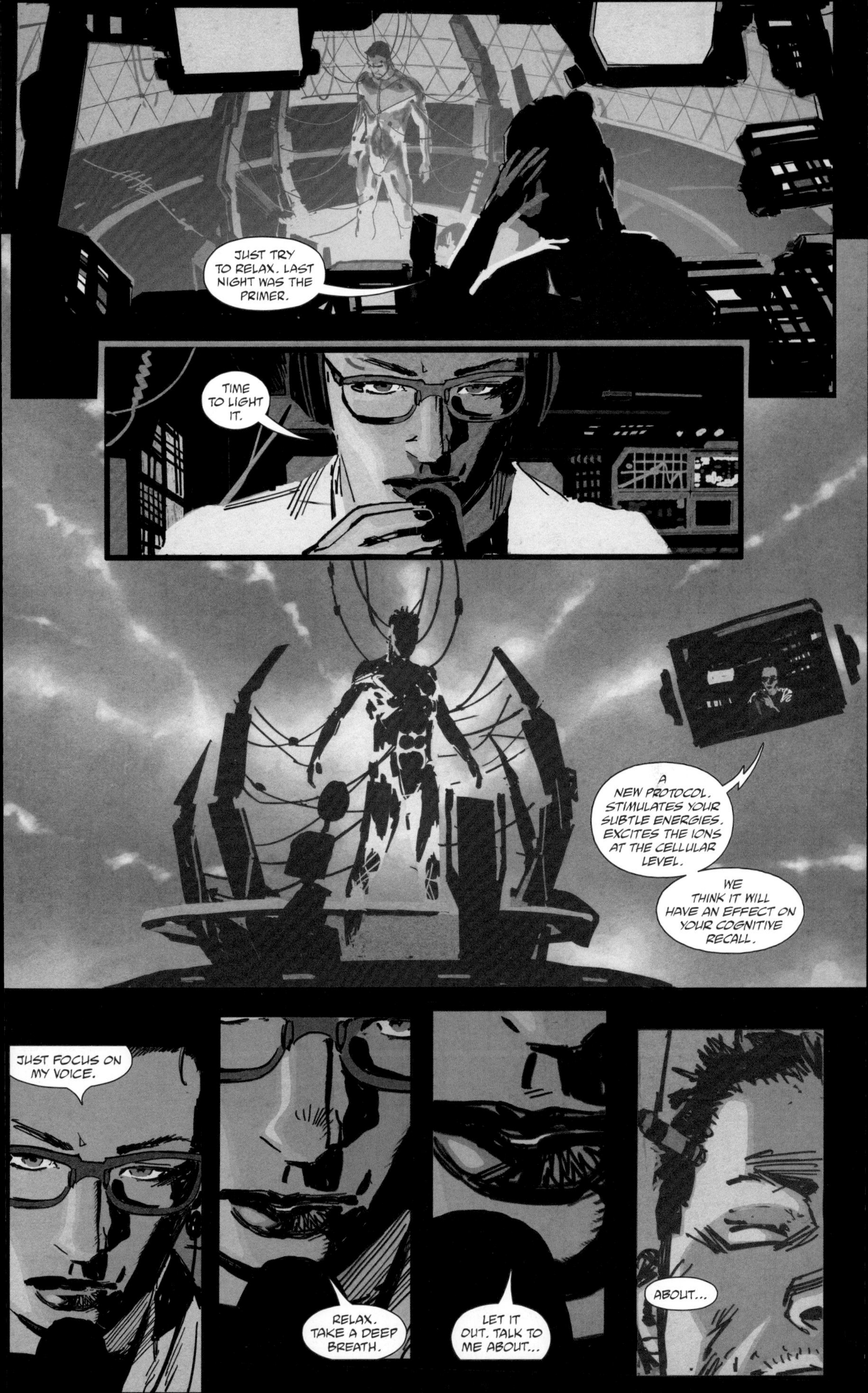
JUST TRY TO RELAX. LAST NIGHT WAS THE PRIMER.
TIME TO LIGHT IT.
A NEW PROTOCOL. STIMULATES YOUR SUBTLE ENERGIES. EXCITES THE IONS AT THE CELLULAR LEVEL.
WE THINK IT WILL HAVE AN EFFECT ON YOUR COGNITIVE RECALL.
JUST FOCUS ON MY VOICE.
RELAX. TAKE A DEEP BREATH.
LET IT OUT. TALK TO ME ABOUT...
ABOUT...

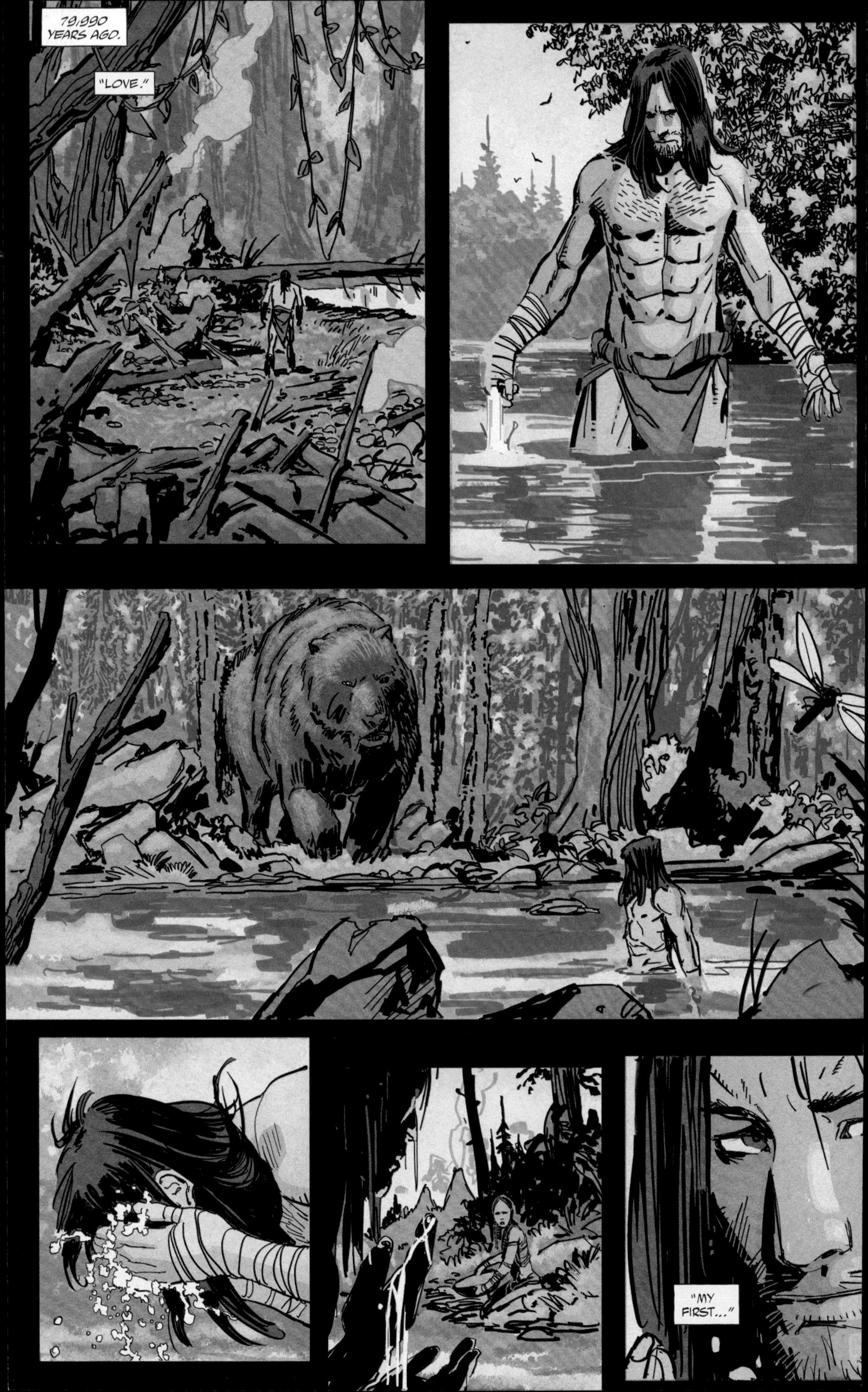
79,990 YEARS AGO.
"LOVE."
"MY FIRST..."

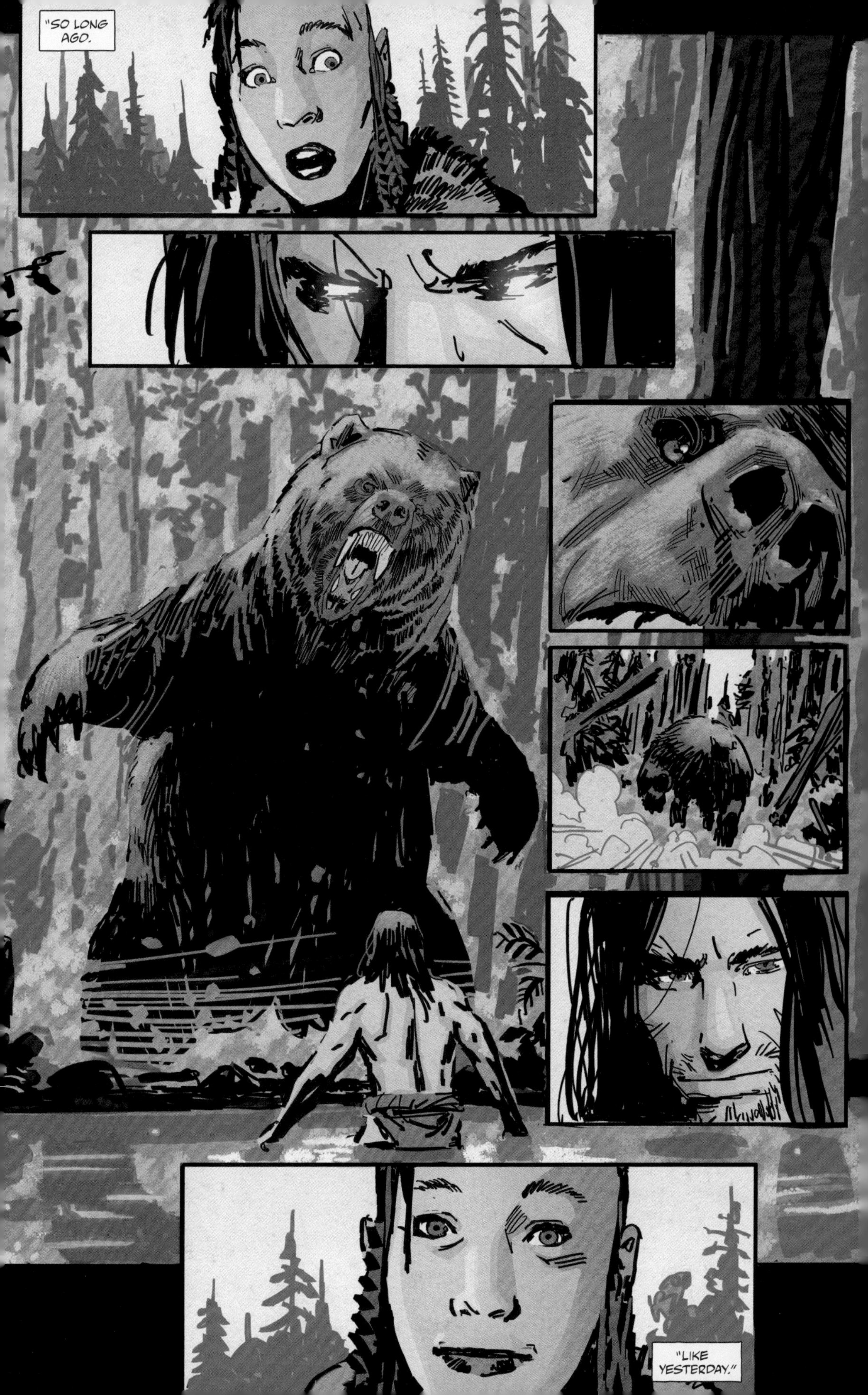
"SO LONG AGO.
"LIKE YESTERDAY."

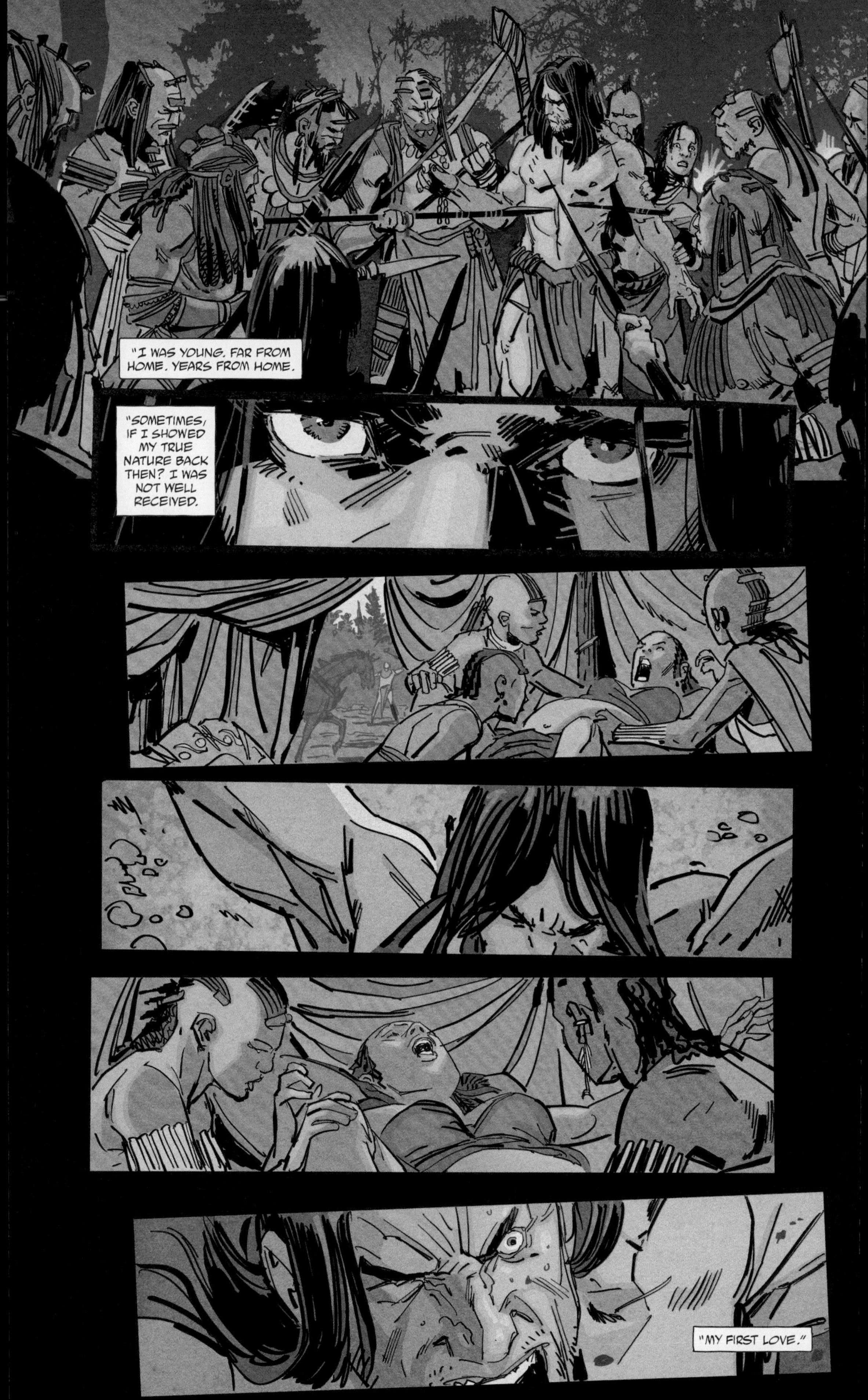
"I WAS YOUNG. FAR FROM HOME. YEARS FROM HOME.
"SOMETIMES, IF I SHOWED MY TRUE NATURE BACK THEN? I WAS NOT WELL RECEIVED.
"MY FIRST LOVE."

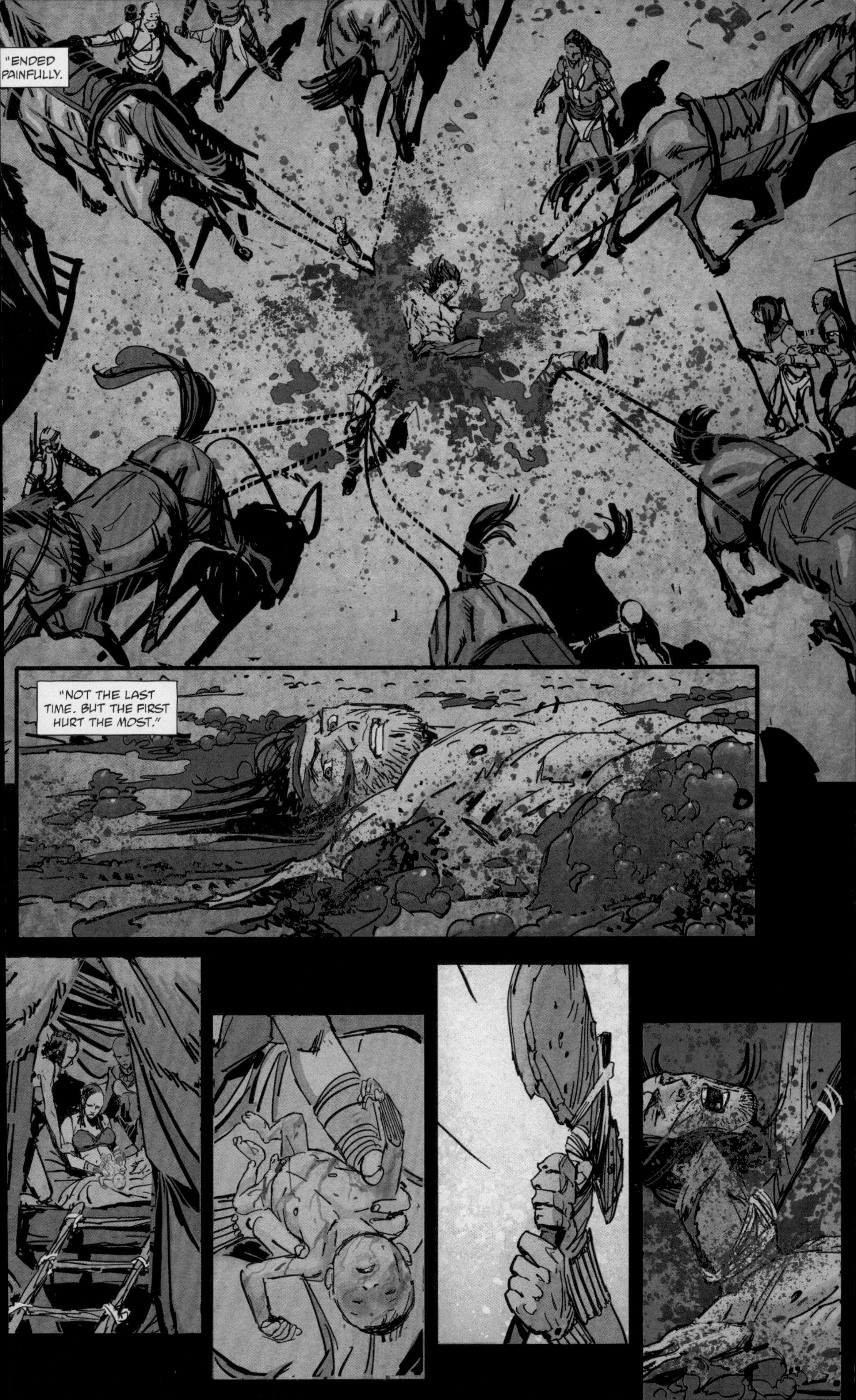
"ENDED PAINFULLY.
"NOT THE LAST TIME. BUT THE FIRST HURT THE MOST."

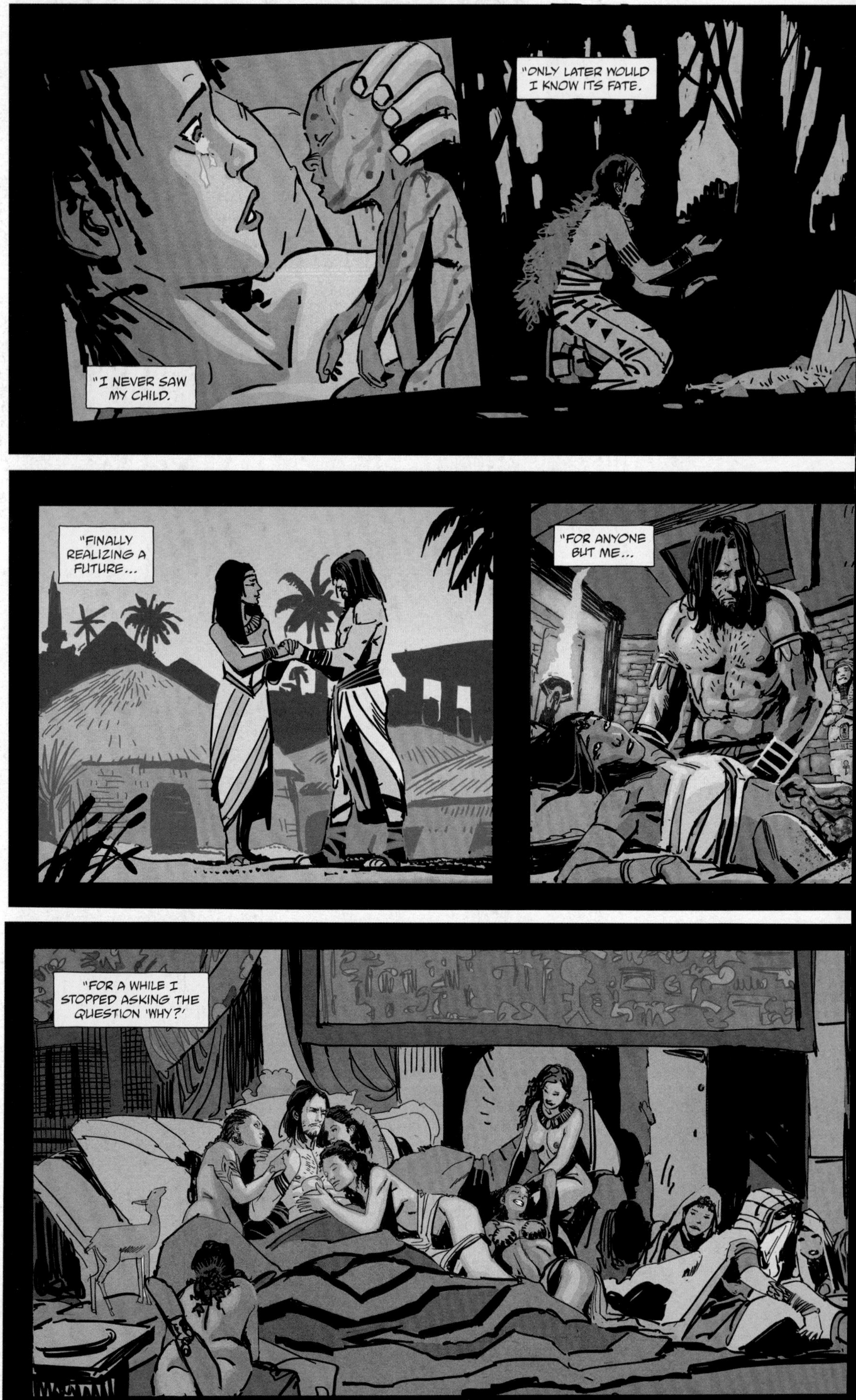
"I NEVER SAW
MY CHILD.
"ONLY LATER WOULD
I KNOW ITS FATE.
"FINALLY
REALIZING A
FUTURE...
"FOR ANYONE
BUT ME...
"FOR A WHILE I
STOPPED ASKING THE
QUESTION 'WHY?'

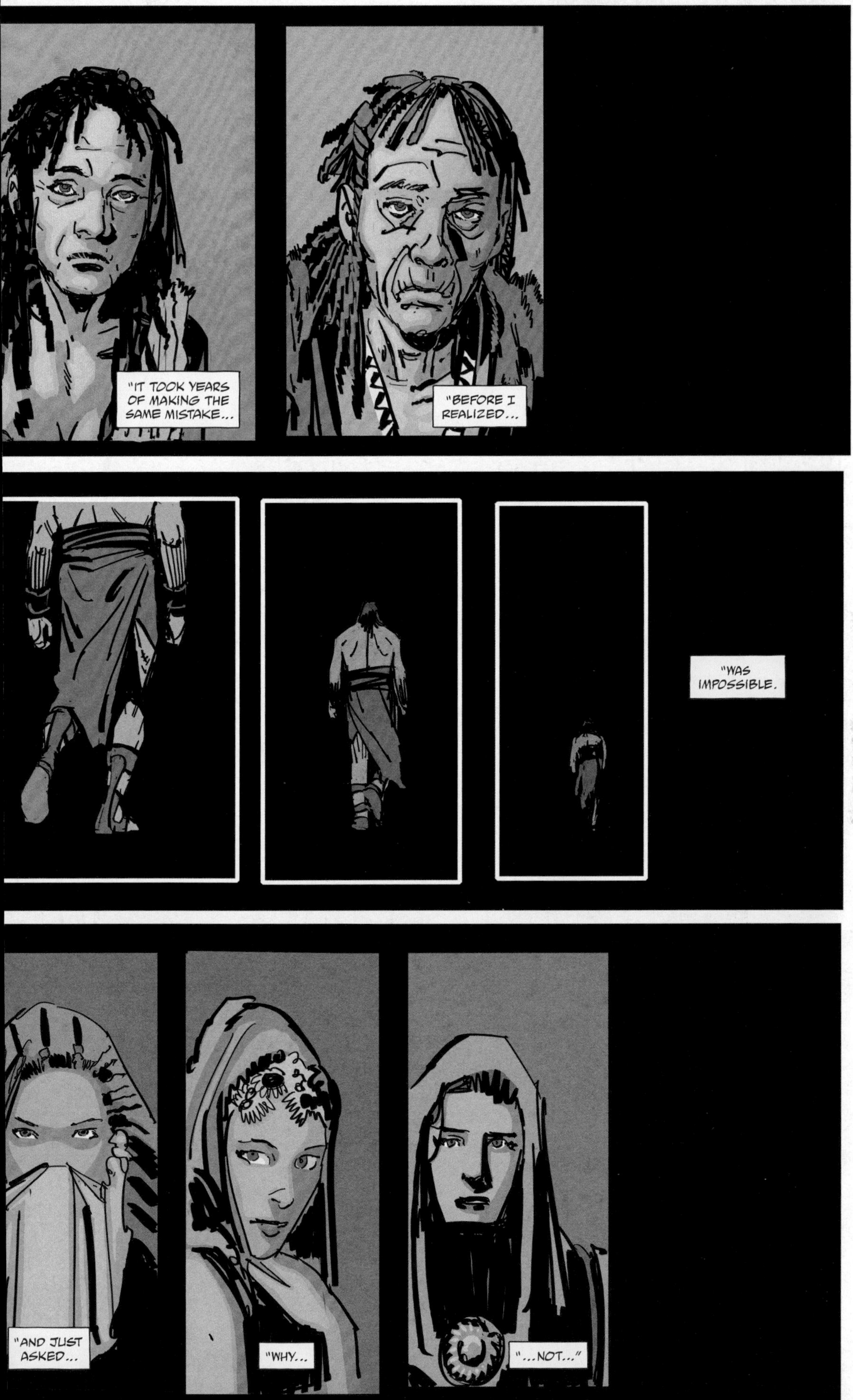
"IT TOOK YEARS OF MAKING THE SAME MISTAKE...
"BEFORE I REALIZED...
"WAS IMPOSSIBLE.
"AND JUST ASKED...
"WHY...
"...NOT..."

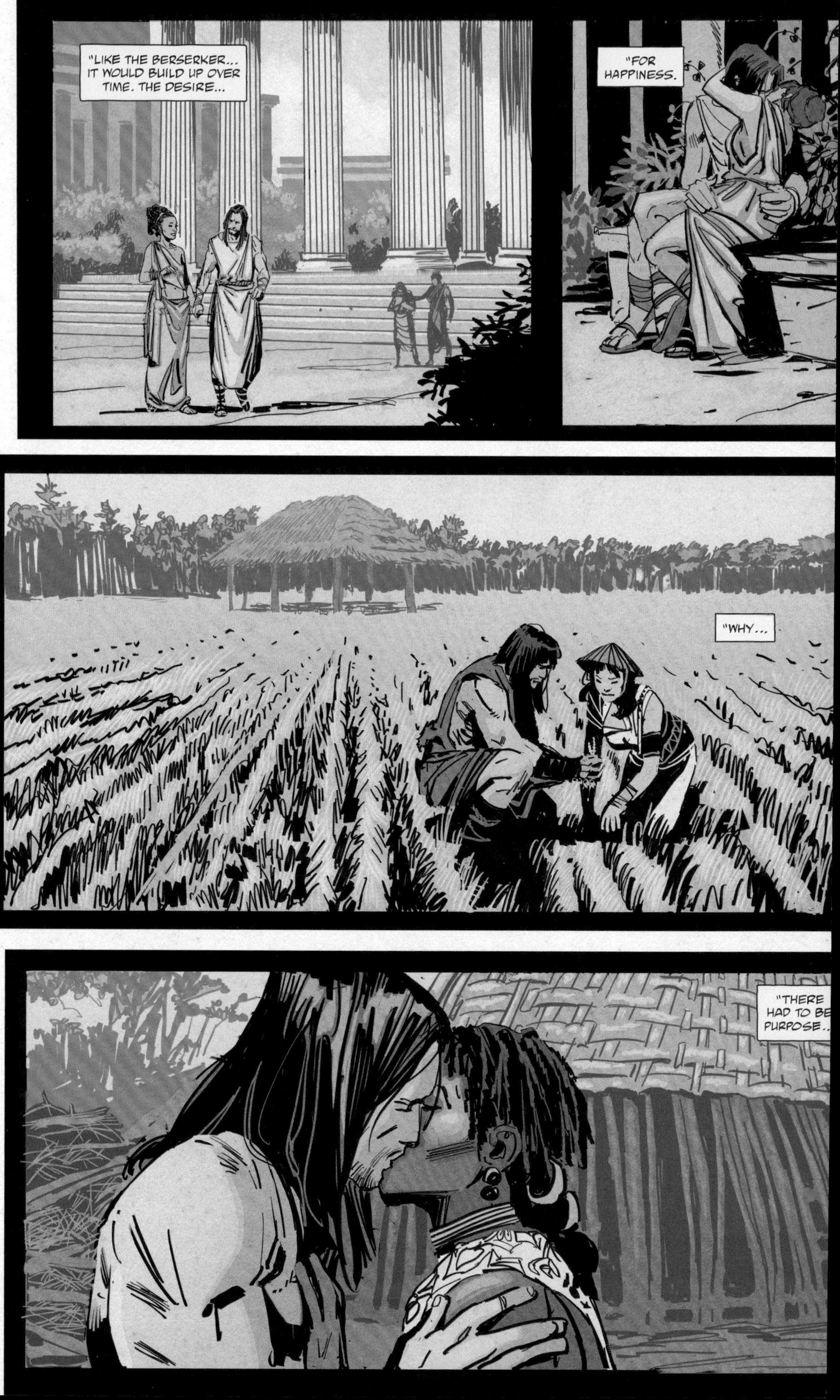
"LIKE THE BERSERKER... IT WOULD BUILD UP OVER TIME. THE DESIRE...
"FOR HAPPINESS.
"WHY...
"THERE HAD TO BE PURPOSE...

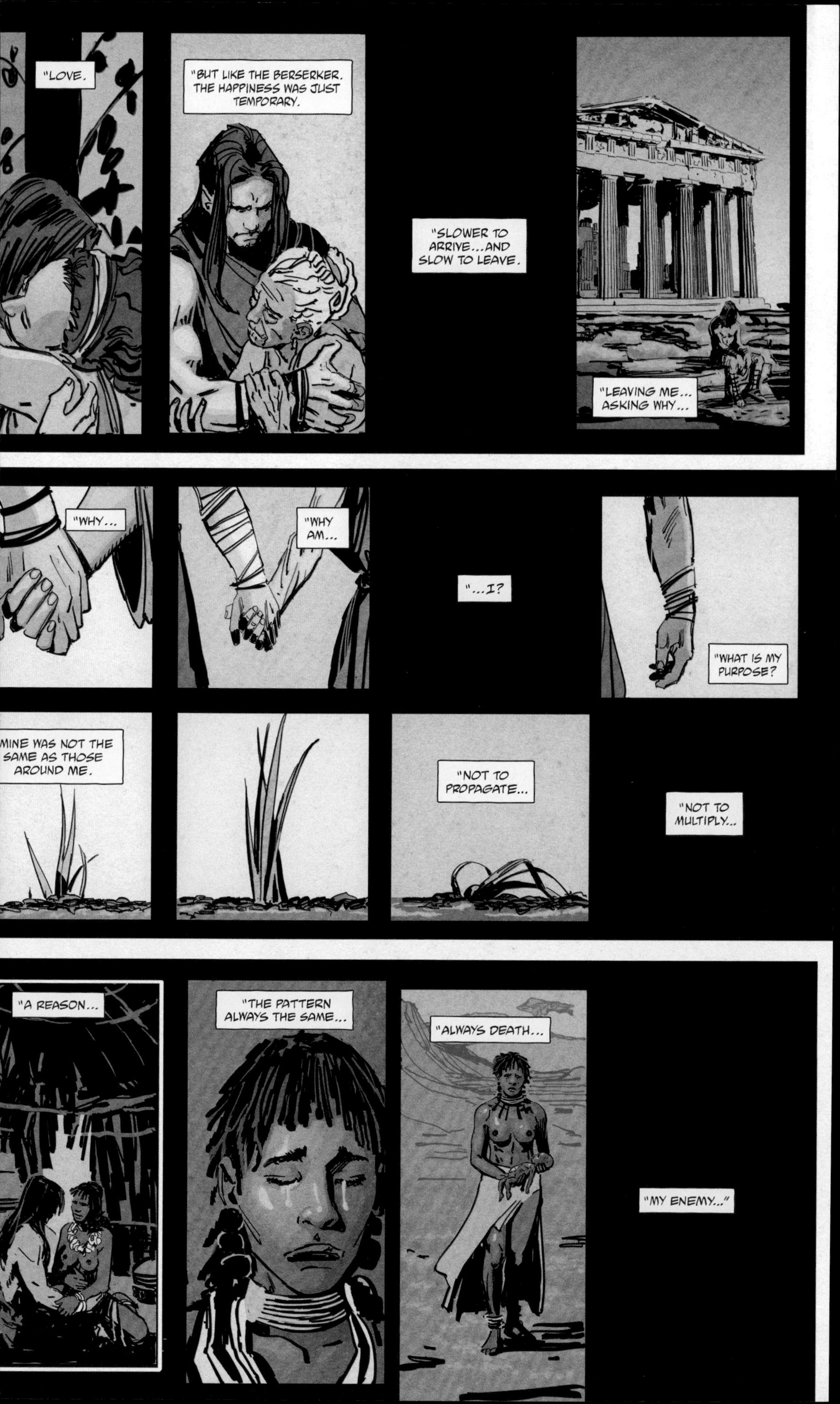
"LOVE.
"BUT LIKE THE BERSERKER. THE HAPPINESS WAS JUST TEMPORARY.
"SLOWER TO ARRIVE...AND SLOW TO LEAVE.
"LEAVING ME... ASKING WHY...
"WHY...
"WHY AM...
"...I?
"WHAT IS MY PURPOSE?
MINE WAS NOT THE SAME AS THOSE AROUND ME.
"NOT TO PROPAGATE...
"NOT TO MULTIPLY...
"A REASON...
"THE PATTERN ALWAYS THE SAME...
"ALWAYS DEATH...
"MY ENEMY..."

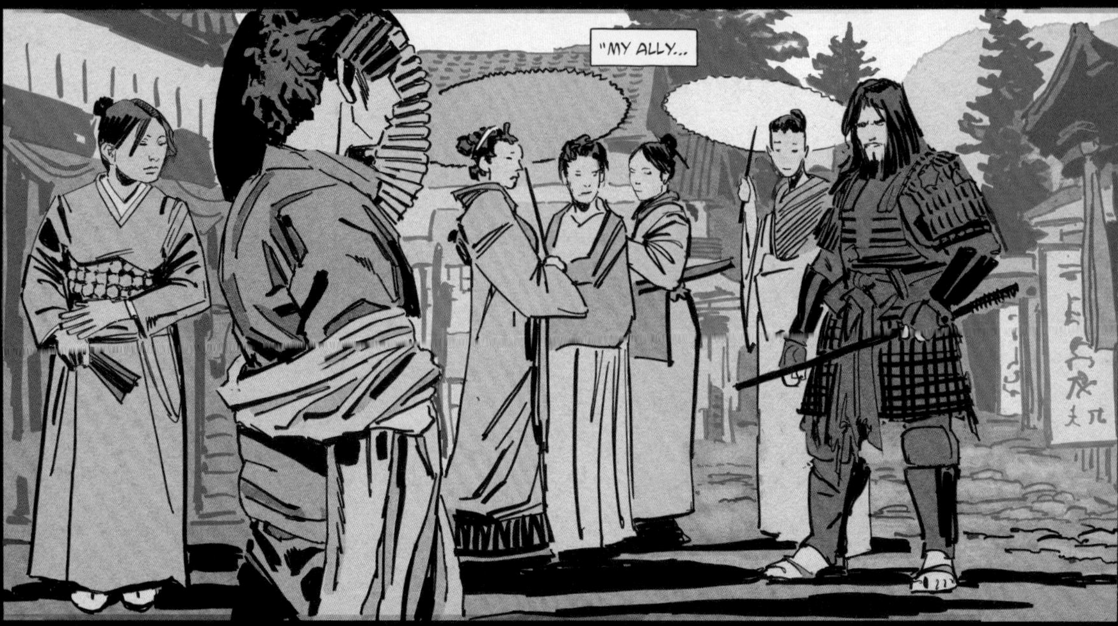
"MY ALLY...

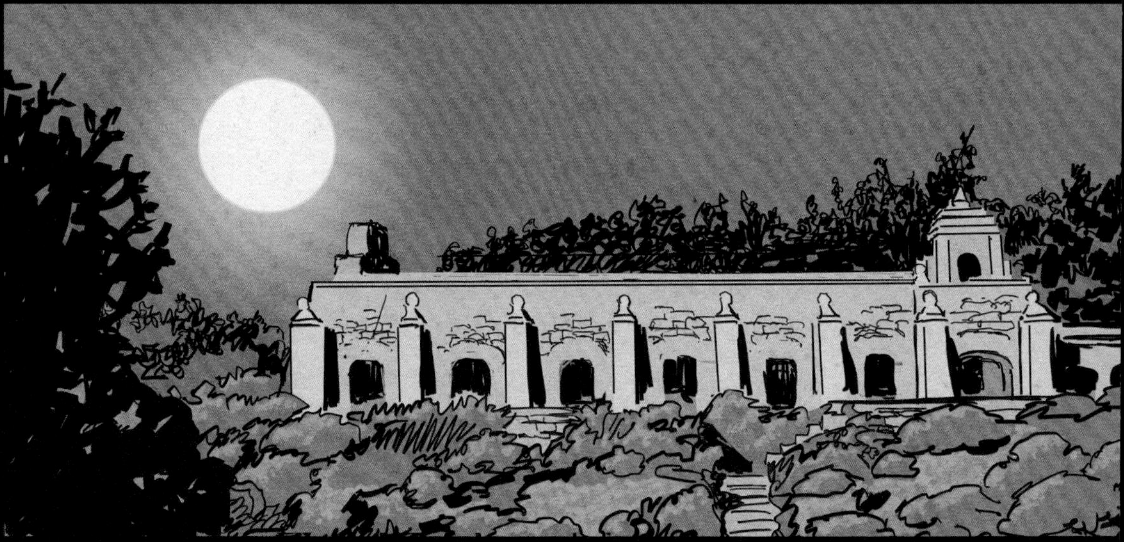

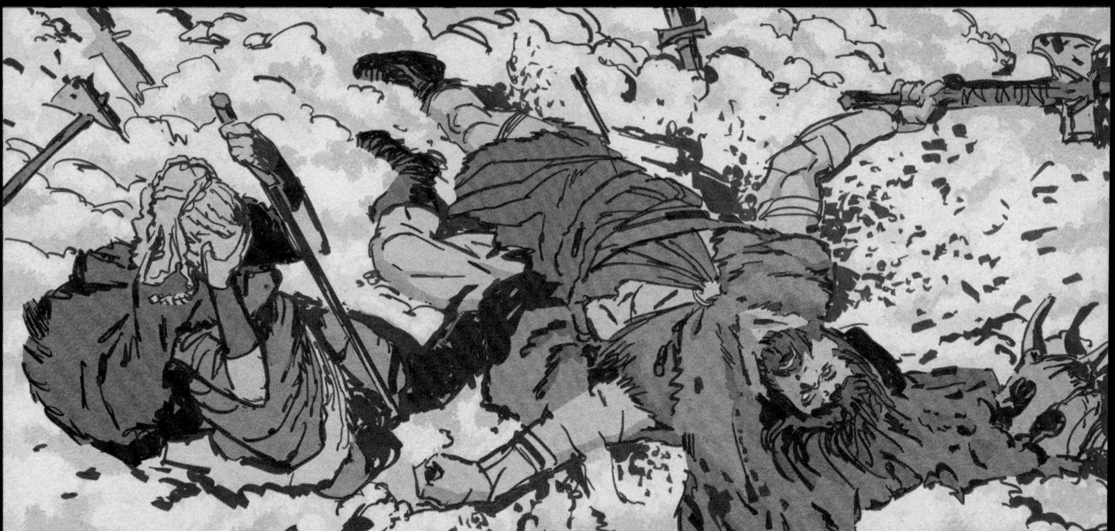

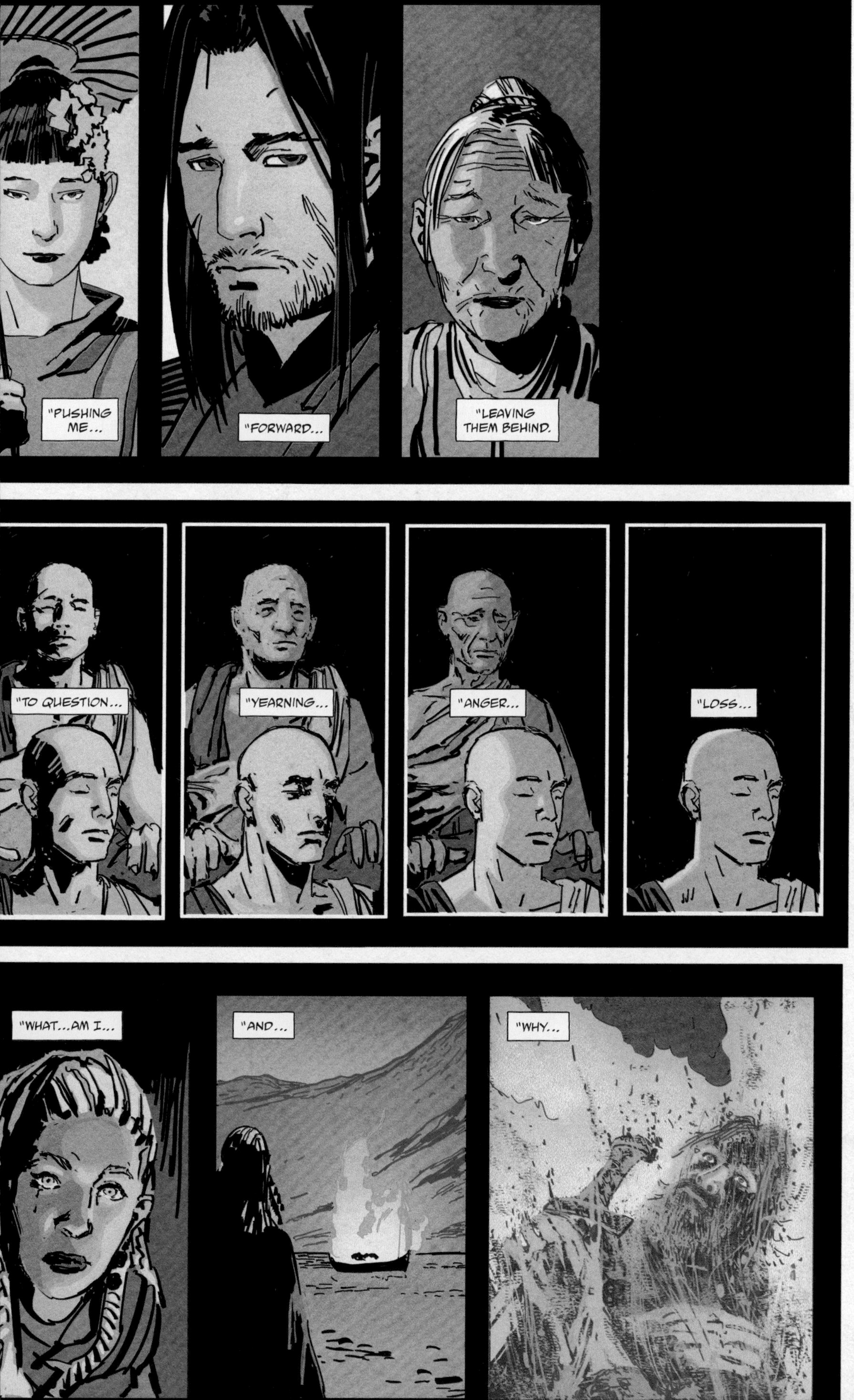
"PUSHING ME...
"FORWARD...
"LEAVING THEM BEHIND.
"TO QUESTION...
"YEARNING...
"ANGER...
"LOSS...
"WHAT...AM I...
"AND...
"WHY...

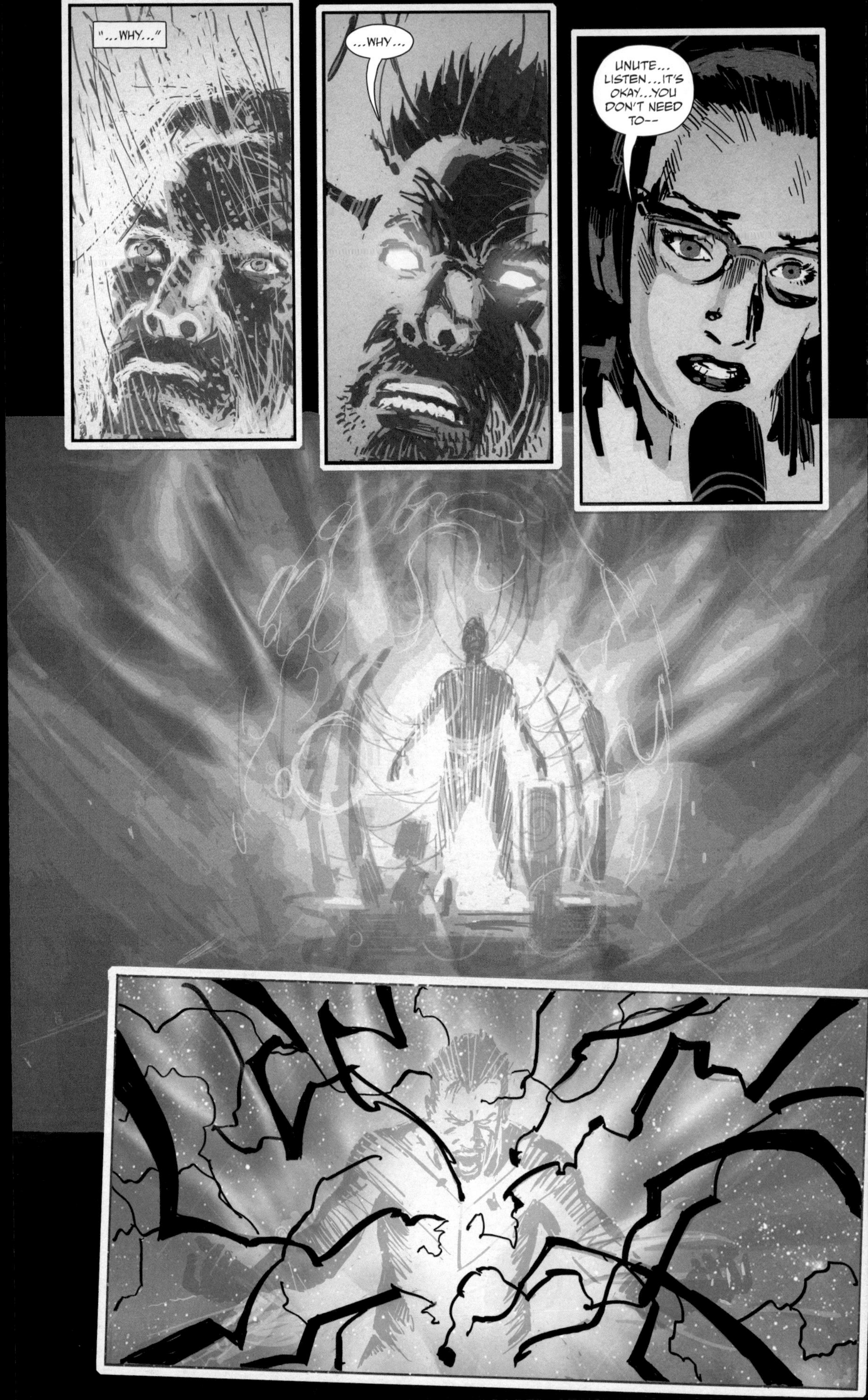
"...WHY..."
...WHY...
UNUTE... LISTEN...IT'S OKAY...YOU DON'T NEED TO--

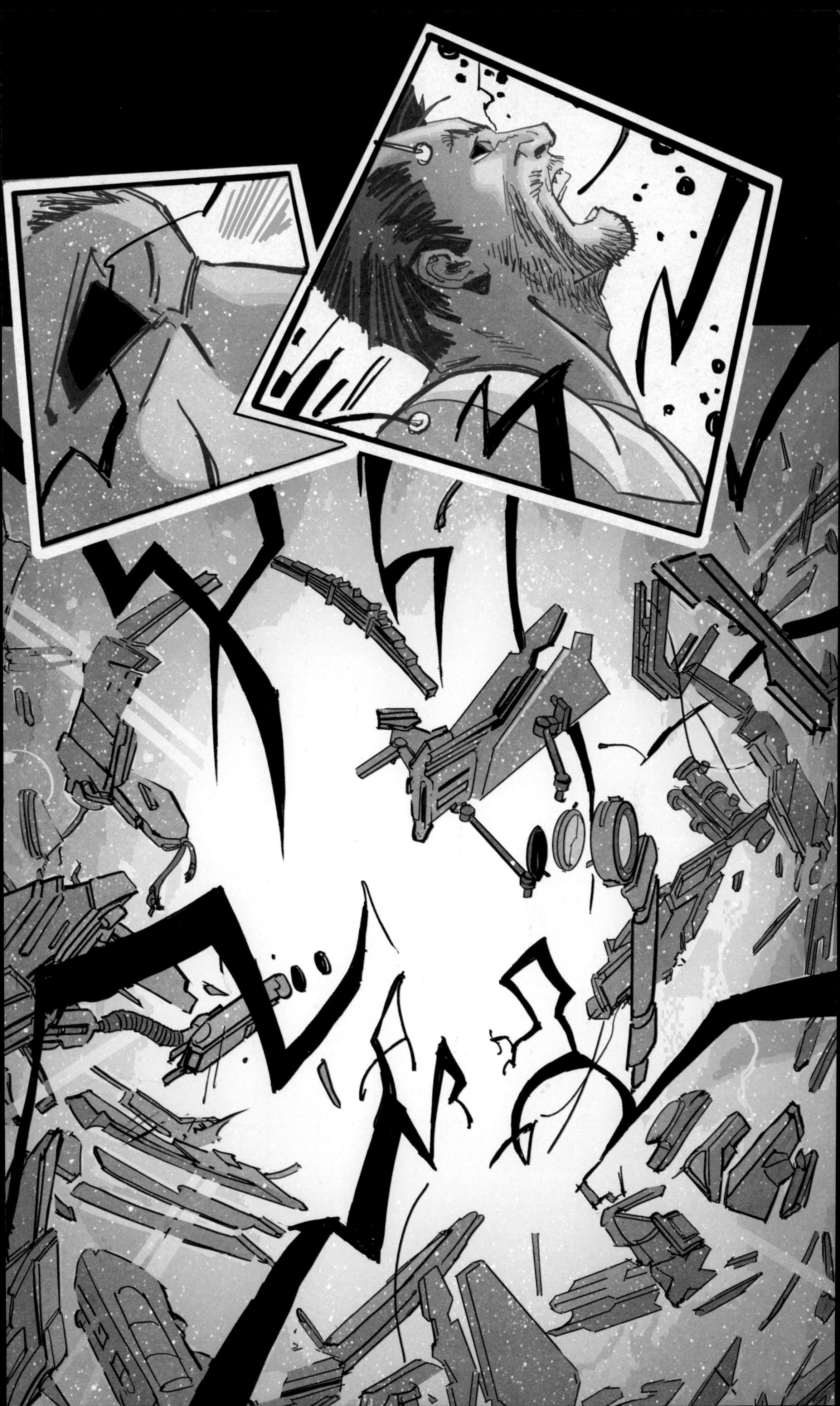

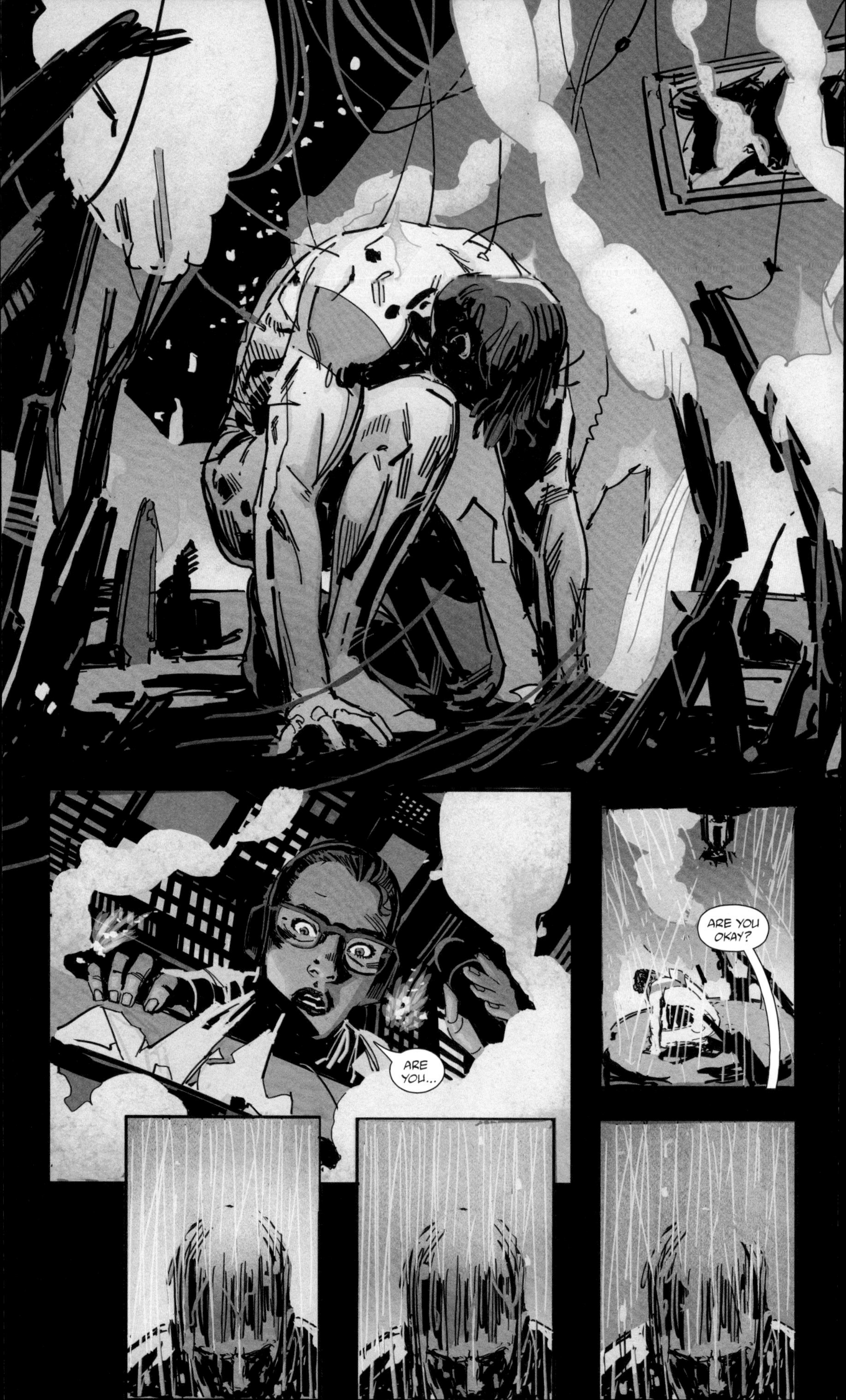
ARE YOU...
ARE YOU OKAY?

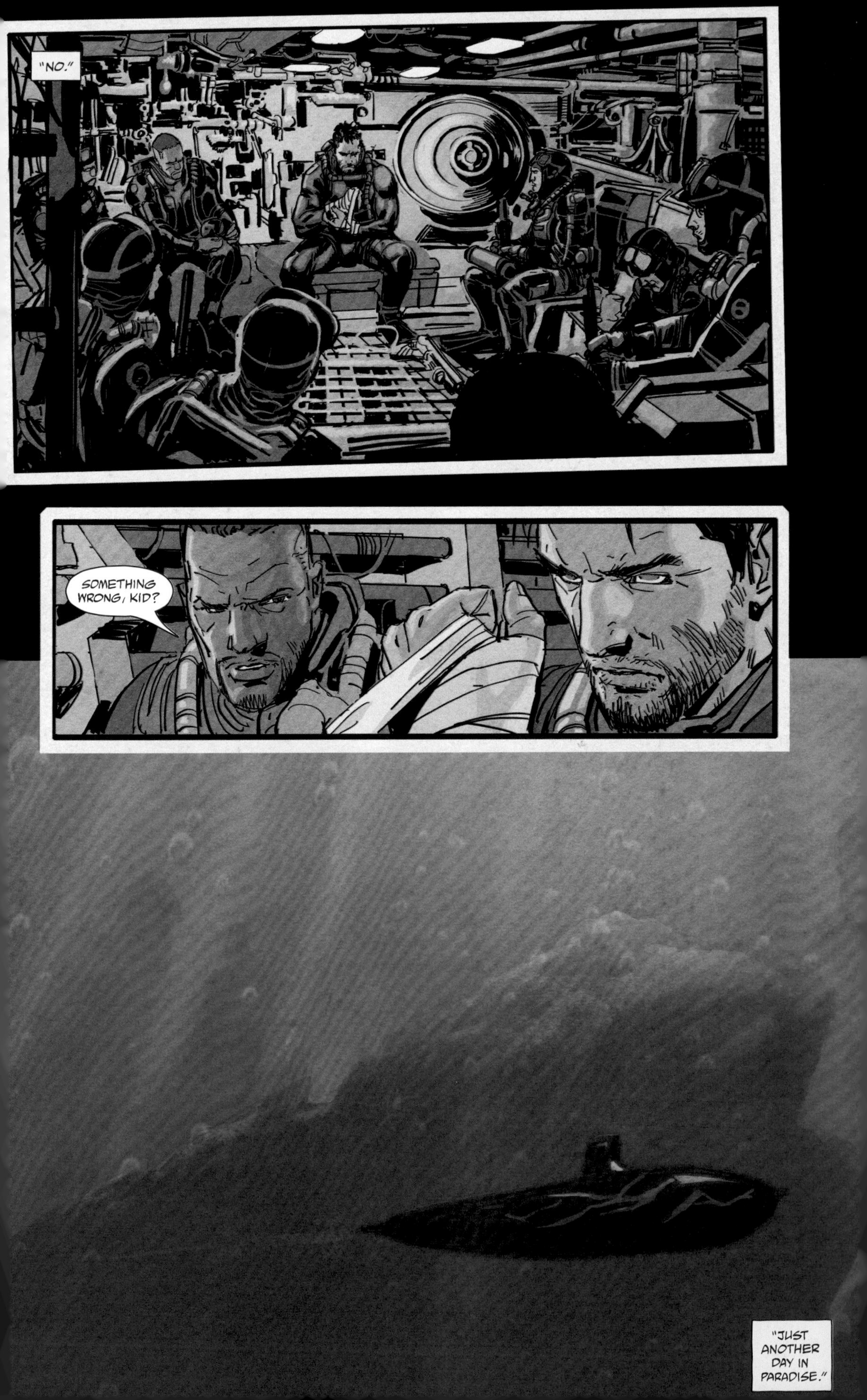
"NO."
SOMETHING WRONG, KID?
"JUST ANOTHER DAY IN PARADISE."

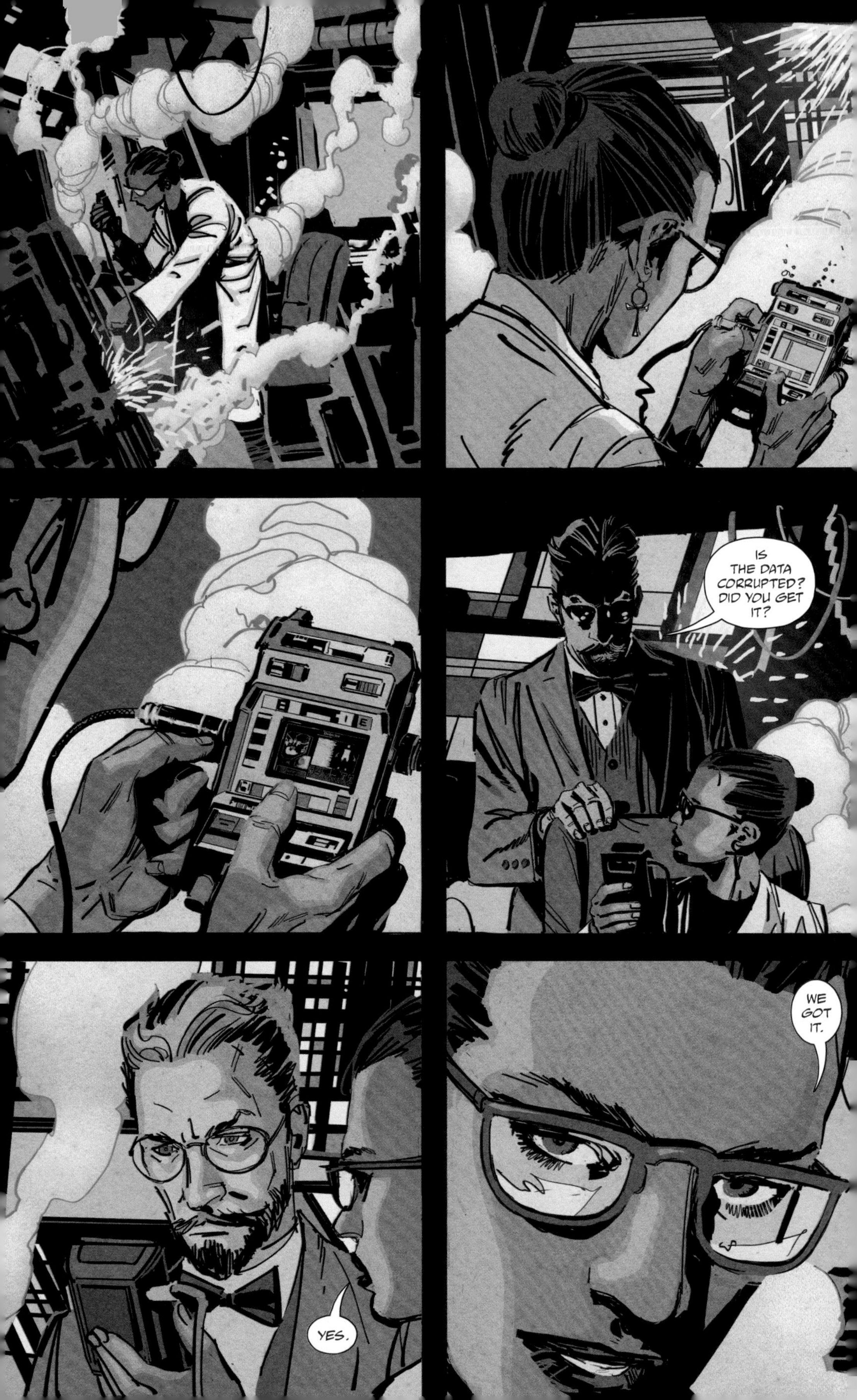
IS THE DATA CORRUPTED? DID YOU GET IT?
YES.
WE GOT IT.

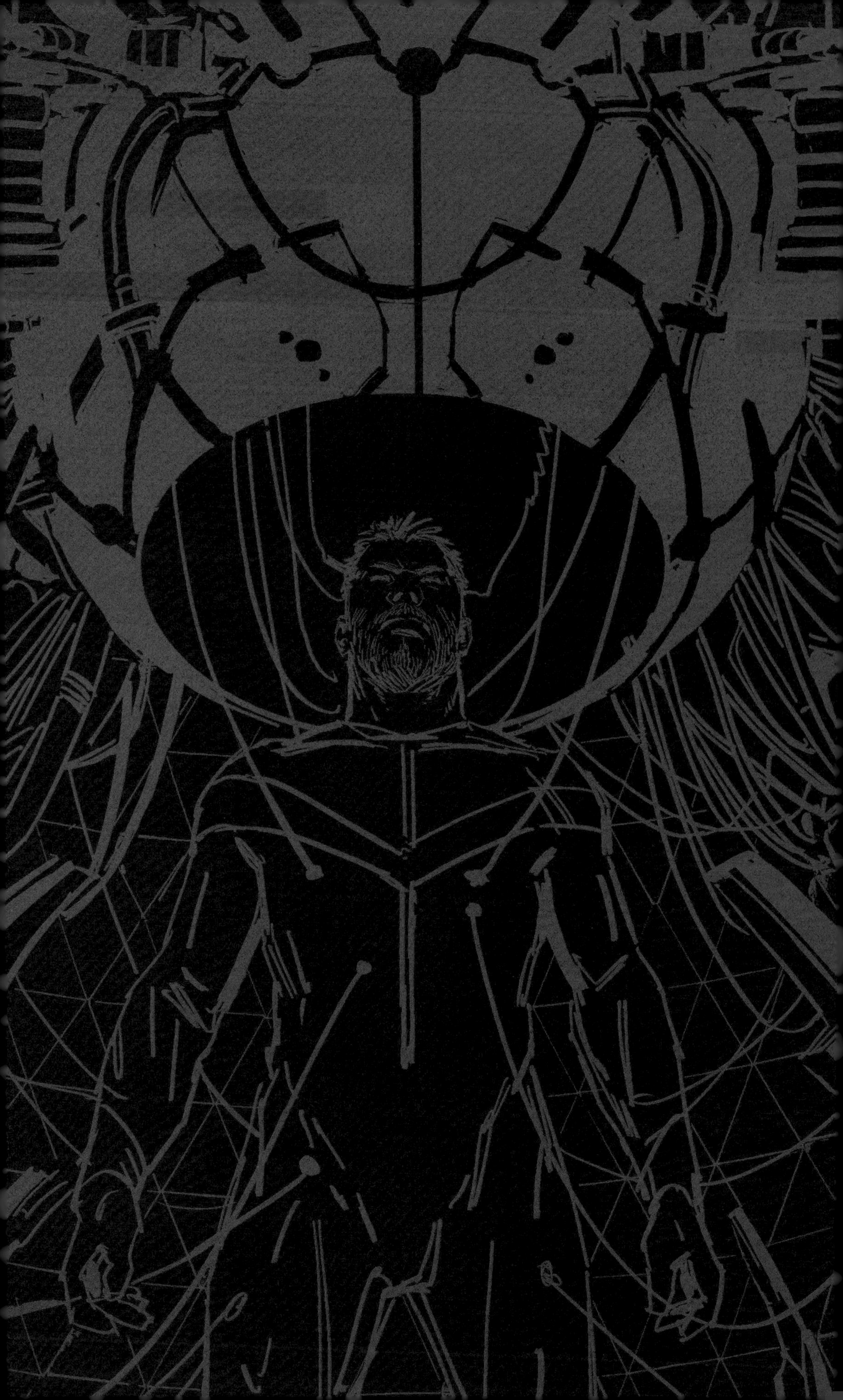

CHAPTER
SIX

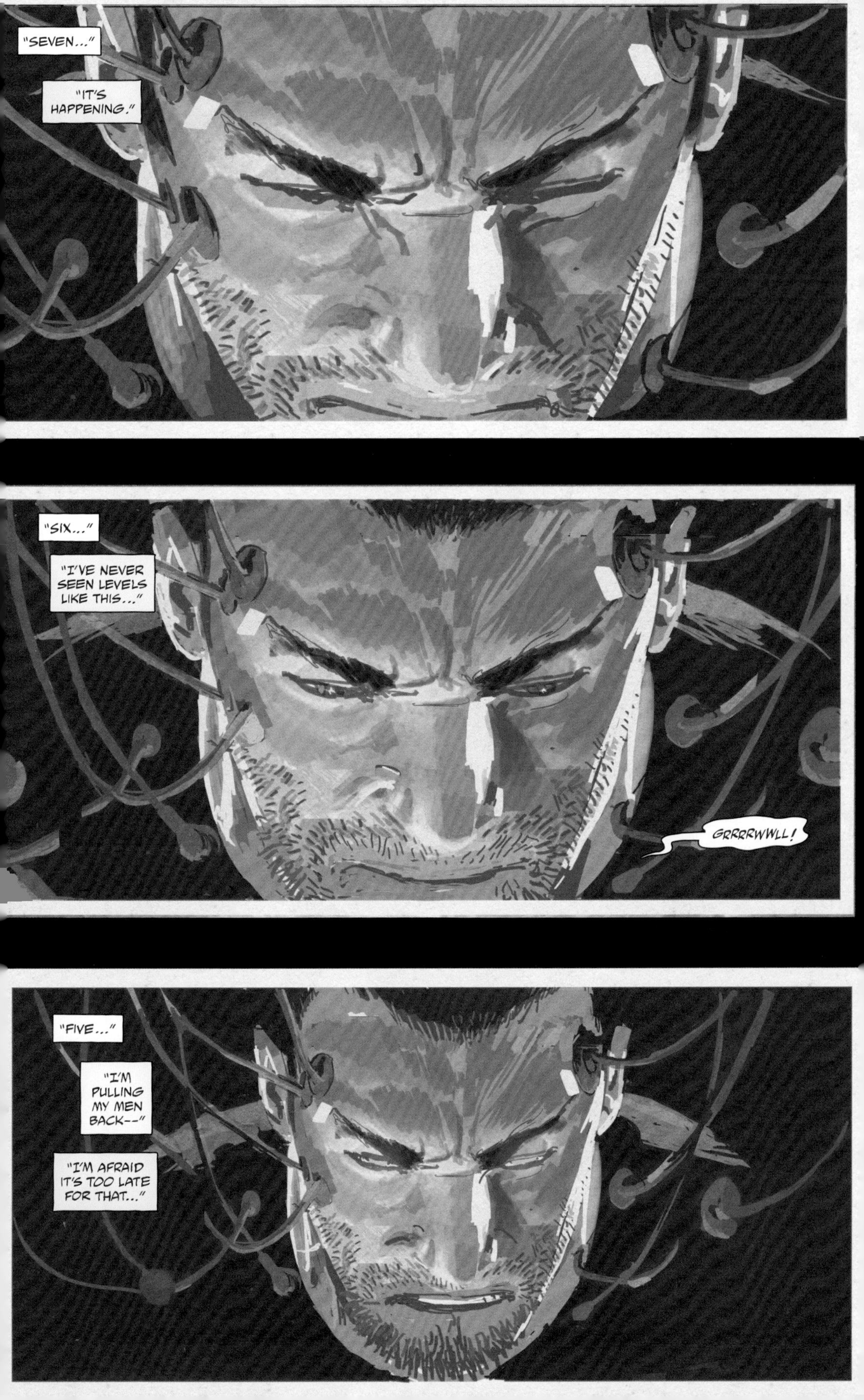
"SEVEN..."
"IT'S HAPPENING."
"SIX..."
"I'VE NEVER SEEN LEVELS LIKE THIS..."
GRRRRWLL!
"FIVE..."
"I'M PULLING MY MEN BACK--"
"I'M AFRAID IT'S TOO LATE FOR THAT..."

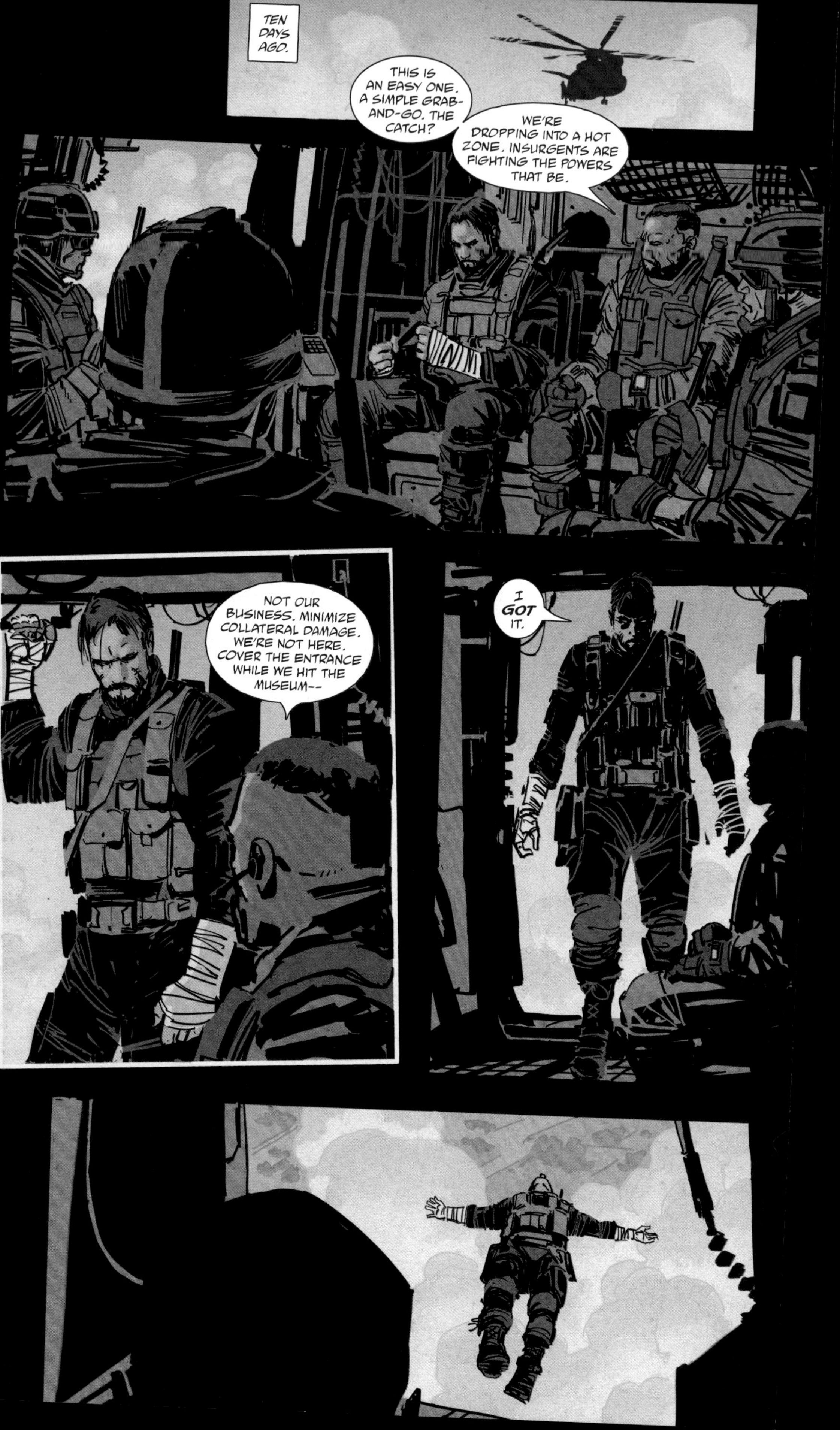
TEN DAYS AGO.
THIS IS AN EASY ONE. A SIMPLE GRAB-AND-GO. THE CATCH?
WE'RE DROPPING INTO A HOT ZONE. INSURGENTS ARE FIGHTING THE POWERS THAT BE.
NOT OUR BUSINESS. MINIMIZE COLLATERAL DAMAGE. WE'RE NOT HERE. COVER THE ENTRANCE WHILE WE HIT THE MUSEUM--
I GOT IT.

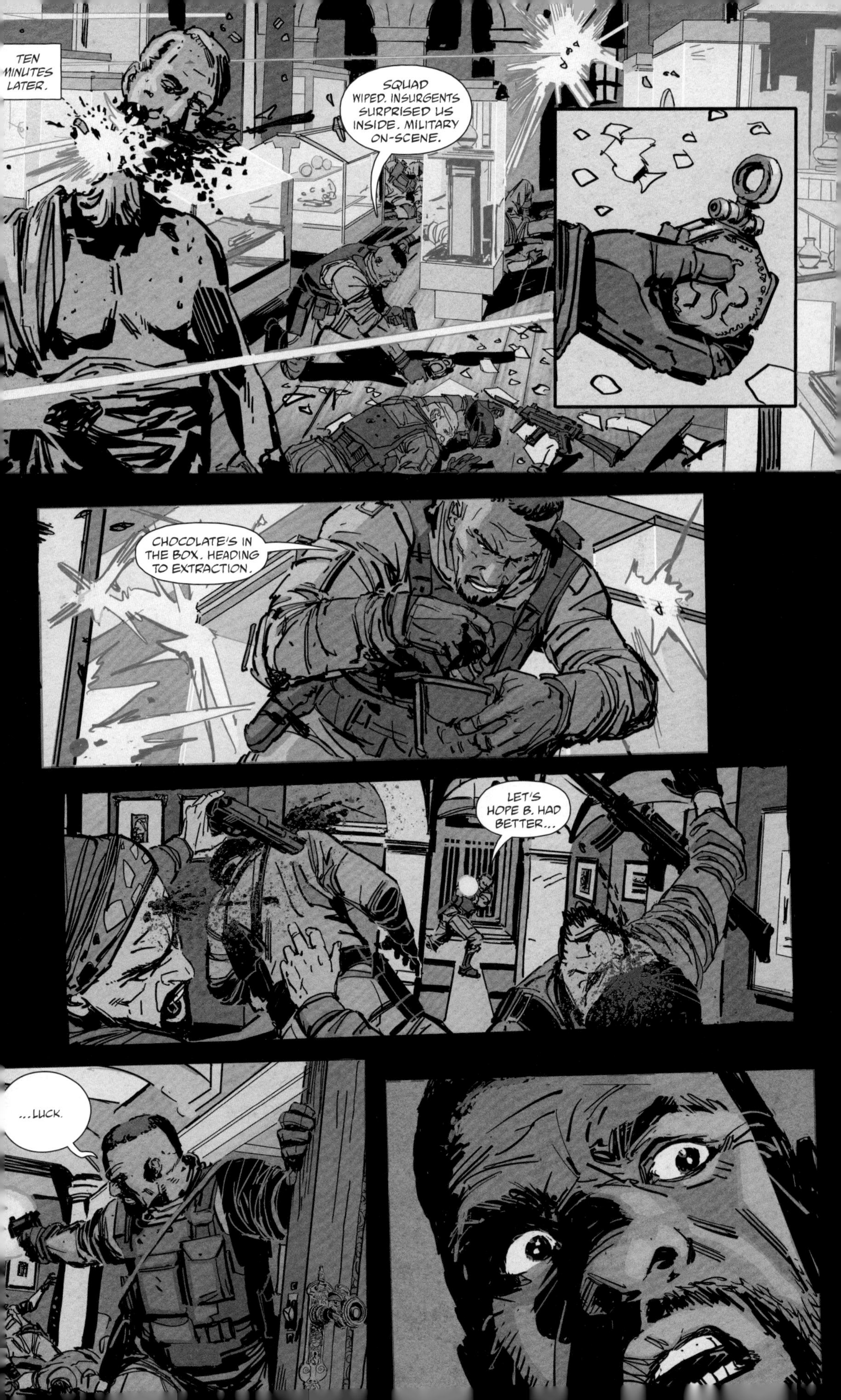
TEN MINUTES LATER.
SQUAD WIPED. INSURGENTS SURPRISED US INSIDE. MILITARY ON-SCENE.
CHOCOLATE'S IN THE BOX. HEADING TO EXTRACTION.
LET'S HOPE B. HAD BETTER...
...LUCK.

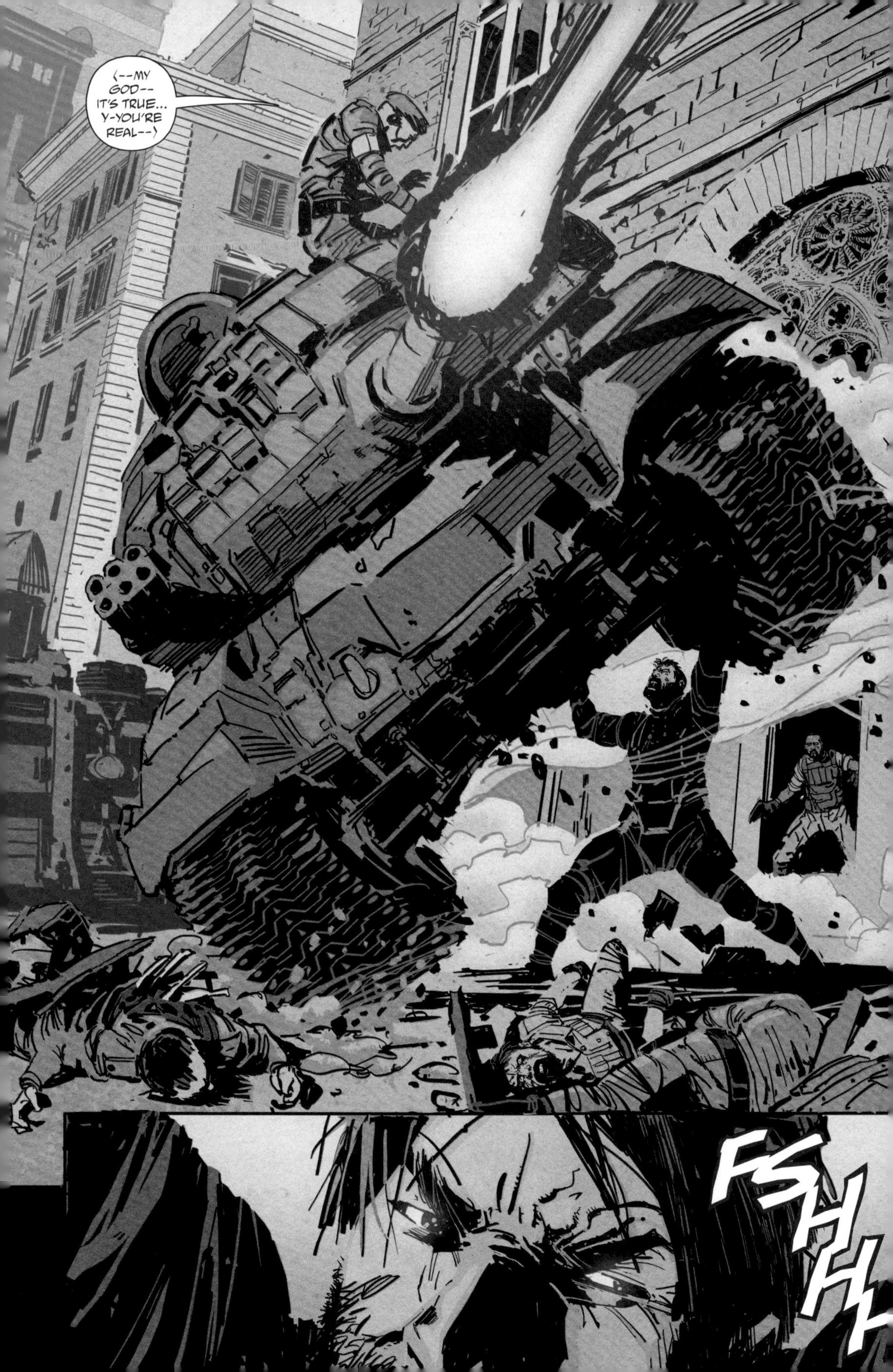
‹--MY GOD-- IT'S TRUE... Y-YOU'RE REAL--›
FSHHH

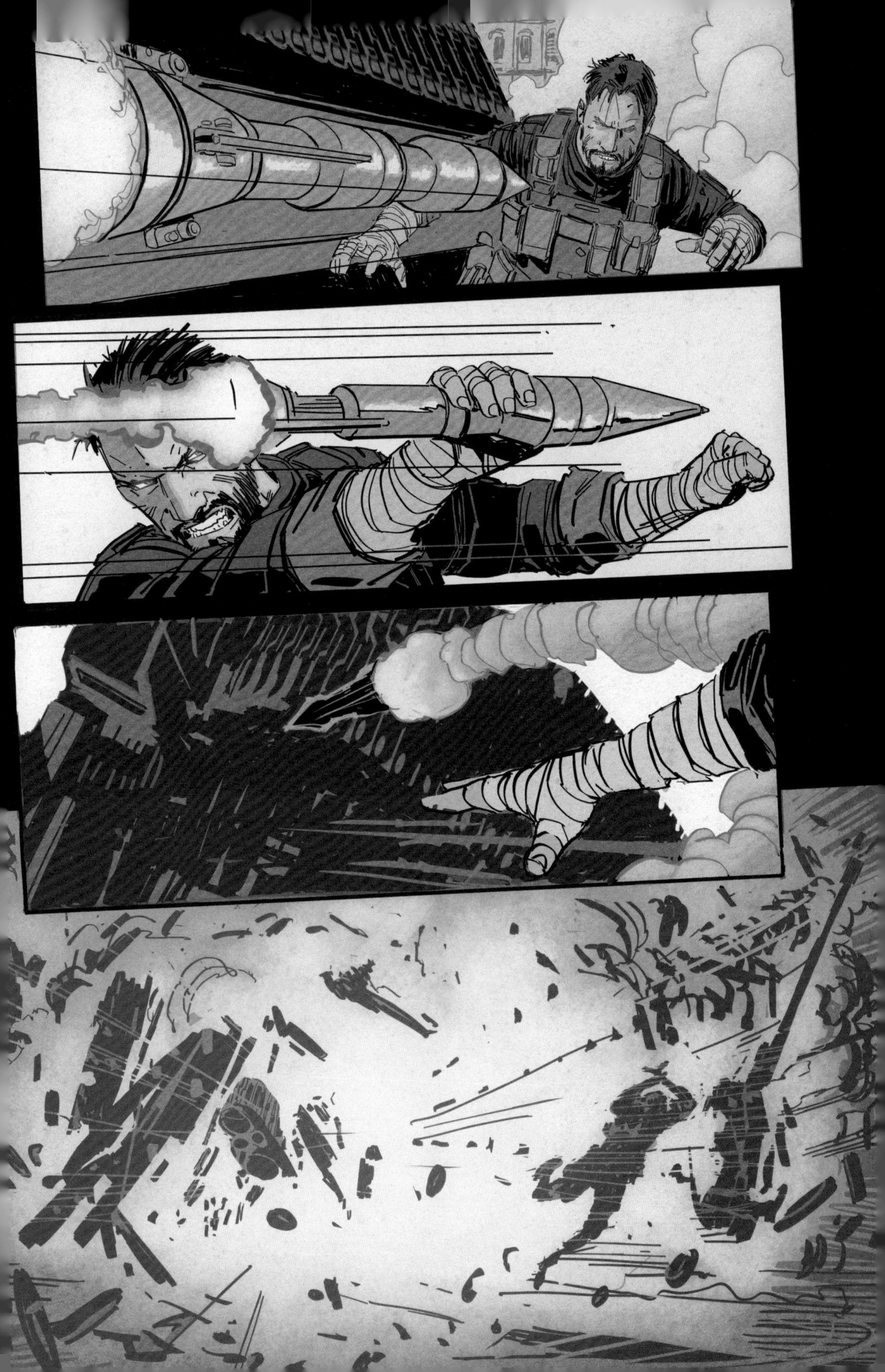

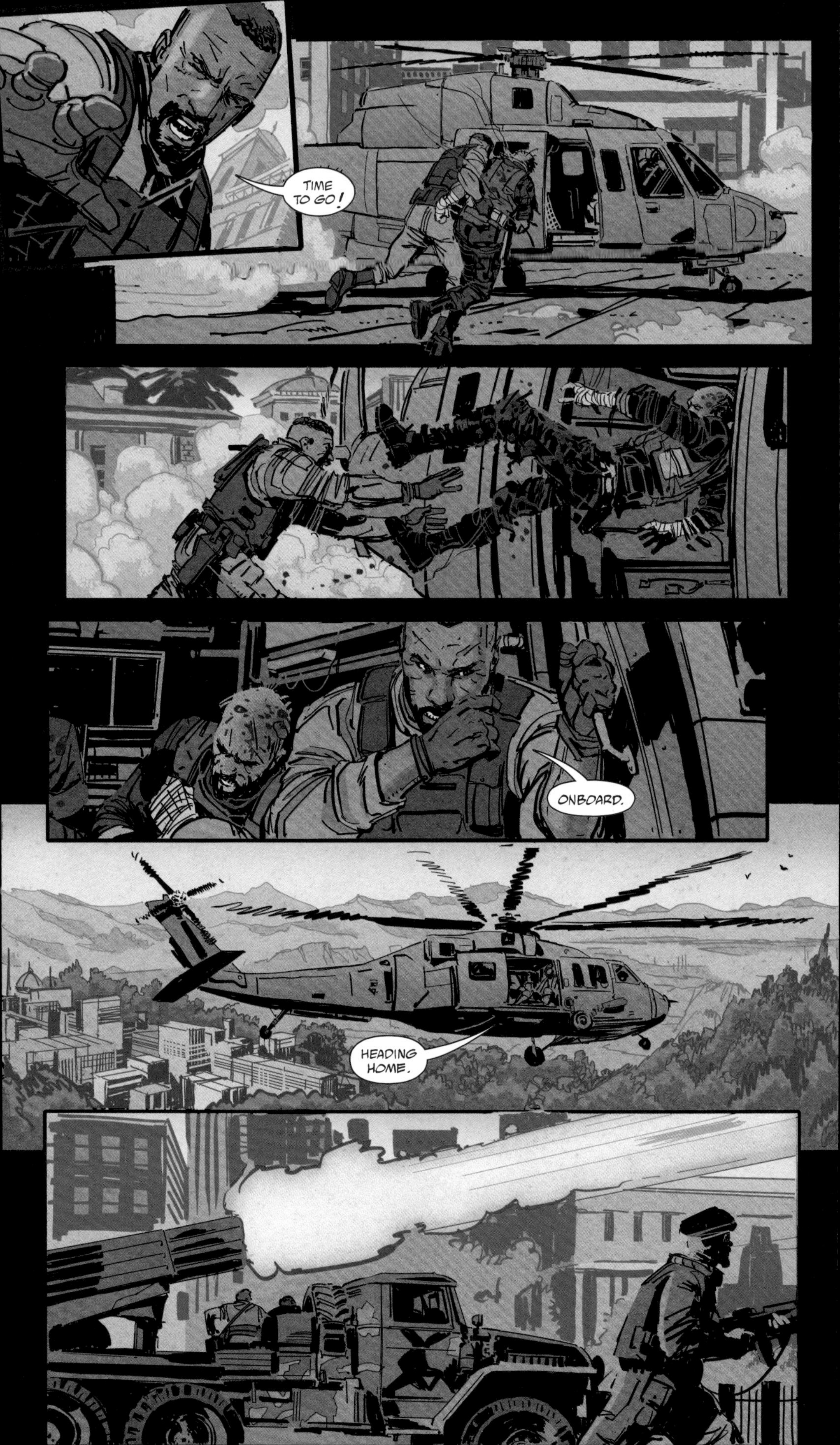
TIME TO GO!
ONBOARD.
HEADING HOME.

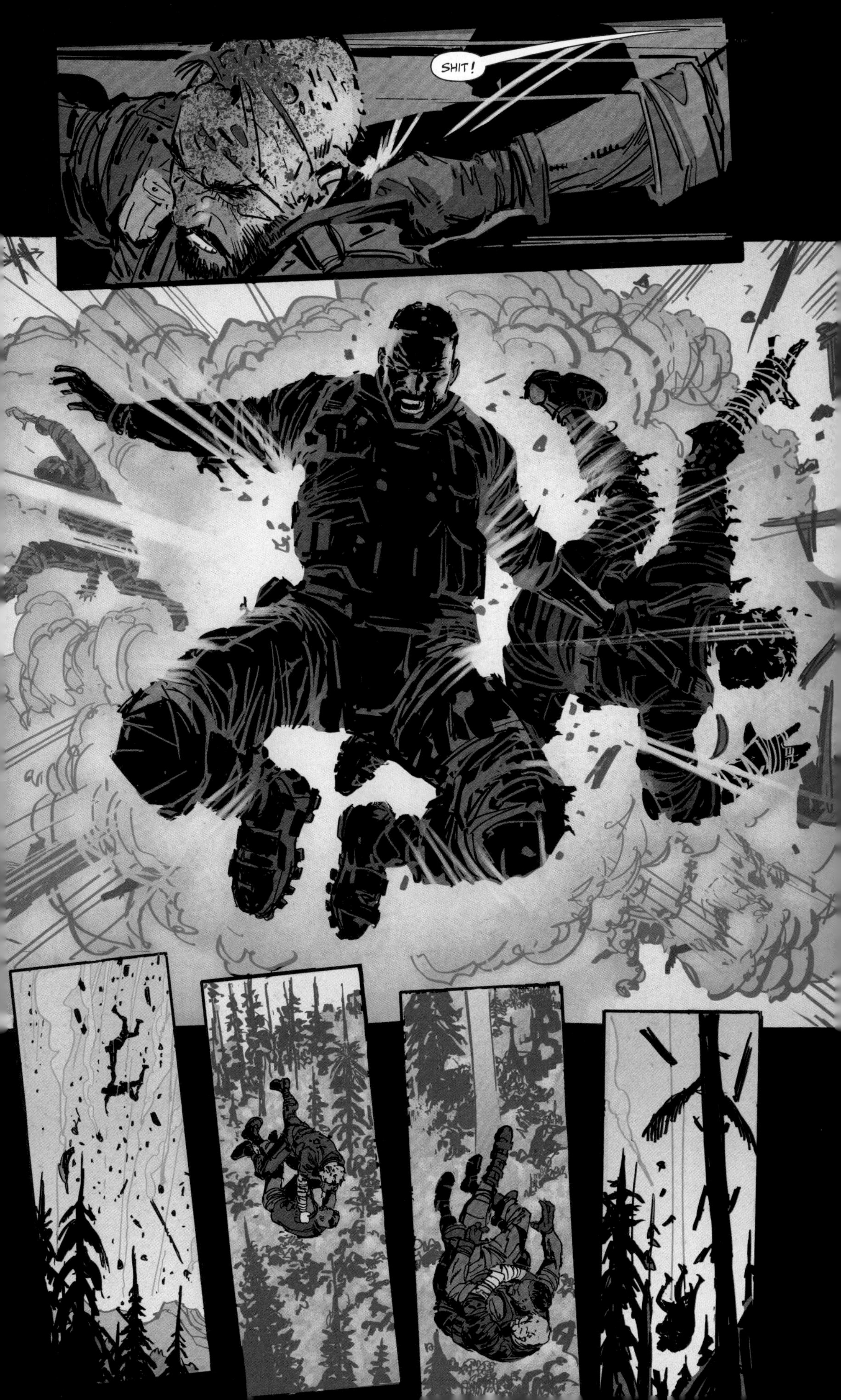
SHIT!

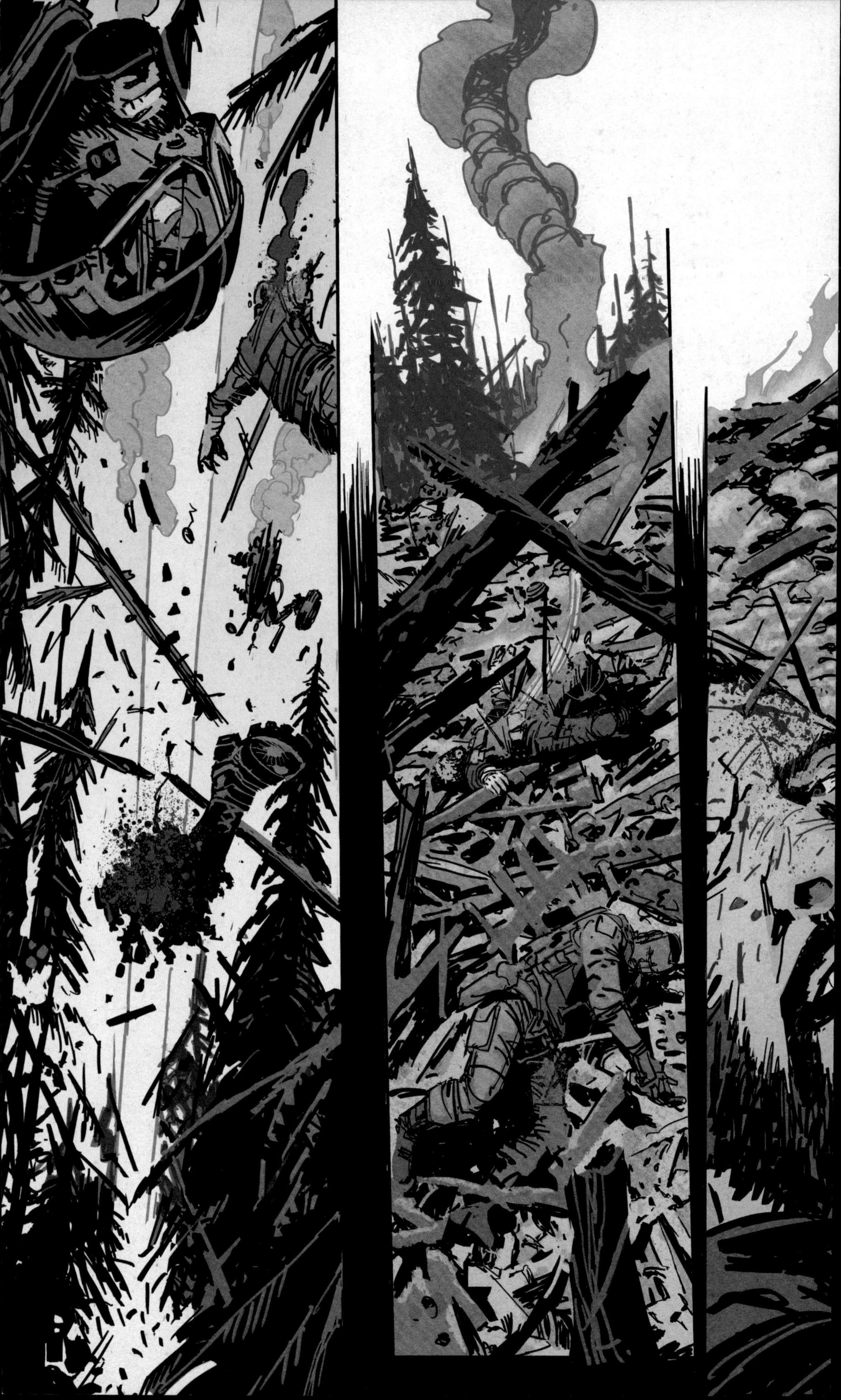

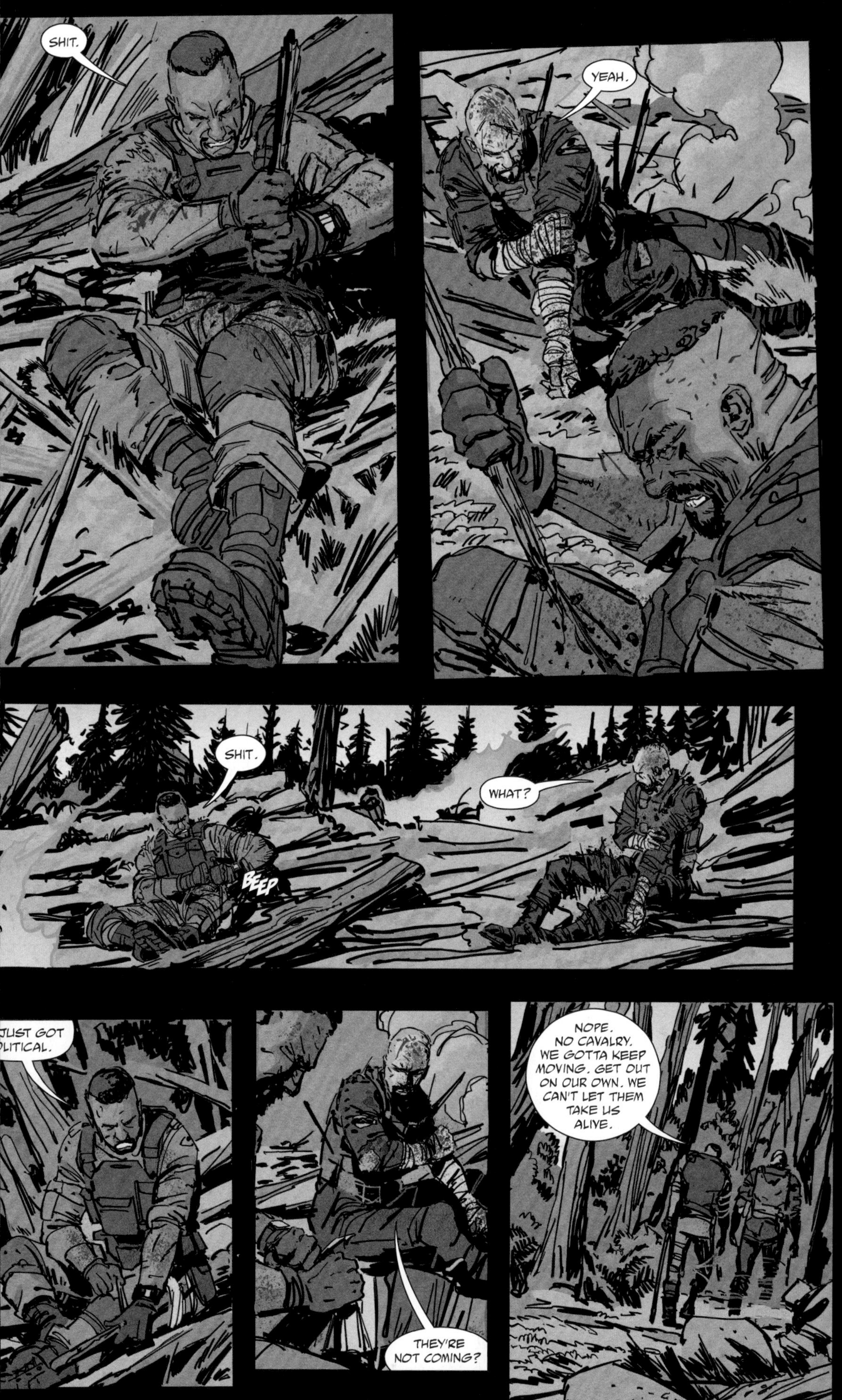
SHIT.
YEAH.
SHIT.
WHAT?
BEEP
JUST GOT
LITICAL.
THEY'RE NOT COMING?
NOPE. NO CAVALRY. WE GOTTA KEEP MOVING. GET OUT ON OUR OWN. WE CAN'T LET THEM TAKE US ALIVE.

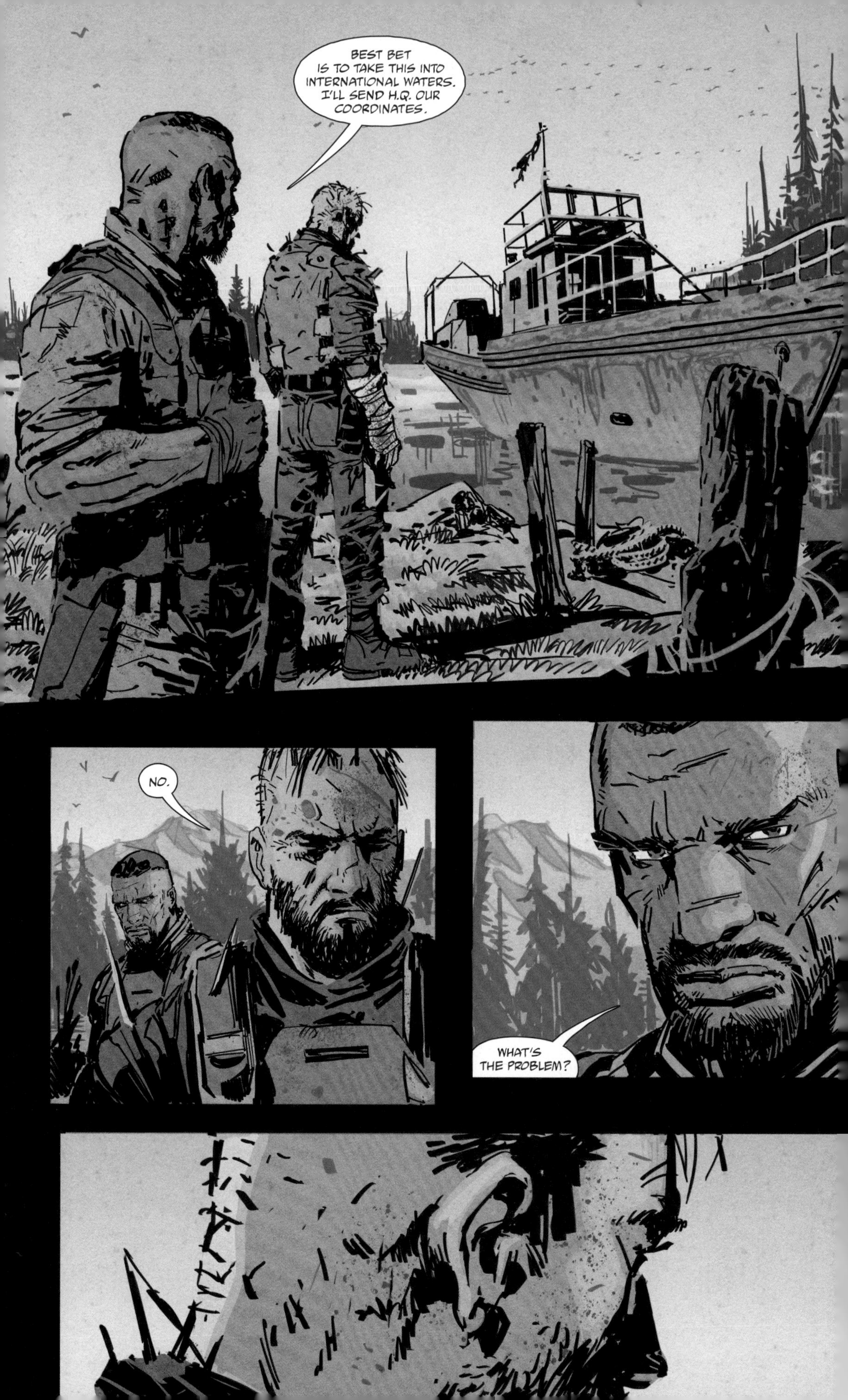
BEST BET IS TO TAKE THIS INTO INTERNATIONAL WATERS. I'LL SEND H.Q. OUR COORDINATES.
NO.
WHAT'S THE PROBLEM?

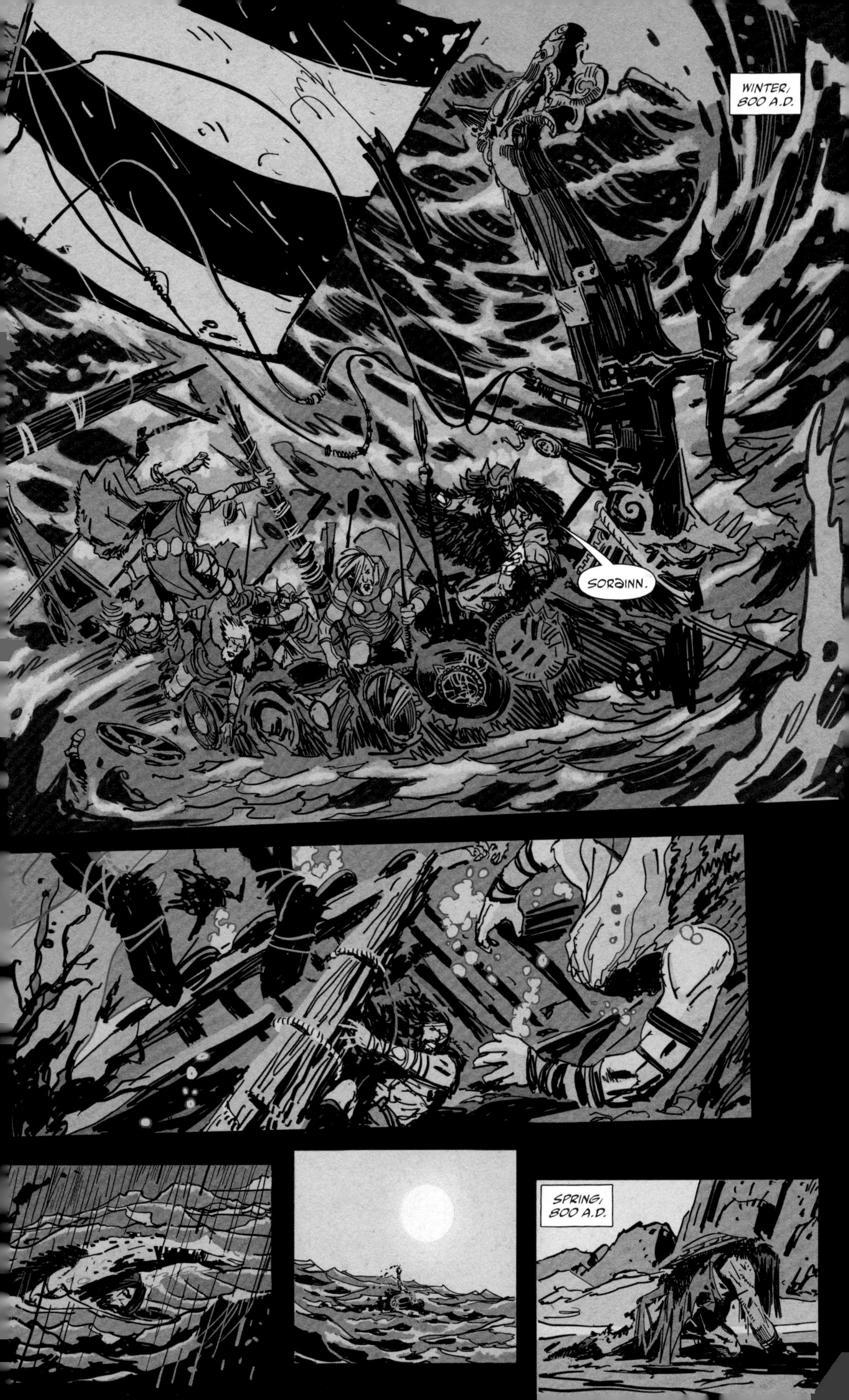
WINTER, 800 A.D.
SORəINN.
SPRING, 800 A.D.

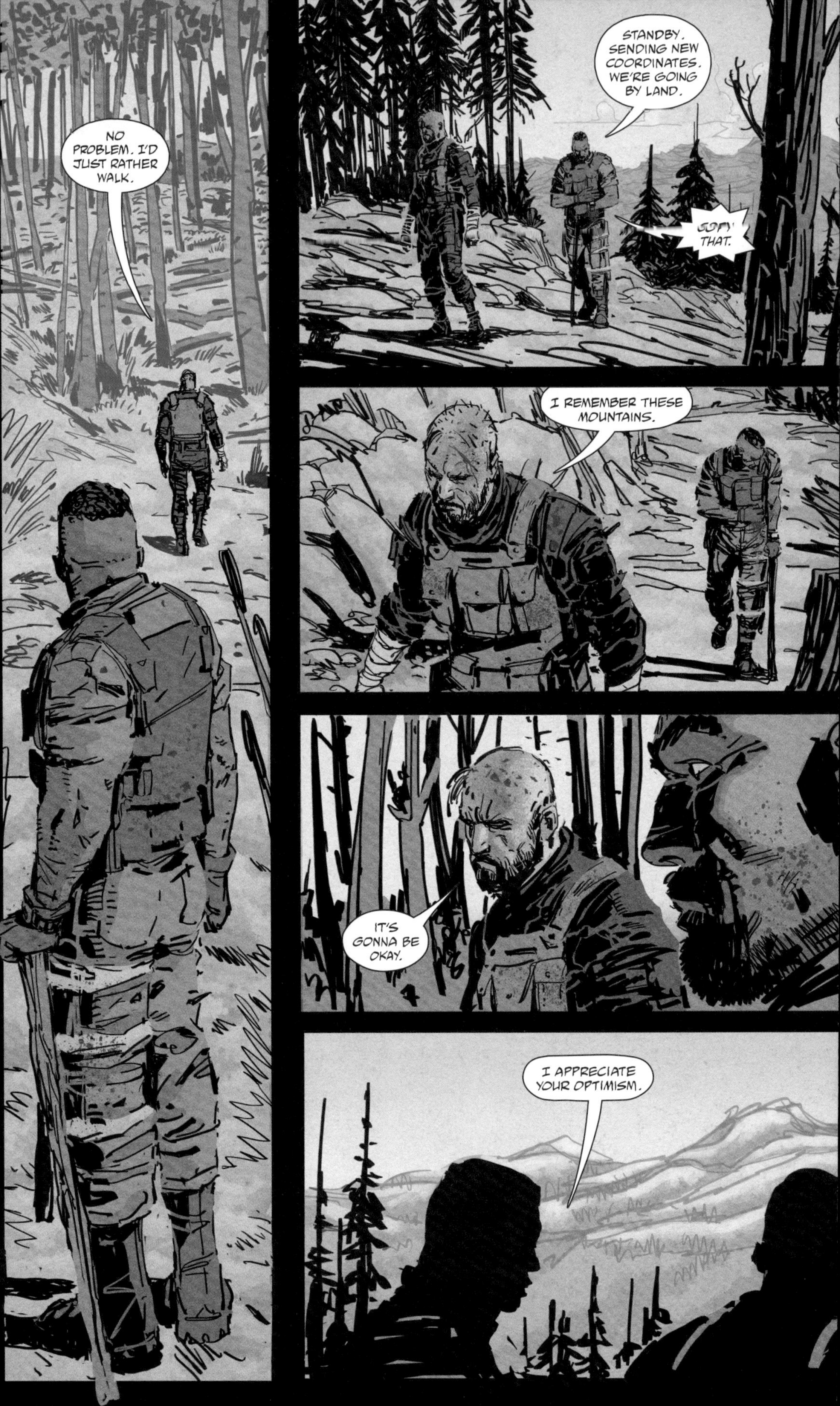
NO PROBLEM. I'D JUST RATHER WALK.
STANDBY. SENDING NEW COORDINATES. WE'RE GOING BY LAND.
THAT.
I REMEMBER THESE MOUNTAINS.
IT'S GONNA BE OKAY.
I APPRECIATE YOUR OPTIMISM.

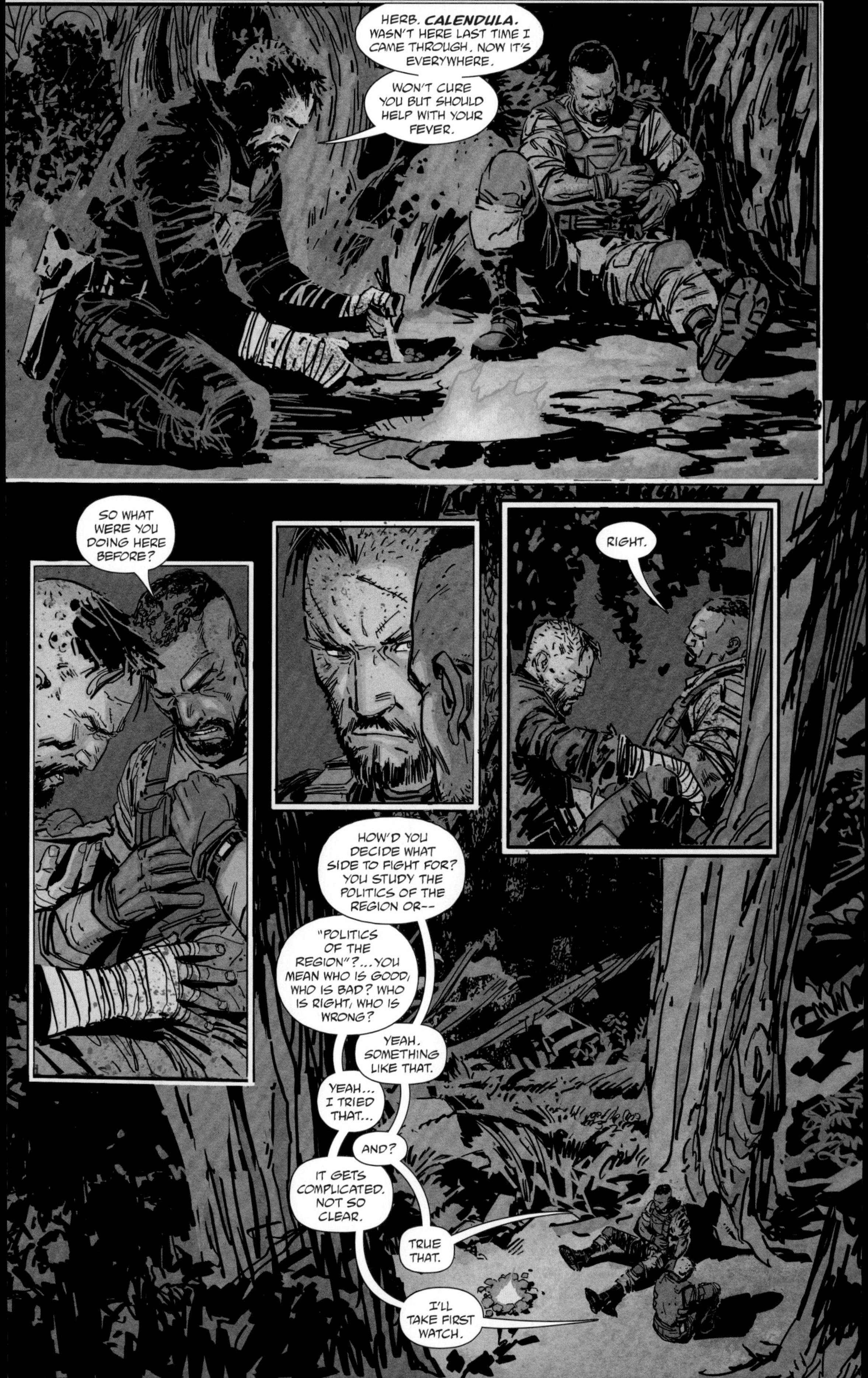
HERB. CALENDULA. WASN'T HERE LAST TIME I CAME THROUGH. NOW IT'S EVERYWHERE.
WON'T CURE YOU BUT SHOULD HELP WITH YOUR FEVER.
SO WHAT WERE YOU DOING HERE BEFORE?
RIGHT.
HOW'D YOU DECIDE WHAT SIDE TO FIGHT FOR? YOU STUDY THE POLITICS OF THE REGION OR--
"POLITICS OF THE REGION"?... YOU MEAN WHO IS GOOD, WHO IS BAD? WHO IS RIGHT, WHO IS WRONG?
YEAH. SOMETHING LIKE THAT.
YEAH... I TRIED THAT...
AND?
IT GETS COMPLICATED. NOT SO CLEAR.
TRUE THAT.
I'LL TAKE FIRST WATCH.

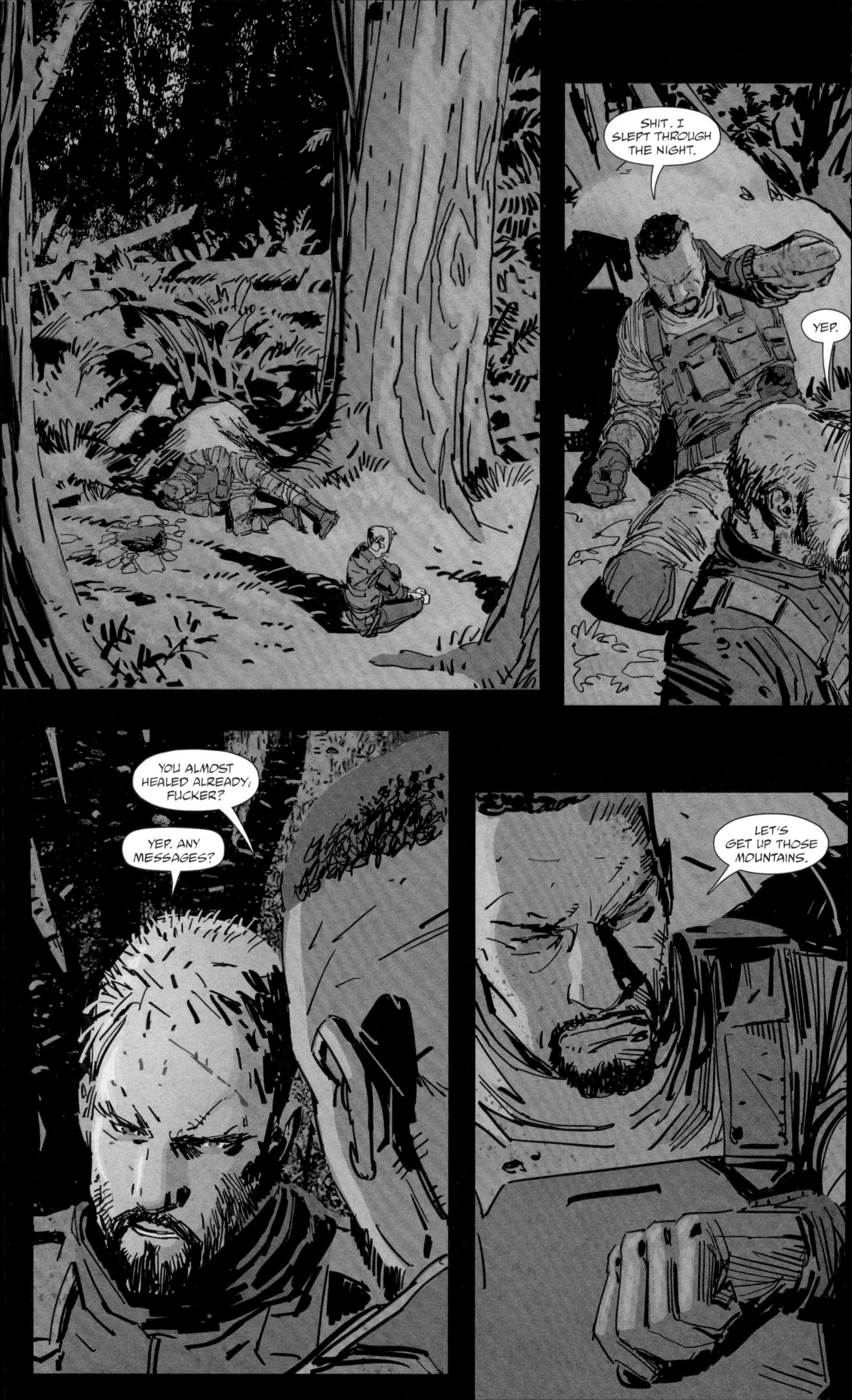
SHIT. I SLEPT THROUGH THE NIGHT.
YEP.
YOU ALMOST HEALED ALREADY, FUCKER?
YEP. ANY MESSAGES?
LET'S GET UP THOSE MOUNTAINS.

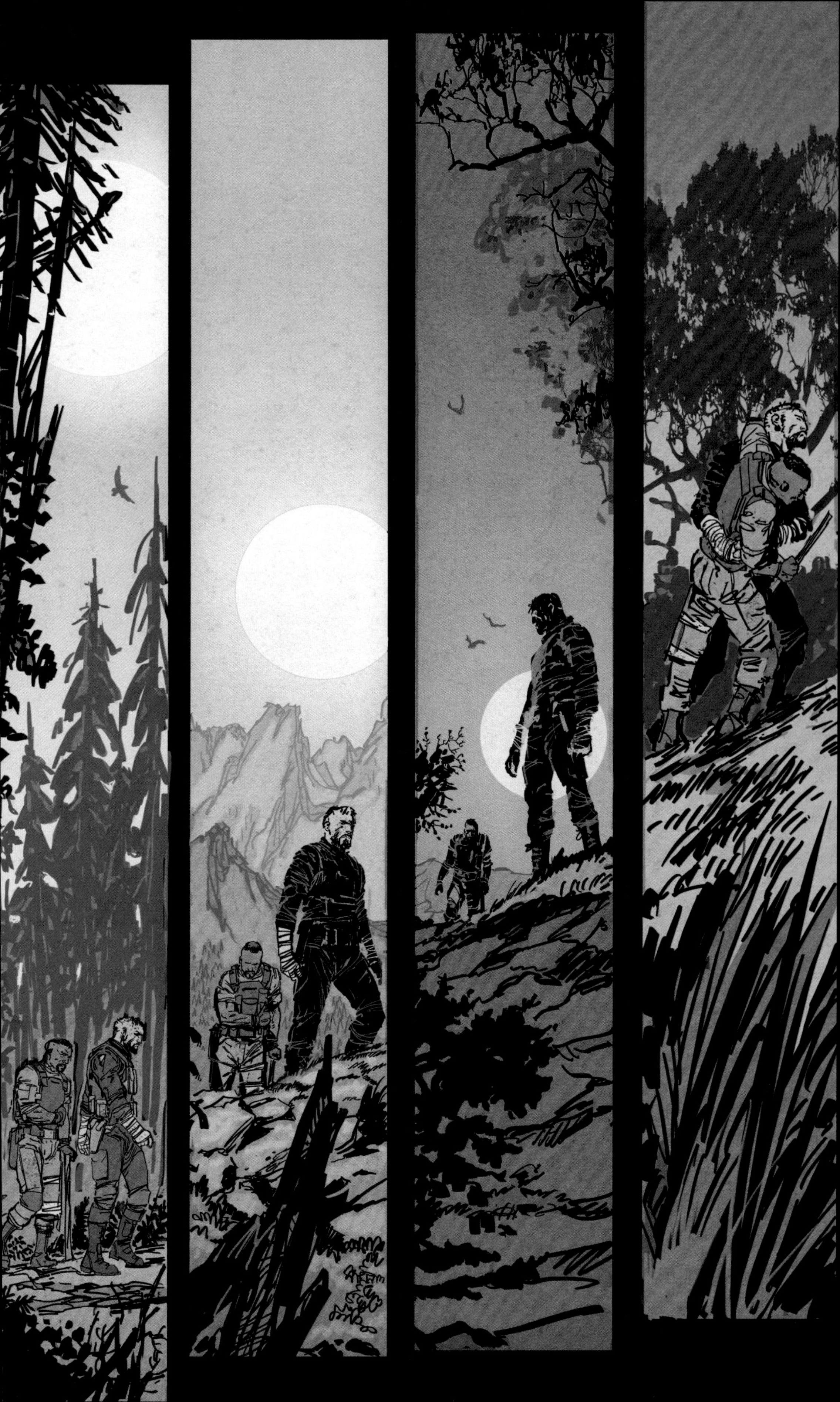

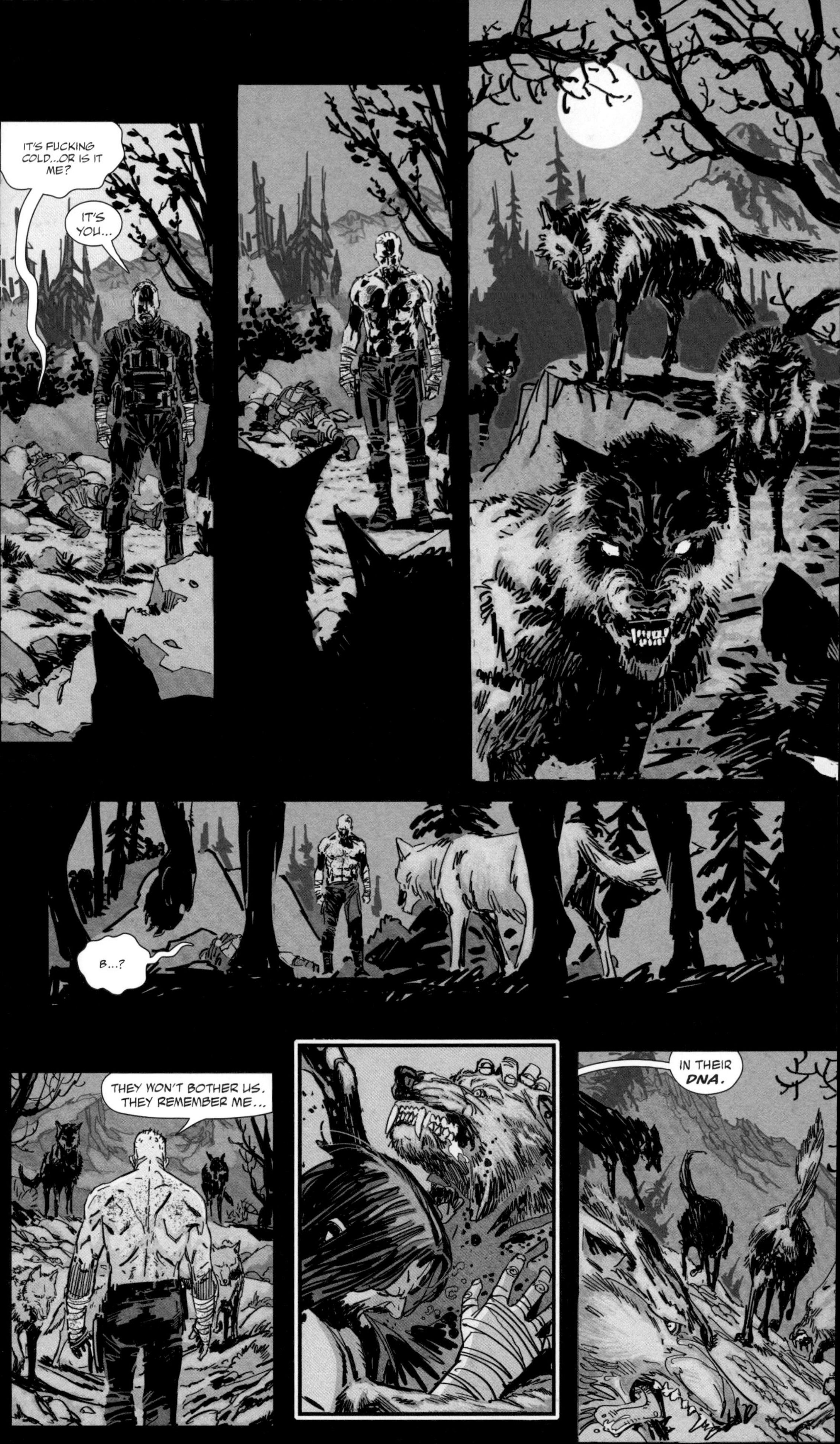
IT'S FUCKING COLD...OR IS IT ME?
IT'S YOU...
B...?
THEY WON'T BOTHER US. THEY REMEMBER ME...
IN THEIR DNA.

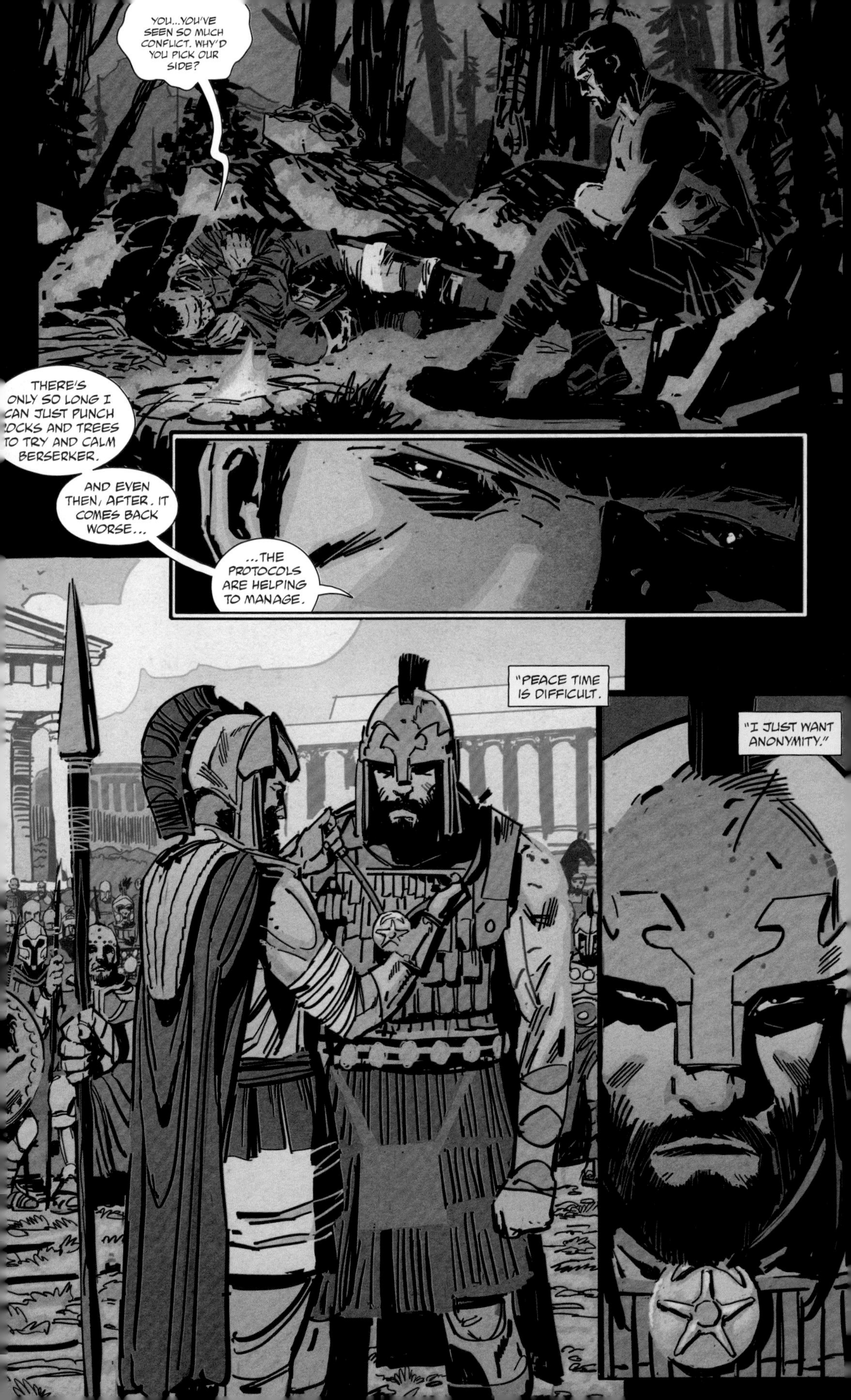
YOU...YOU'VE SEEN SO MUCH CONFLICT. WHY'D YOU PICK OUR SIDE?
THERE'S ONLY SO LONG I CAN JUST PUNCH ROCKS AND TREES TO TRY AND CALM BERSERKER.
AND EVEN THEN, AFTER. IT COMES BACK WORSE...
...THE PROTOCOLS ARE HELPING TO MANAGE.
"PEACE TIME IS DIFFICULT.
"I JUST WANT ANONYMITY."

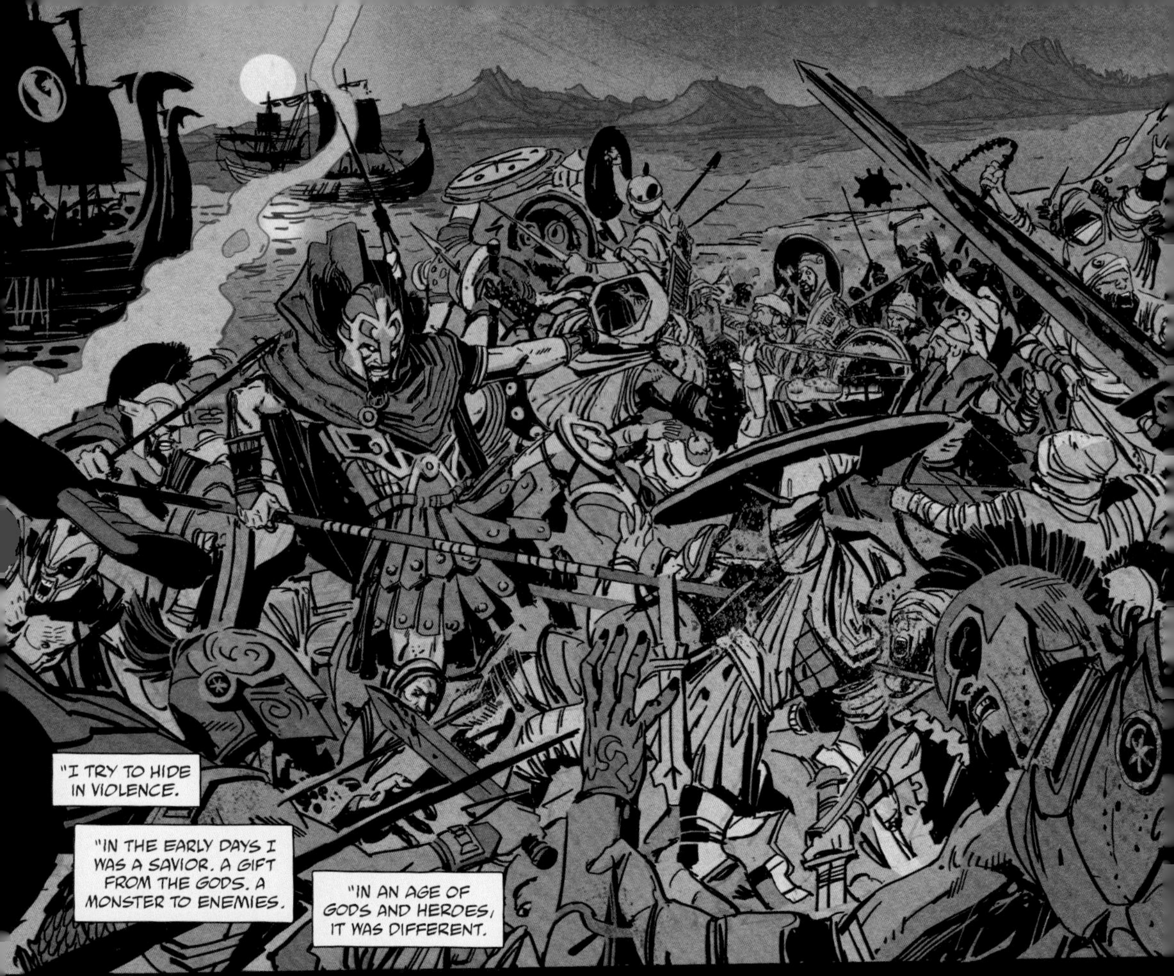
"I TRY TO HIDE IN VIOLENCE.
"IN THE EARLY DAYS I WAS A SAVIOR. A GIFT FROM THE GODS. A MONSTER TO ENEMIES.
"IN AN AGE OF GODS AND HEROES, IT WAS DIFFERENT.

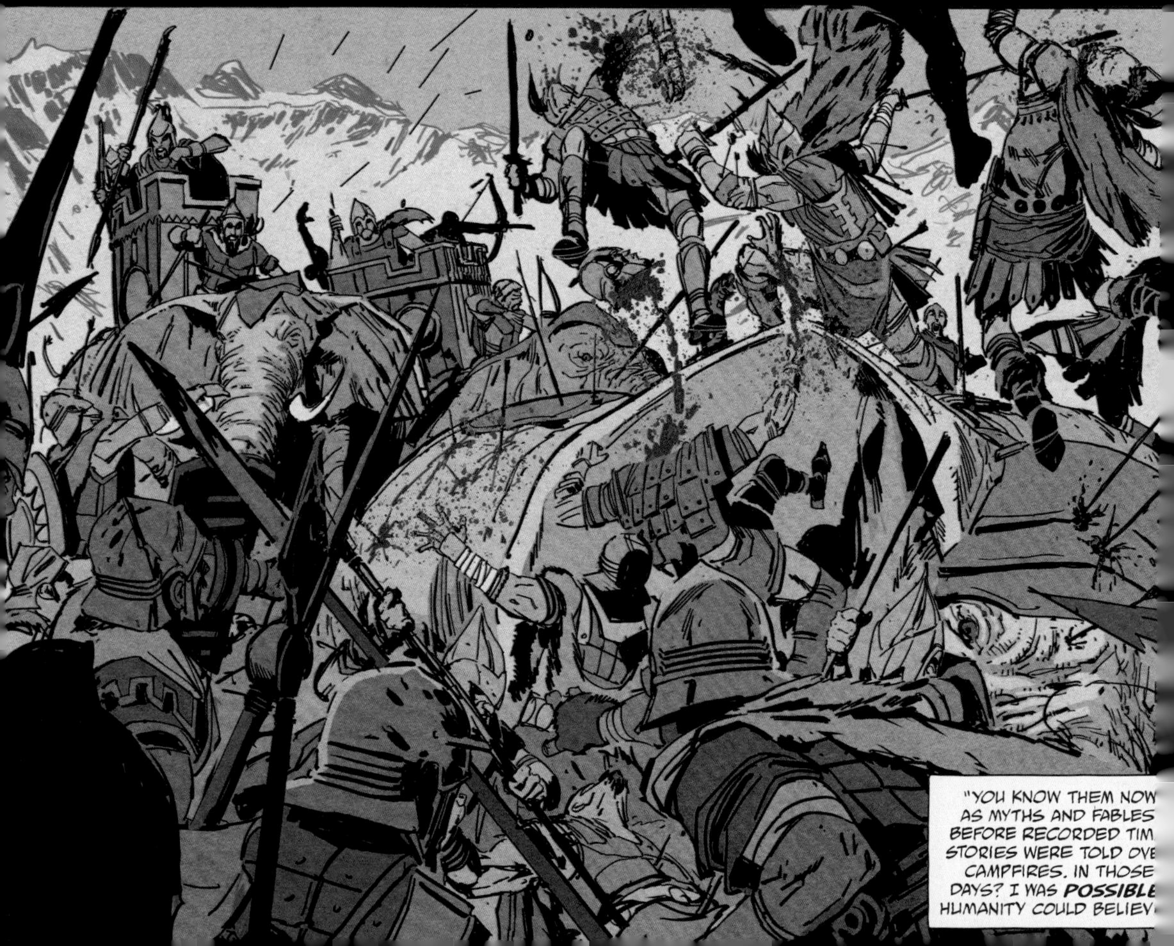
"YOU KNOW THEM NOW AS MYTHS AND FABLES. BEFORE RECORDED TIM STORIES WERE TOLD OVE CAMPFIRES. IN THOSE DAYS? I WAS POSSIBLE HUMANITY COULD BELIEV

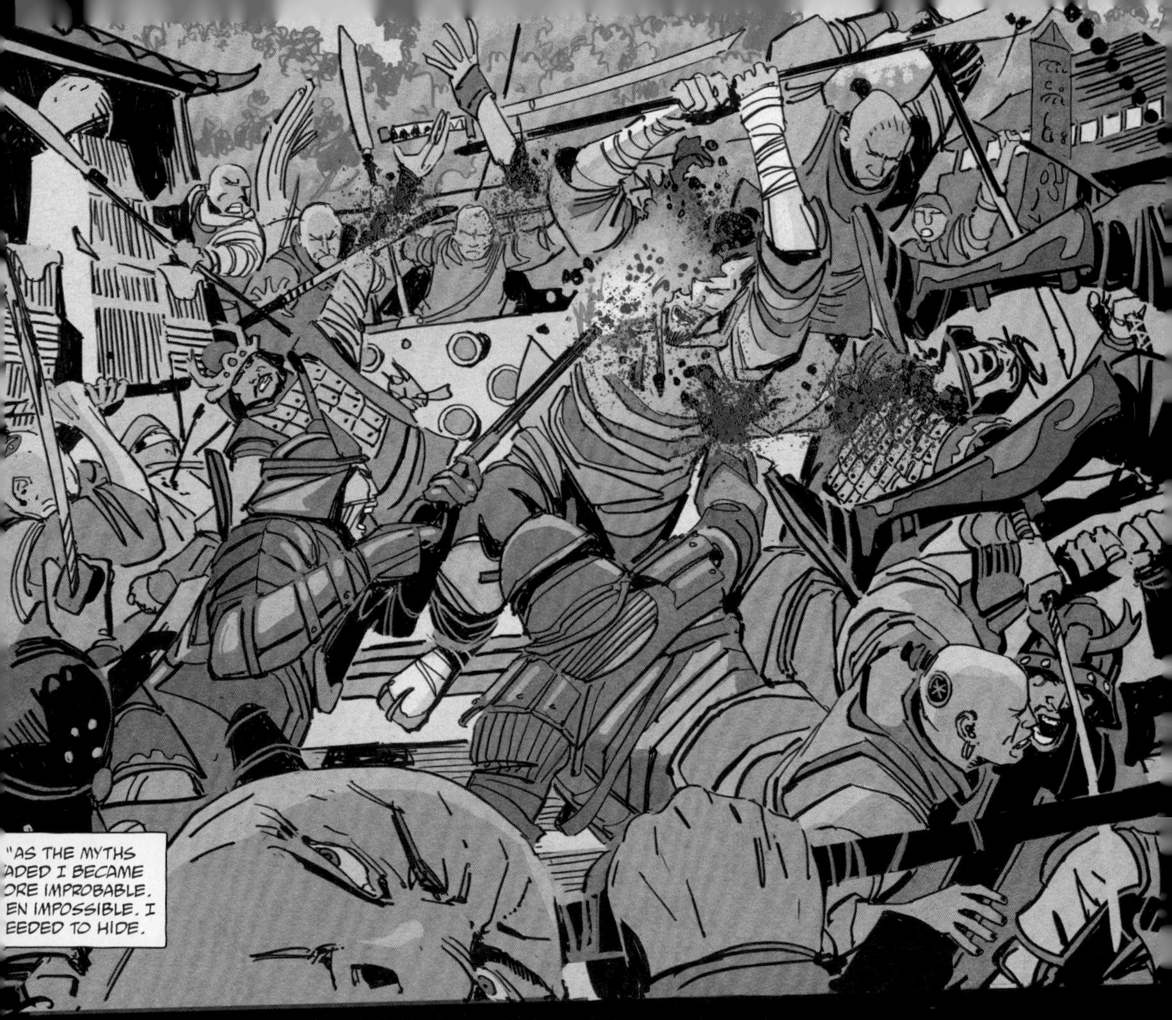
"AS THE MYTHS
ADED I BECAME
ORE IMPROBABLE.
EN IMPOSSIBLE. I
EEDED TO HIDE.

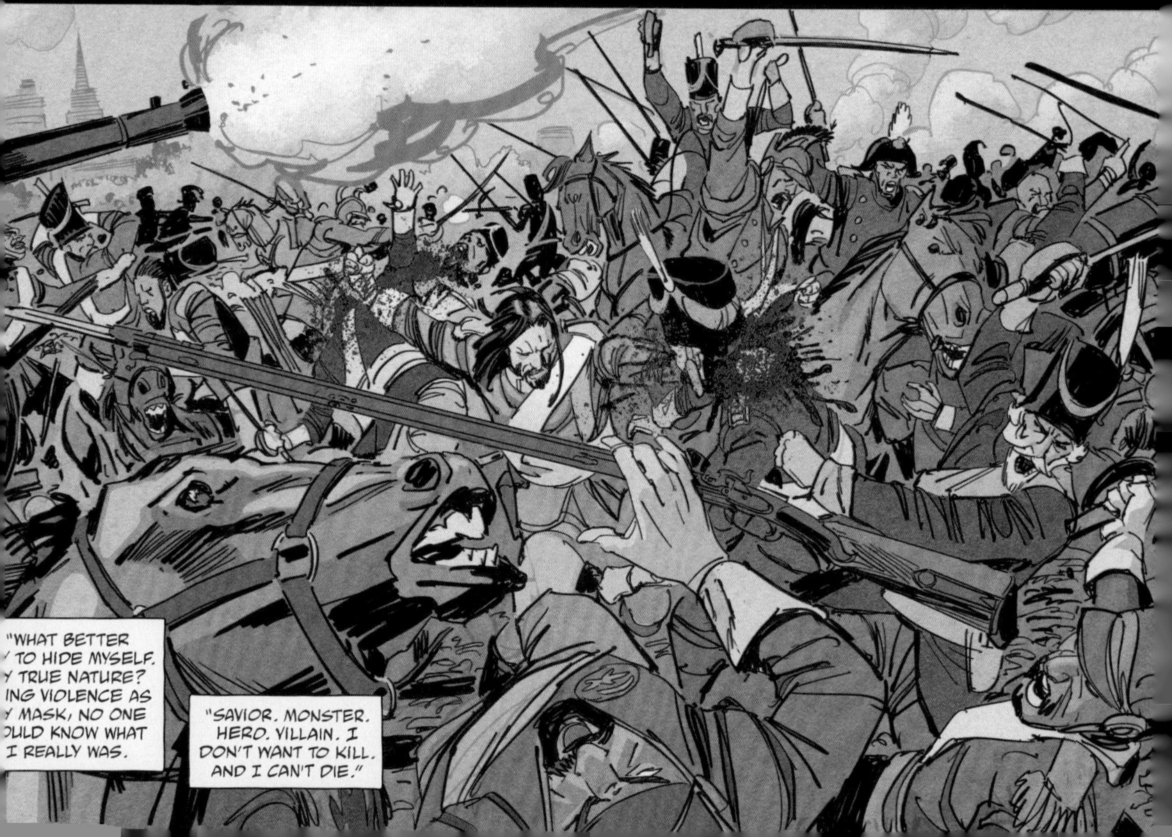
"WHAT BETTER
TO HIDE MYSELF.
TRUE NATURE?
ING VIOLENCE AS
MASK, NO ONE
OULD KNOW WHAT
I REALLY WAS.
"SAVIOR. MONSTER. HERO. VILLAIN. I DON'T WANT TO KILL. AND I CAN'T DIE."

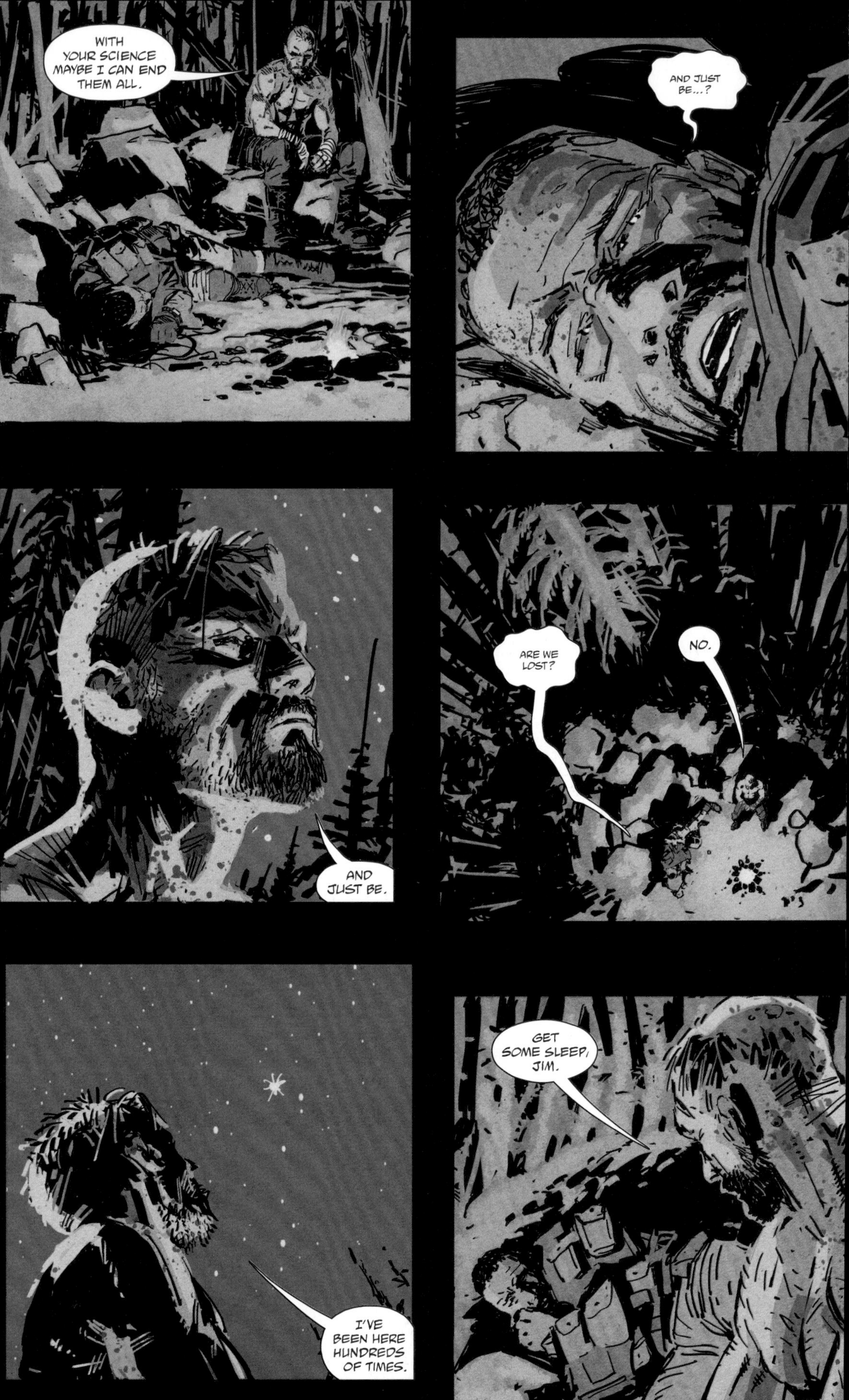
WITH YOUR SCIENCE MAYBE I CAN END THEM ALL.
AND JUST BE...?
AND JUST BE.
ARE WE LOST?
NO.
I'VE BEEN HERE HUNDREDS OF TIMES.
GET SOME SLEEP, JIM.

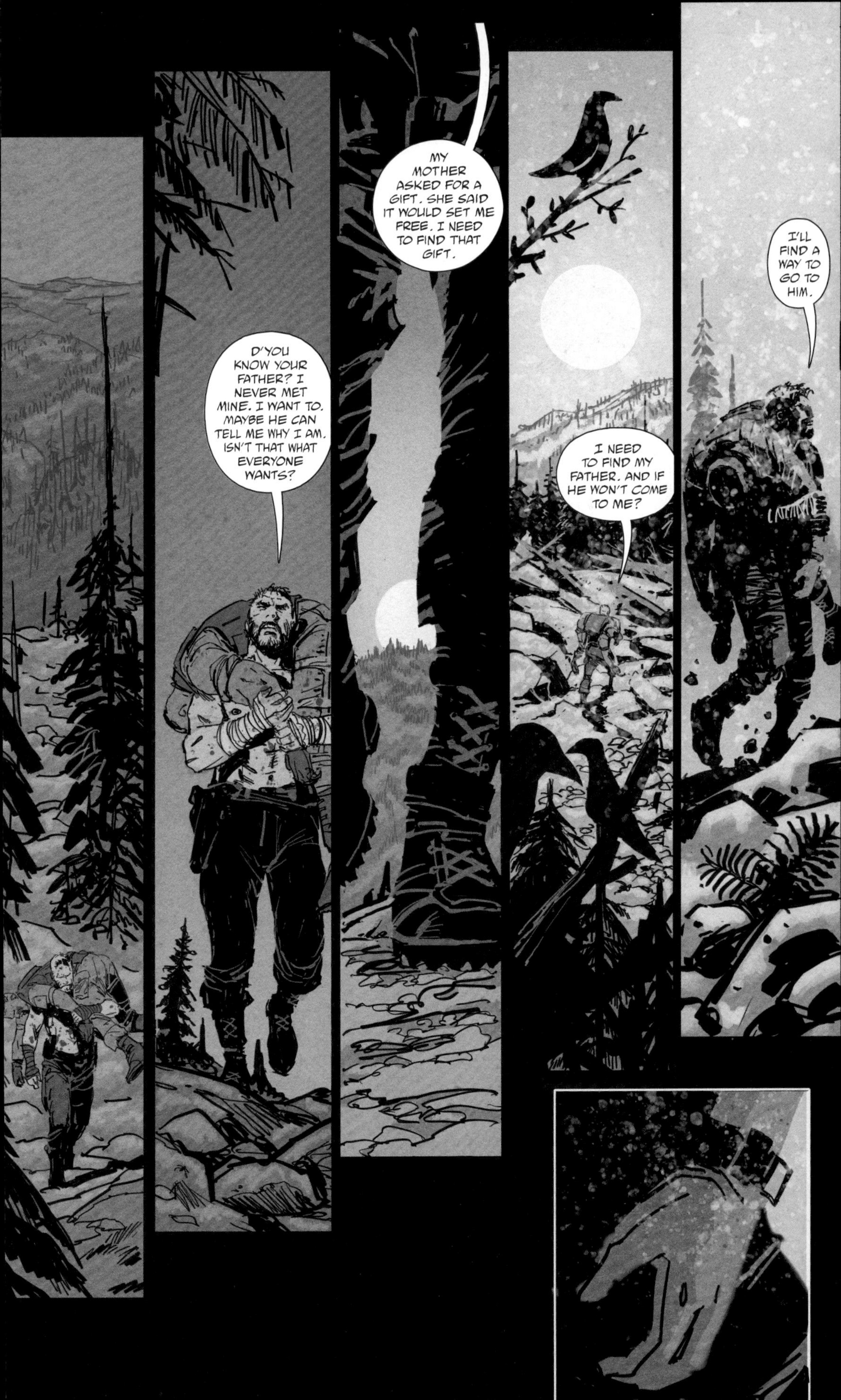
D'YOU KNOW YOUR FATHER? I NEVER MET MINE. I WANT TO. MAYBE HE CAN TELL ME WHY I AM. ISN'T THAT WHAT EVERYONE WANTS?
MY MOTHER ASKED FOR A GIFT. SHE SAID IT WOULD SET ME FREE. I NEED TO FIND THAT GIFT.
I NEED TO FIND MY FATHER. AND IF HE WON'T COME TO ME?
I'LL FIND A WAY TO GO TO HIM.

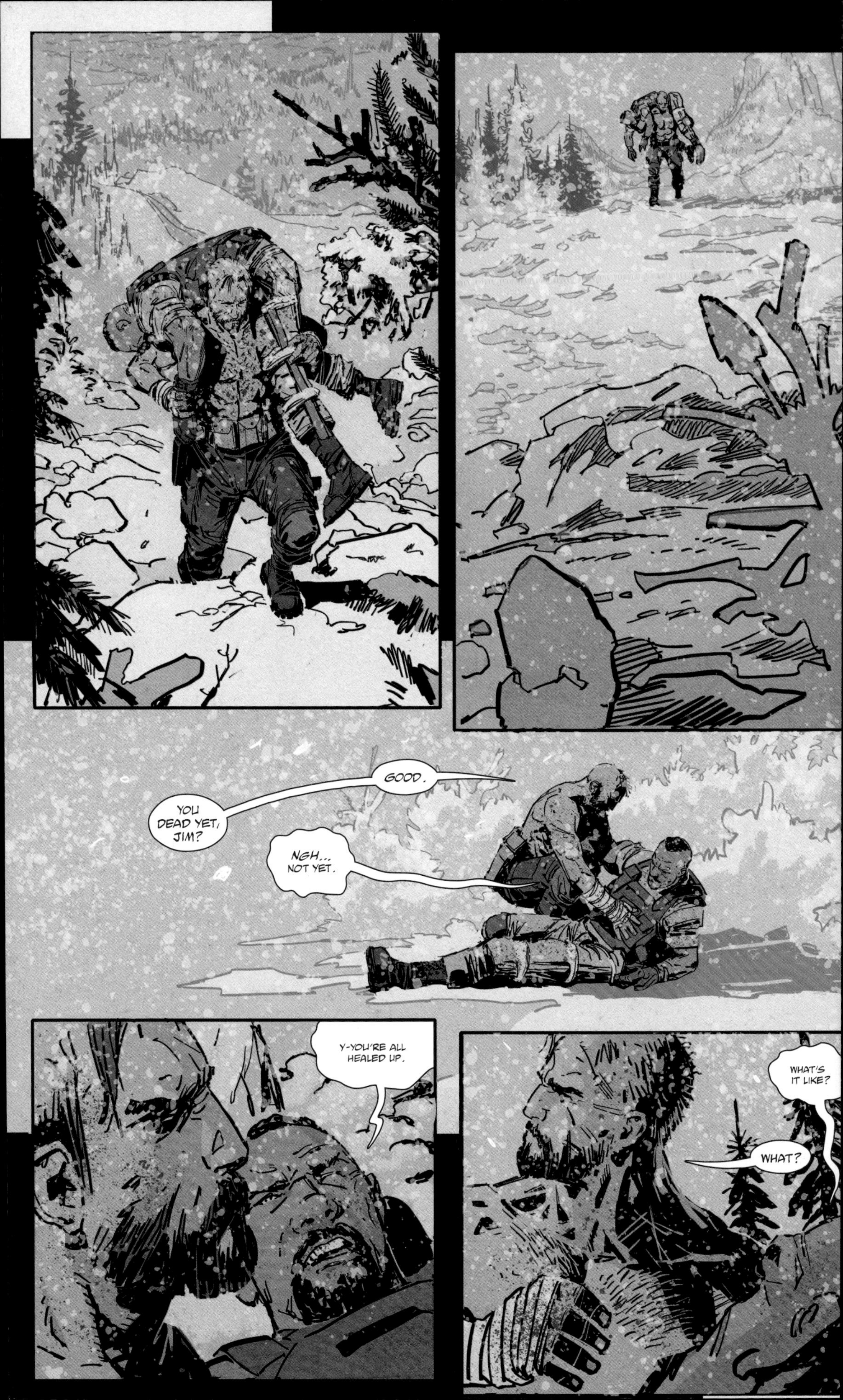

YOU DEAD YET, JIM?
GOOD.
NGH... NOT YET.
Y-YOU'RE ALL HEALED UP.
WHAT'S IT LIKE?
WHAT?

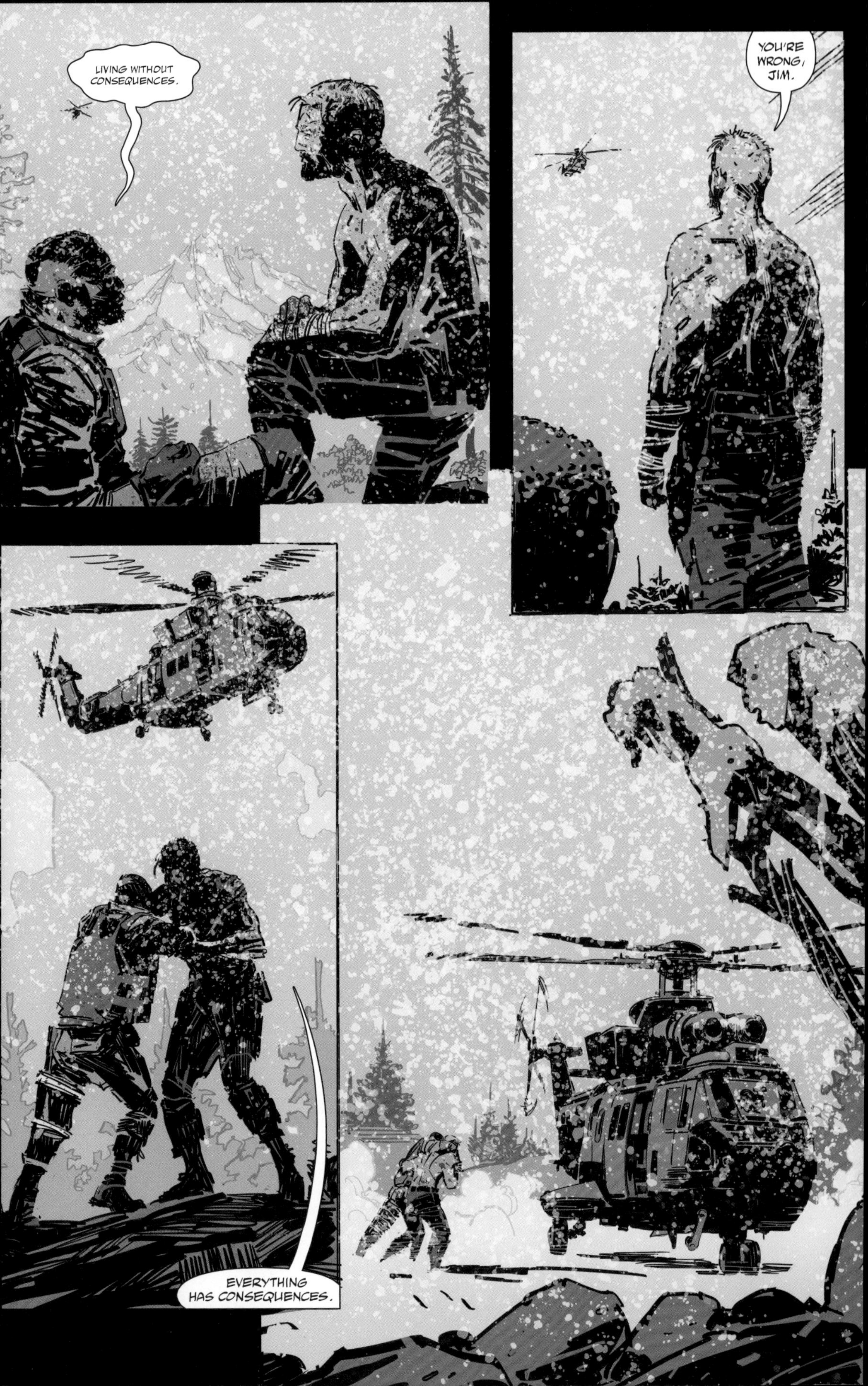
LIVING WITHOUT CONSEQUENCES.
YOU'RE WRONG, JIM.
EVERYTHING HAS CONSEQUENCES.

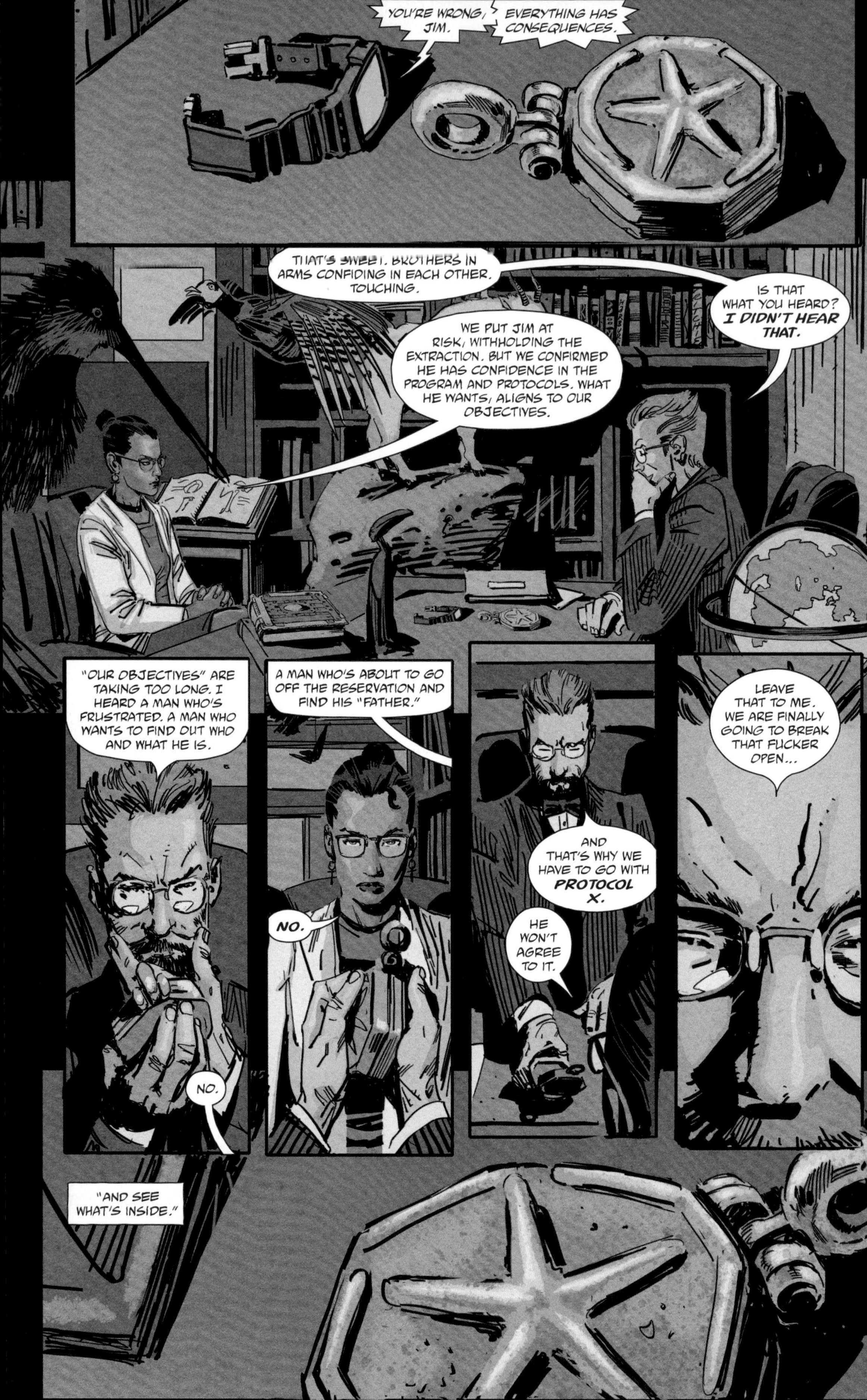

YOU'RE WRONG, JIM.
EVERYTHING HAS CONSEQUENCES.
THAT'S SWEET. BROTHERS IN ARMS CONFIDING IN EACH OTHER. TOUCHING.
WE PUT JIM AT RISK, WITHHOLDING THE EXTRACTION. BUT WE CONFIRMED HE HAS CONFIDENCE IN THE PROGRAM AND PROTOCOLS. WHAT HE WANTS, ALIGNS TO OUR OBJECTIVES.
IS THAT WHAT YOU HEARD? I DIDN'T HEAR THAT.
"OUR OBJECTIVES" ARE TAKING TOO LONG. I HEARD A MAN WHO'S FRUSTRATED. A MAN WHO WANTS TO FIND OUT WHO AND WHAT HE IS.
NO.
A MAN WHO'S ABOUT TO GO OFF THE RESERVATION AND FIND HIS "FATHER."
NO.
AND THAT'S WHY WE HAVE TO GO WITH PROTOCOL X.
HE WON'T AGREE TO IT.
LEAVE THAT TO ME. WE ARE FINALLY GOING TO BREAK THAT FUCKER OPEN...
"AND SEE WHAT'S INSIDE."

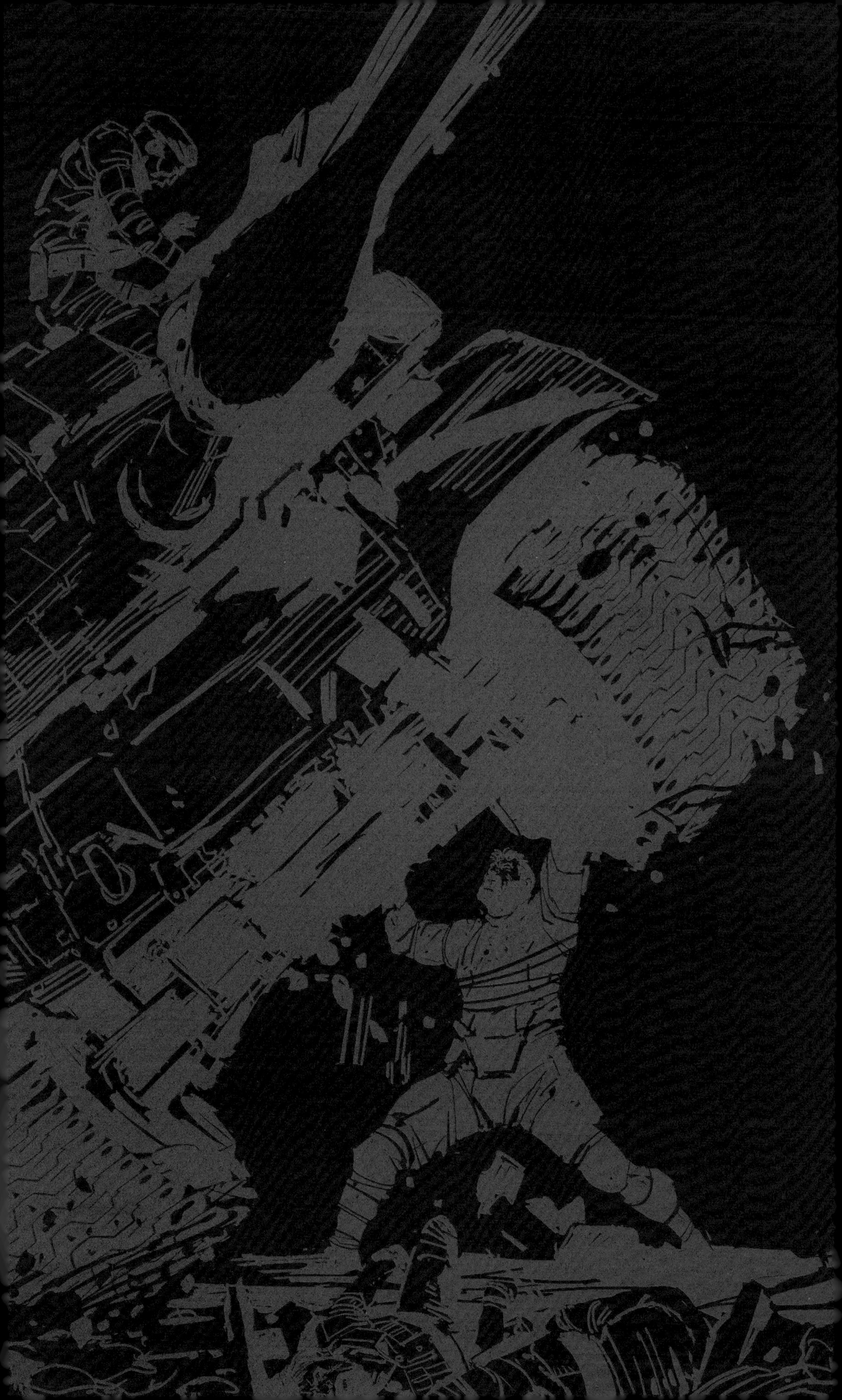

CHAPTER
SEVEN

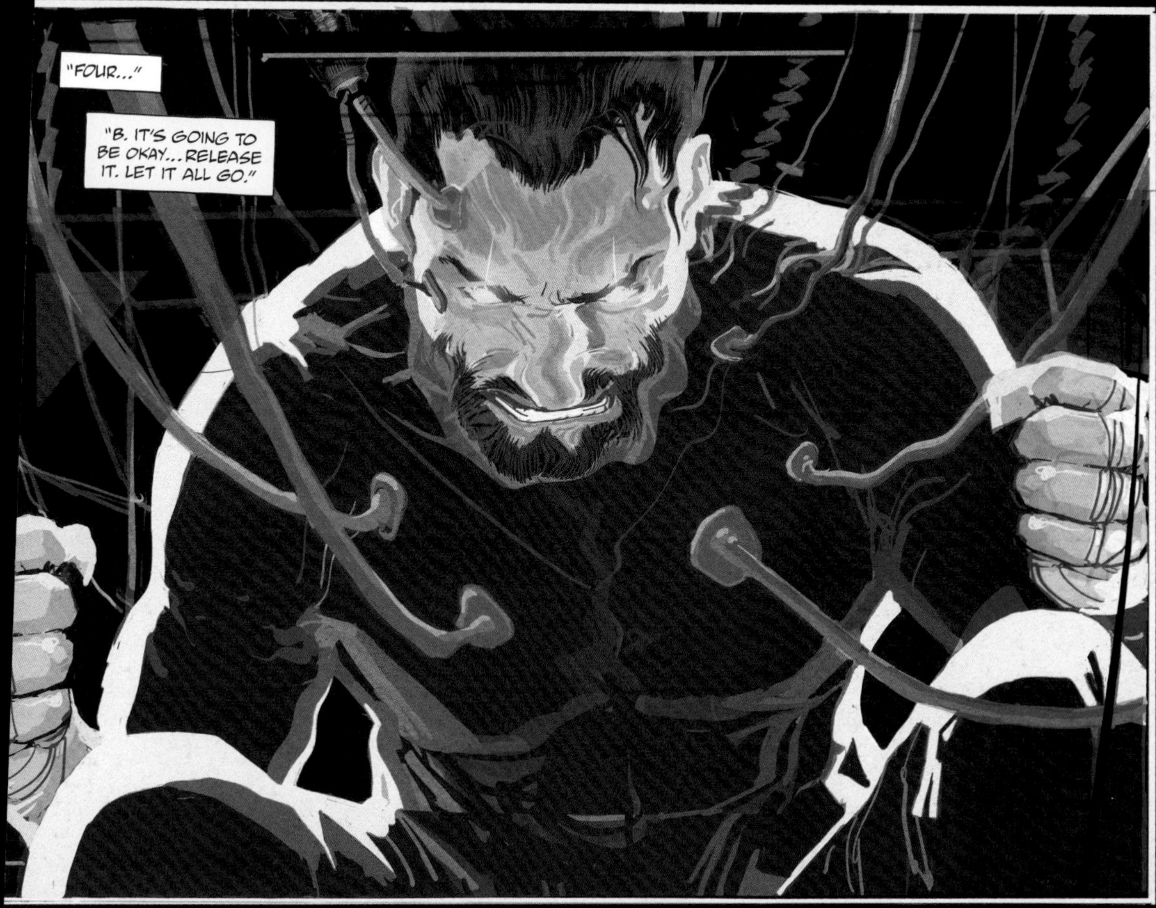
"FOUR..."
"B. IT'S GOING TO BE OKAY... RELEASE IT. LET IT ALL GO."

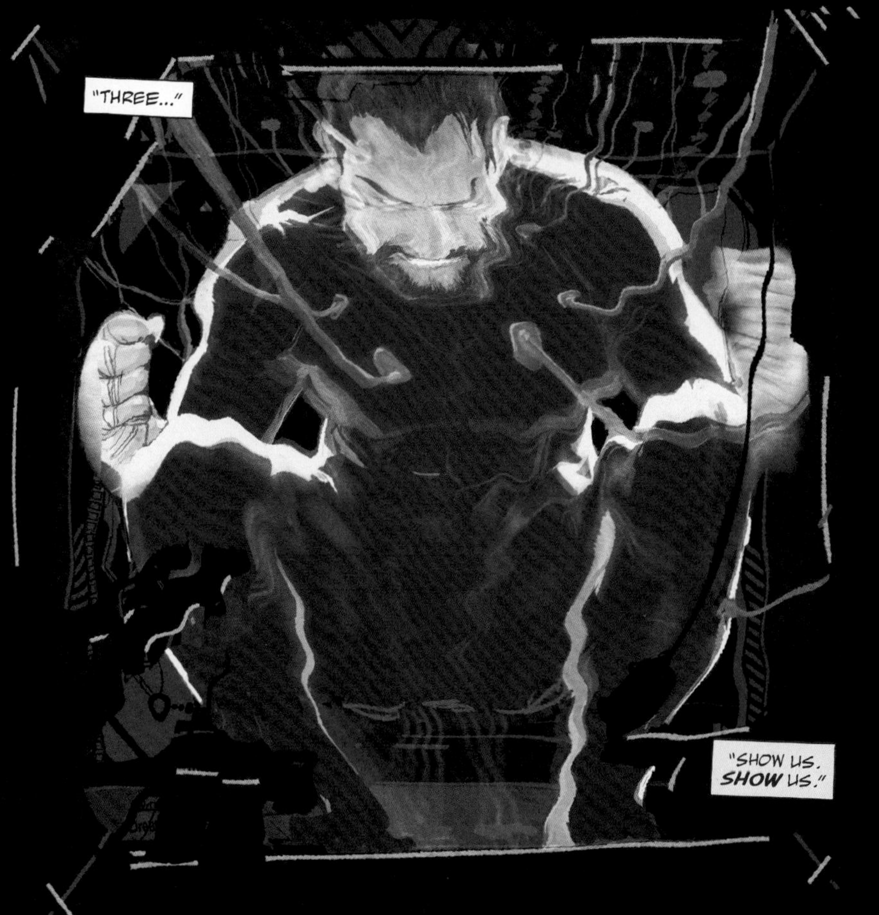
"THREE..."
"SHOW US. **SHOW** US."

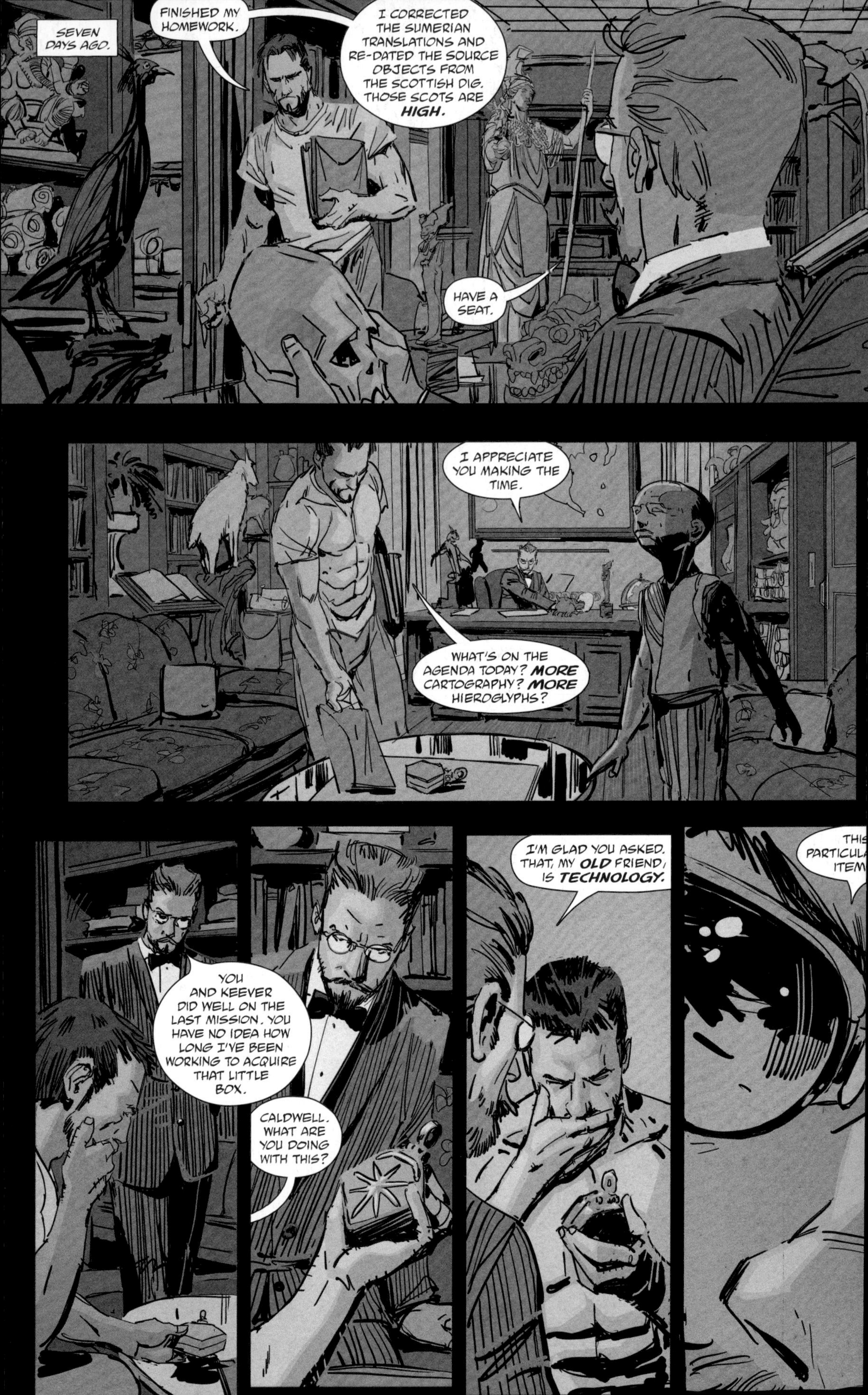
SEVEN DAYS AGO.
FINISHED MY HOMEWORK.
I CORRECTED THE SUMERIAN TRANSLATIONS AND RE-DATED THE SOURCE OBJECTS FROM THE SCOTTISH DIG. THOSE SCOTS ARE **HIGH.**
HAVE A SEAT.
I APPRECIATE YOU MAKING THE TIME.
WHAT'S ON THE AGENDA TODAY? **MORE** CARTOGRAPHY? **MORE** HIEROGLYPHS?
YOU AND KEEVER DID WELL ON THE LAST MISSION. YOU HAVE NO IDEA HOW LONG I'VE BEEN WORKING TO ACQUIRE THAT LITTLE BOX.
CALDWELL. WHAT ARE YOU DOING WITH THIS?
I'M GLAD YOU ASKED. THAT, MY **OLD** FRIEND, IS **TECHNOLOGY.**

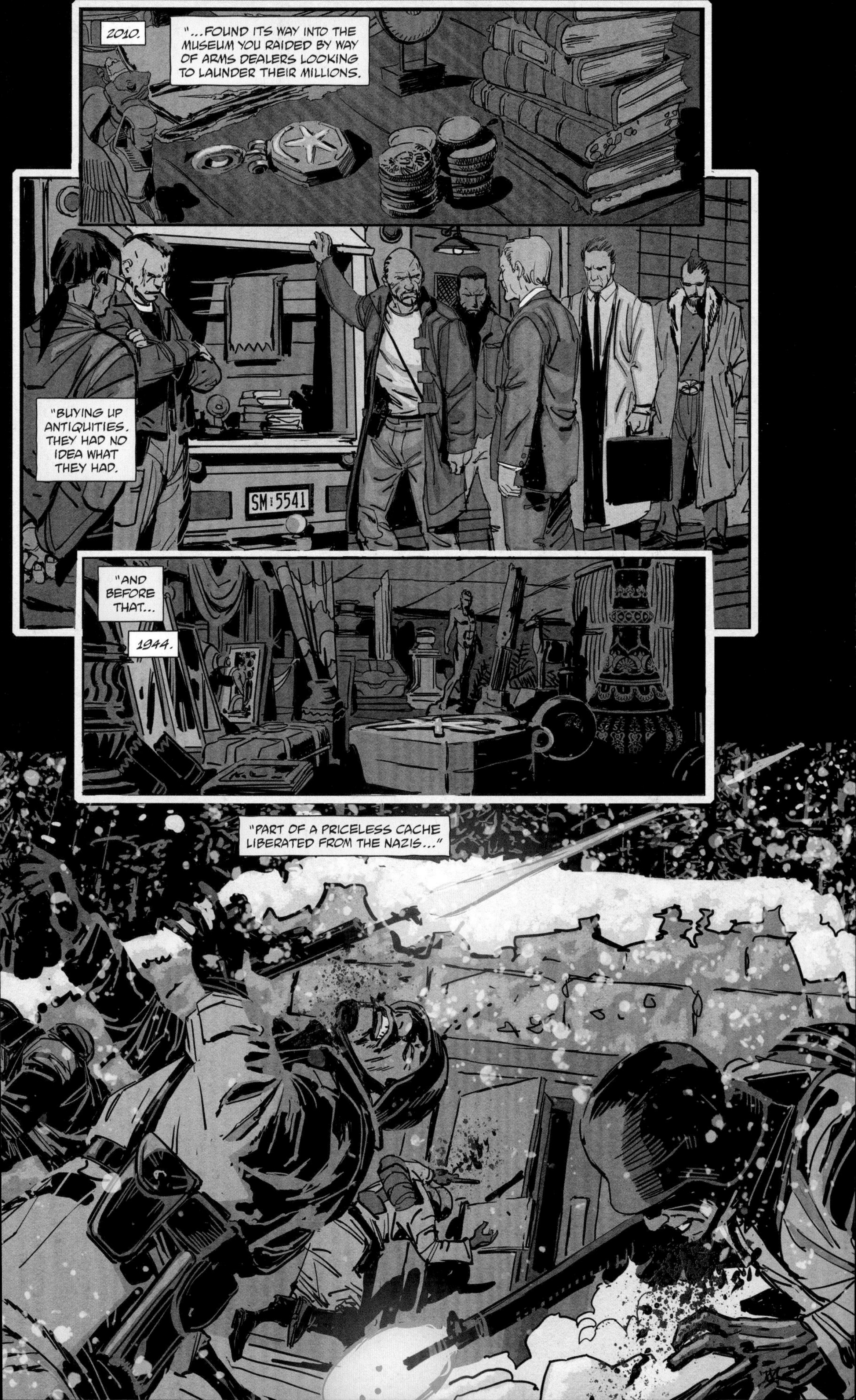
2010.
"...FOUND ITS WAY INTO THE MUSEUM YOU RAIDED BY WAY OF ARMS DEALERS LOOKING TO LAUNDER THEIR MILLIONS.
"BUYING UP ANTIQUITIES. THEY HAD NO IDEA WHAT THEY HAD.
SM 5541
"AND BEFORE THAT...
1944.
"PART OF A PRICELESS CACHE LIBERATED FROM THE NAZIS..."

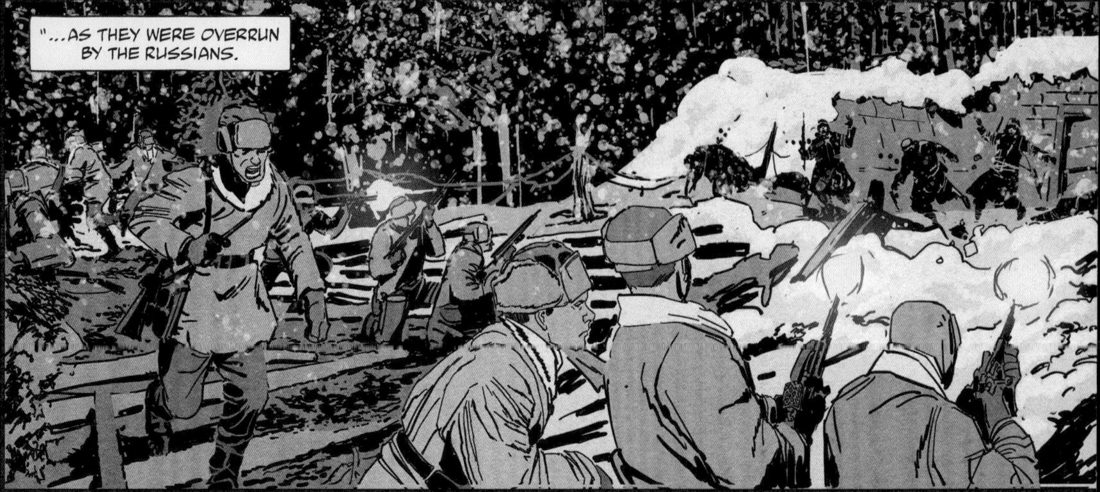
"...AS THEY WERE OVERRUN BY THE RUSSIANS.

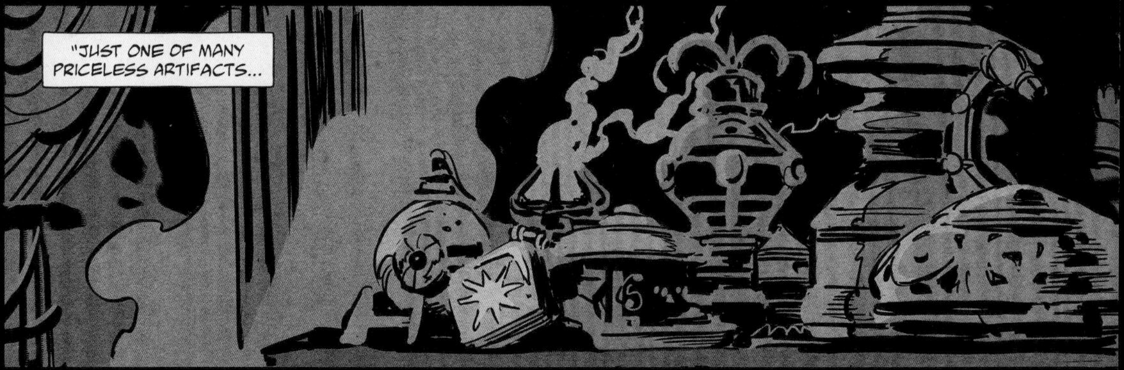
"JUST ONE OF MANY PRICELESS ARTIFACTS...

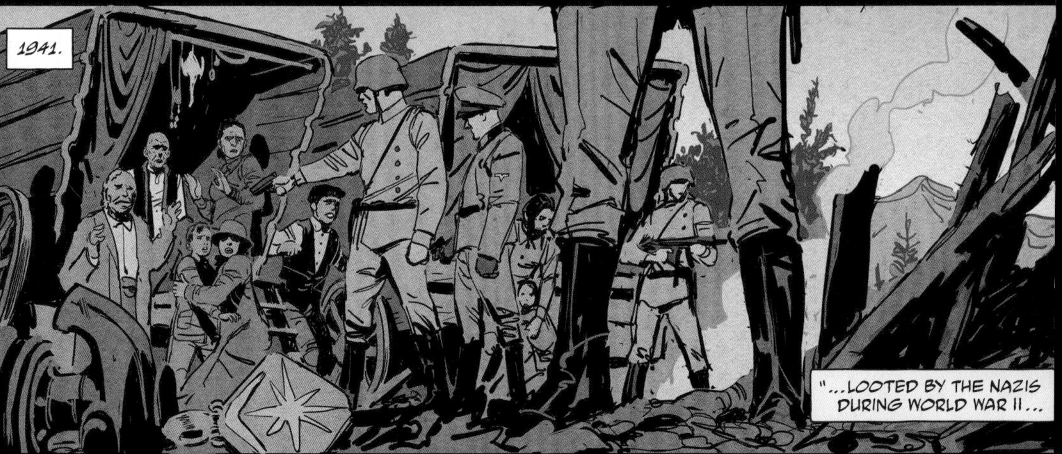
1941.
"...LOOTED BY THE NAZIS DURING WORLD WAR II...

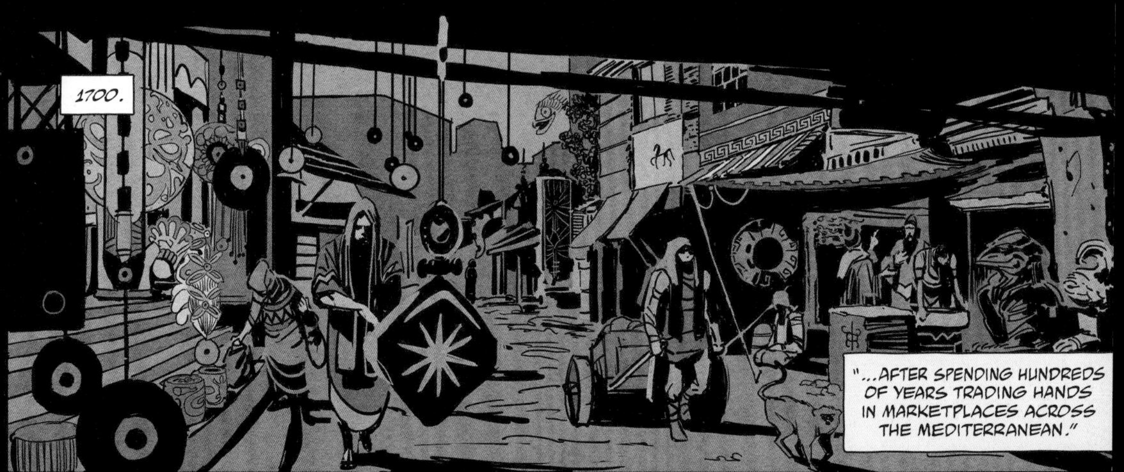
1700.
"...AFTER SPENDING HUNDREDS OF YEARS TRADING HANDS IN MARKETPLACES ACROSS THE MEDITERRANEAN."

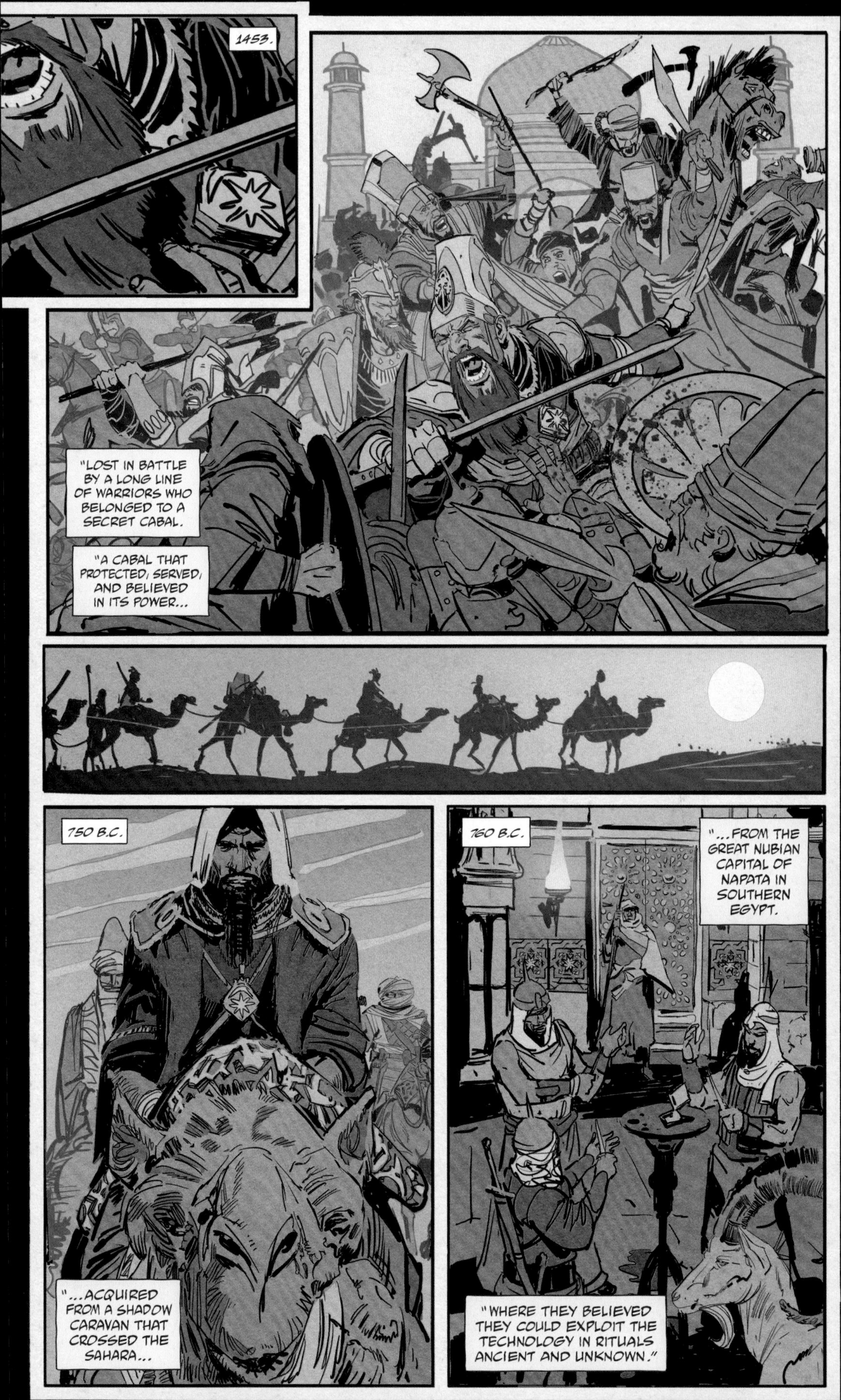
1453.
"LOST IN BATTLE BY A LONG LINE OF WARRIORS WHO BELONGED TO A SECRET CABAL.
"A CABAL THAT PROTECTED, SERVED, AND BELIEVED IN ITS POWER...
750 B.C.
"...ACQUIRED FROM A SHADOW CARAVAN THAT CROSSED THE SAHARA...
760 B.C.
"...FROM THE GREAT NUBIAN CAPITAL OF NAPATA IN SOUTHERN EGYPT.
"WHERE THEY BELIEVED THEY COULD EXPLOIT THE TECHNOLOGY IN RITUALS ANCIENT AND UNKNOWN."

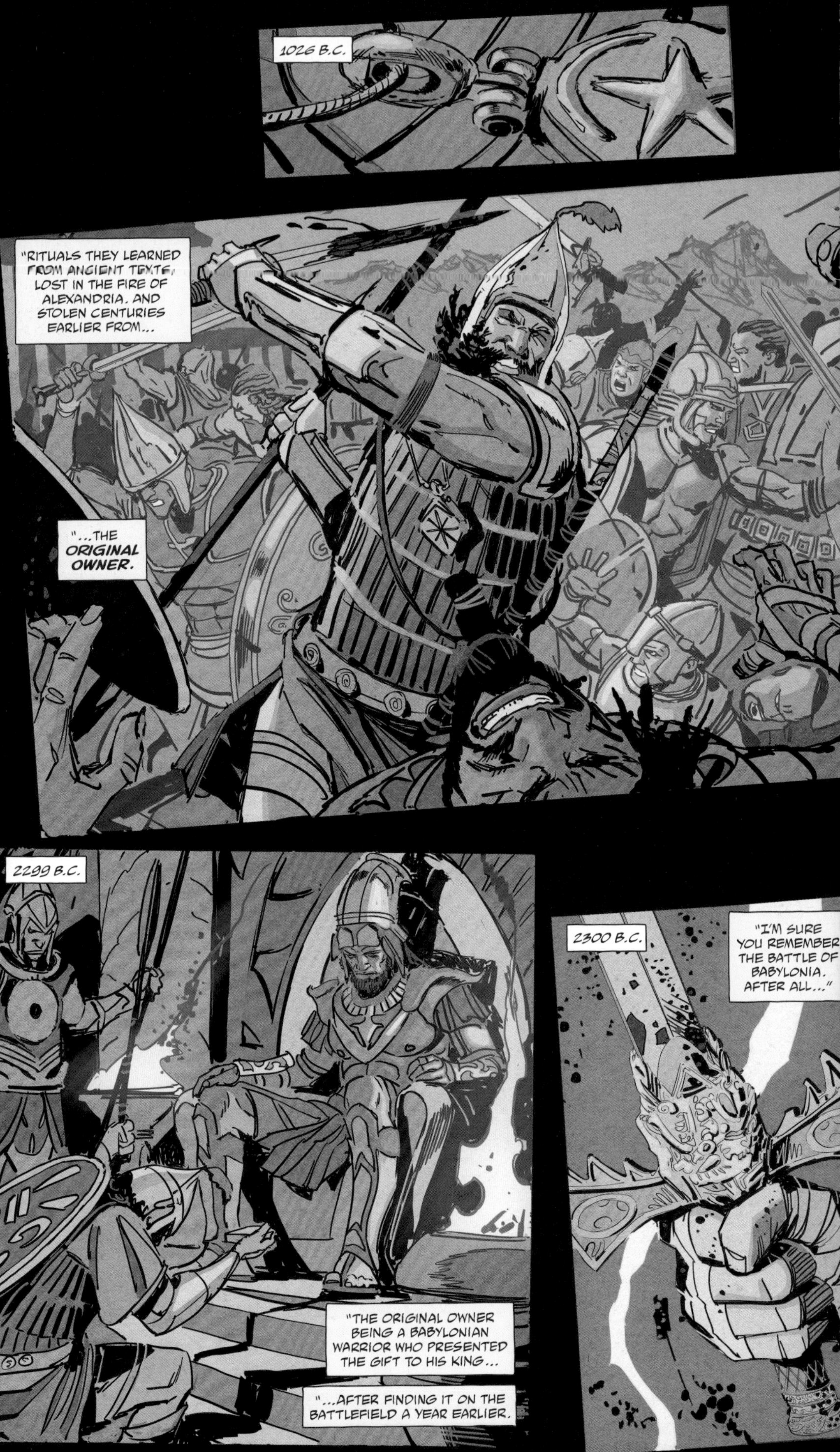
1026 B.C.
"RITUALS THEY LEARNED FROM ANCIENT TEXTS, LOST IN THE FIRE OF ALEXANDRIA. AND STOLEN CENTURIES EARLIER FROM...
"...THE *ORIGINAL OWNER.*
2299 B.C.
"THE ORIGINAL OWNER BEING A BABYLONIAN WARRIOR WHO PRESENTED THE GIFT TO HIS KING...
"...AFTER FINDING IT ON THE BATTLEFIELD A YEAR EARLIER.
2300 B.C.
"I'M SURE YOU REMEMBER THE BATTLE OF BABYLONIA. AFTER ALL..."

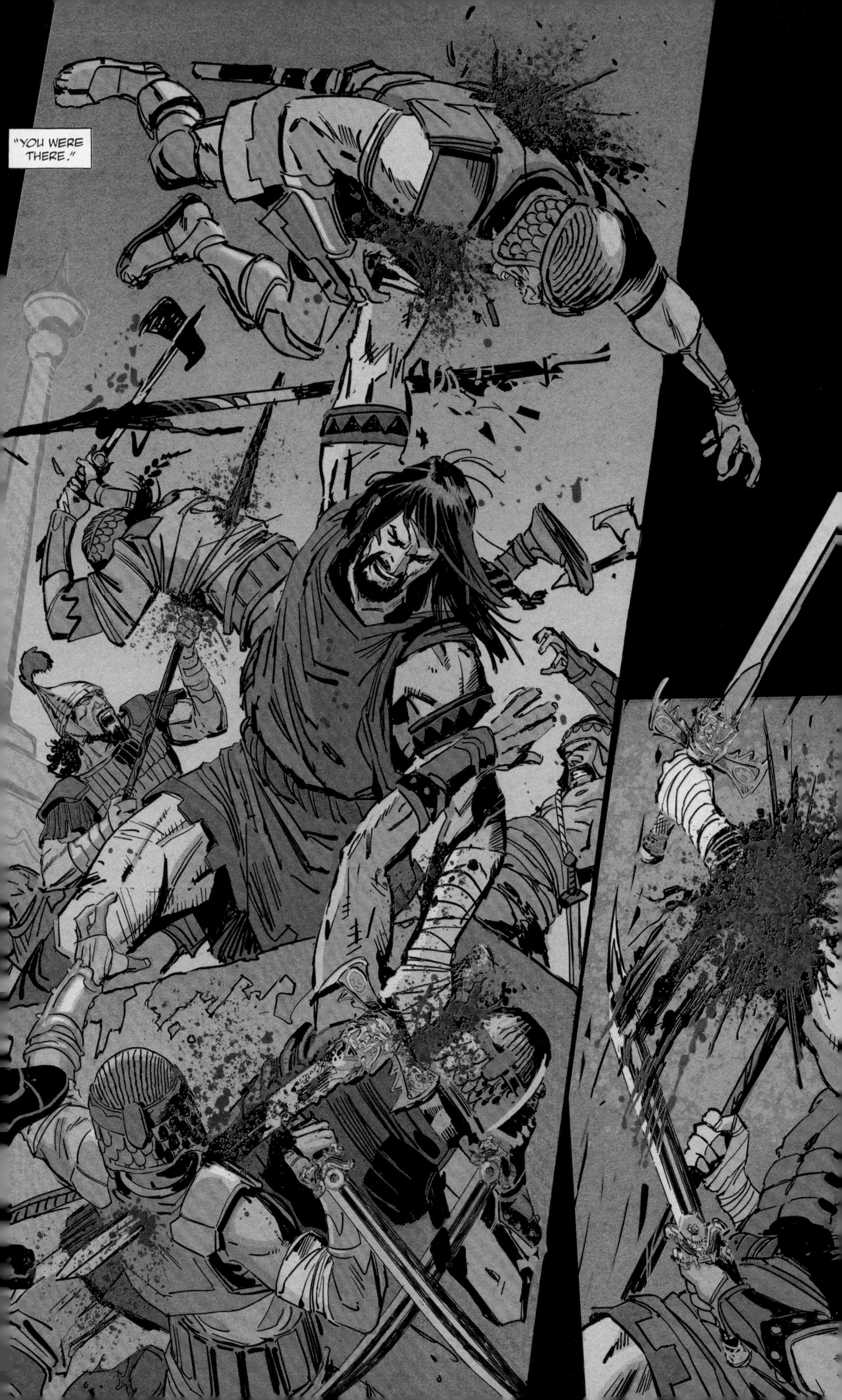
"YOU WERE THERE."

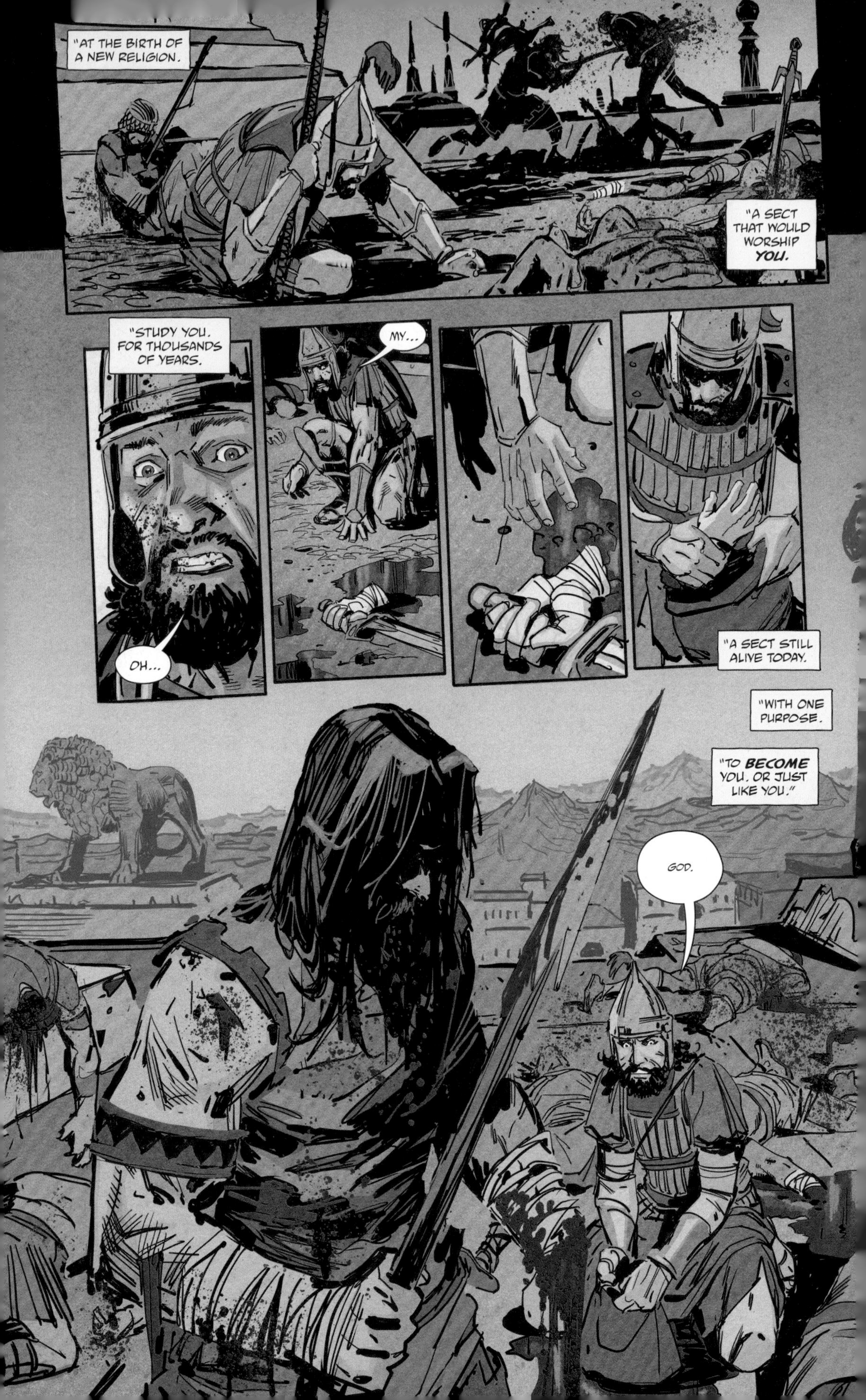
"AT THE BIRTH OF A NEW RELIGION.
"A SECT THAT WOULD WORSHIP ***YOU.***
"STUDY YOU. FOR THOUSANDS OF YEARS.
OH...
MY...
"A SECT STILL ALIVE TODAY.
"WITH ONE PURPOSE.
"TO ***BECOME*** YOU. OR JUST LIKE YOU."
GOD.

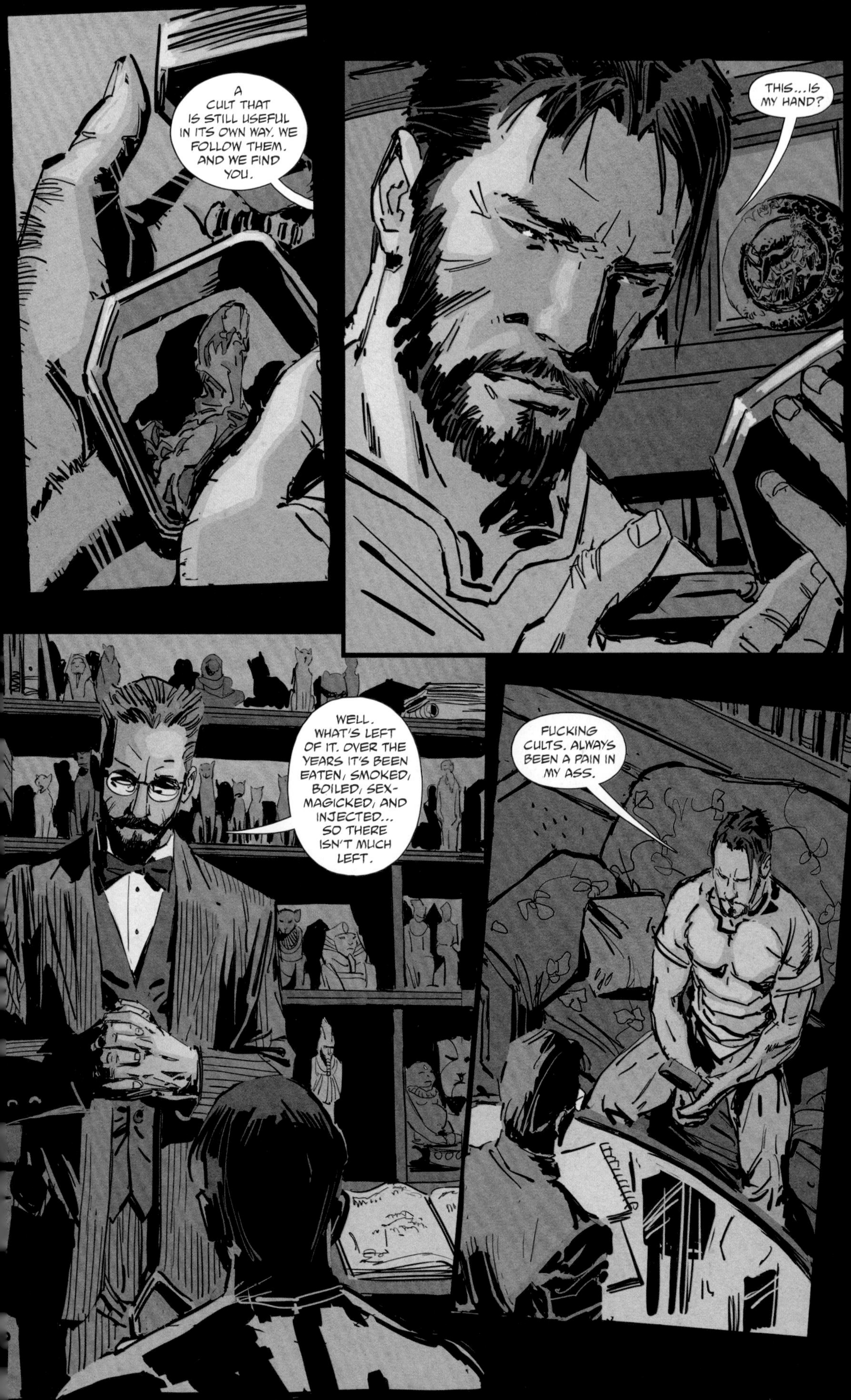
A CULT THAT IS STILL USEFUL IN ITS OWN WAY. WE FOLLOW THEM. AND WE FIND YOU.
THIS... IS MY HAND?
WELL. WHAT'S LEFT OF IT. OVER THE YEARS IT'S BEEN EATEN, SMOKED, BOILED, SEX-MAGICKED, AND INJECTED... SO THERE ISN'T MUCH LEFT.
FUCKING CULTS. ALWAYS BEEN A PAIN IN MY ASS.

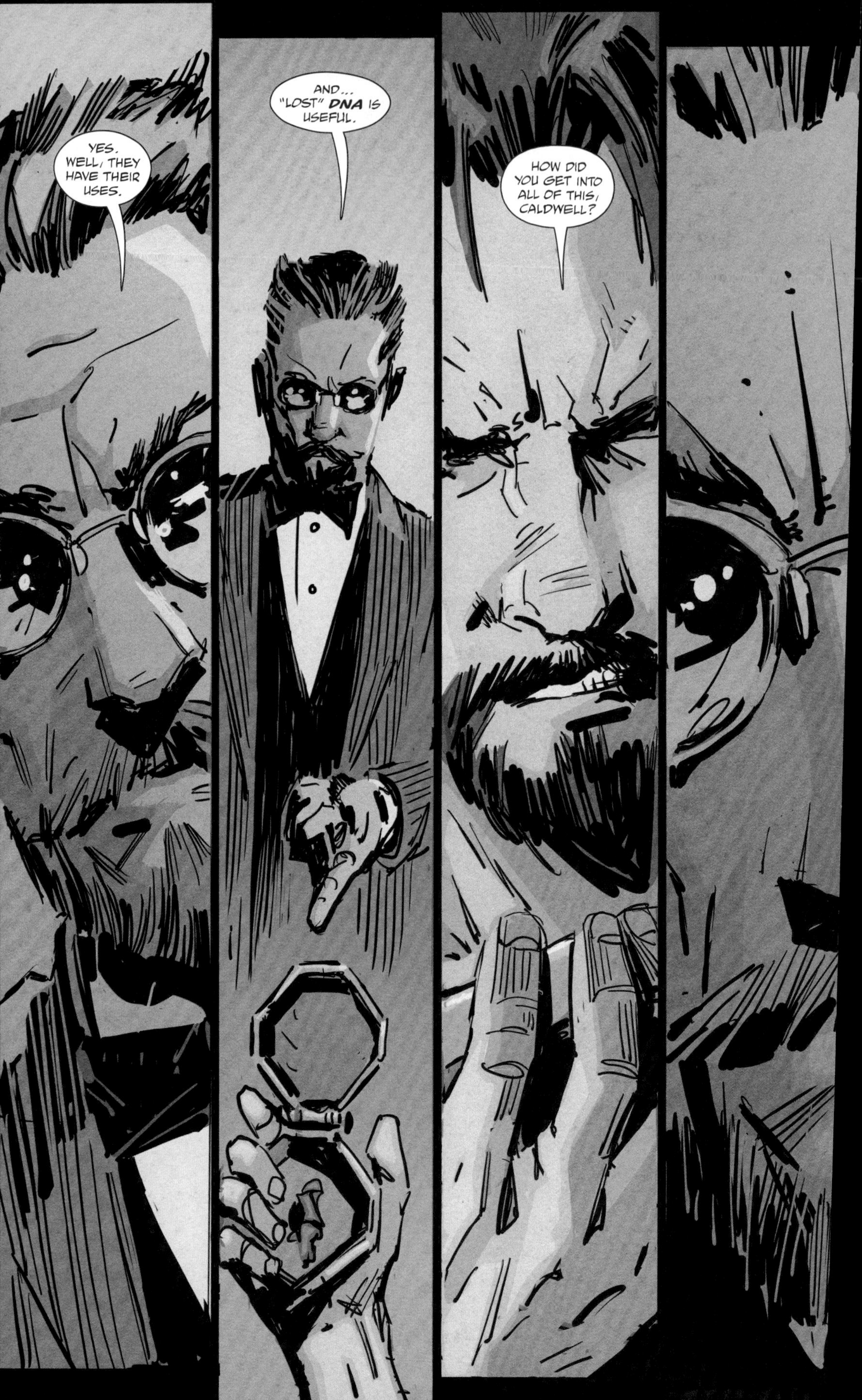
YES. WELL, THEY HAVE THEIR USES.
AND... "LOST" **DNA** IS USEFUL.
HOW DID YOU GET INTO ALL OF THIS, CALDWELL?

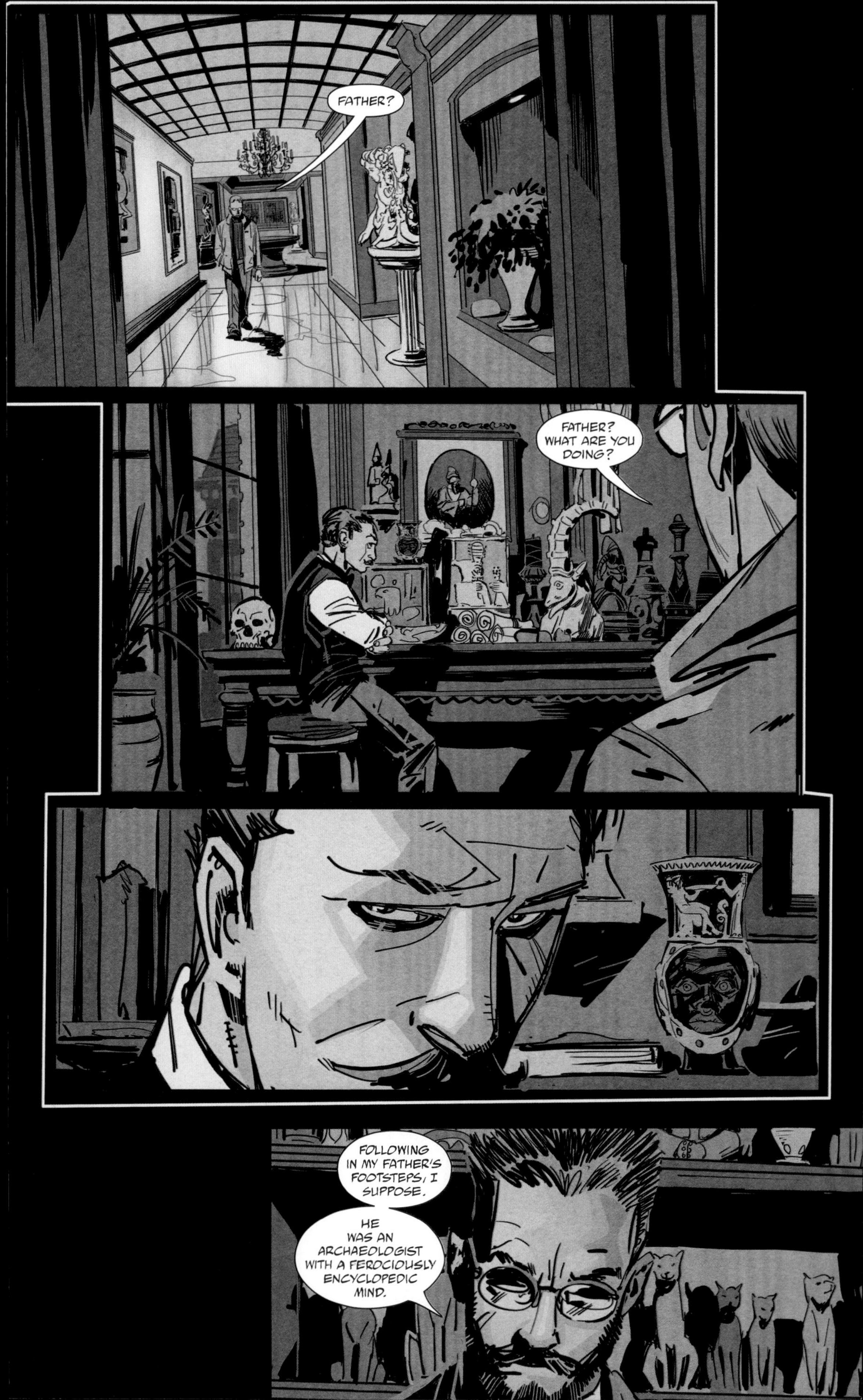
FATHER?
FATHER? WHAT ARE YOU DOING?
FOLLOWING IN MY FATHER'S FOOTSTEPS, I SUPPOSE.
HE WAS AN ARCHAEOLOGIST WITH A FEROCIOUSLY ENCYCLOPEDIC MIND.

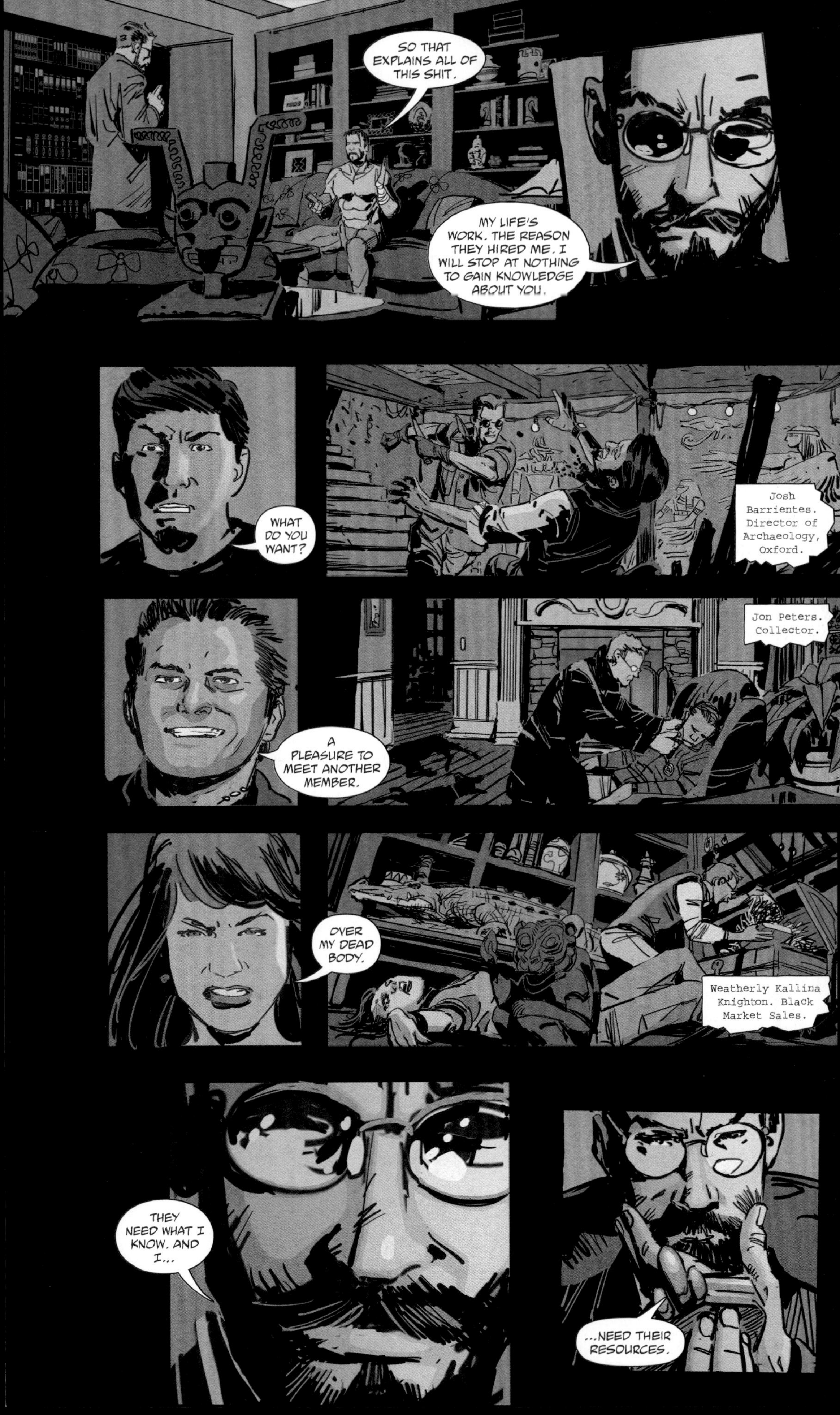
SO THAT EXPLAINS ALL OF THIS SHIT.
MY LIFE'S WORK. THE REASON THEY HIRED ME. I WILL STOP AT NOTHING TO GAIN KNOWLEDGE ABOUT YOU.
WHAT DO YOU WANT?
Josh Barrientes. Director of Archaeology, Oxford.
A PLEASURE TO MEET ANOTHER MEMBER.
Jon Peters. Collector.
OVER MY DEAD BODY.
Weatherly Kallina Knighton. Black Market Sales.
THEY NEED WHAT I KNOW. AND I...
...NEED THEIR RESOURCES.

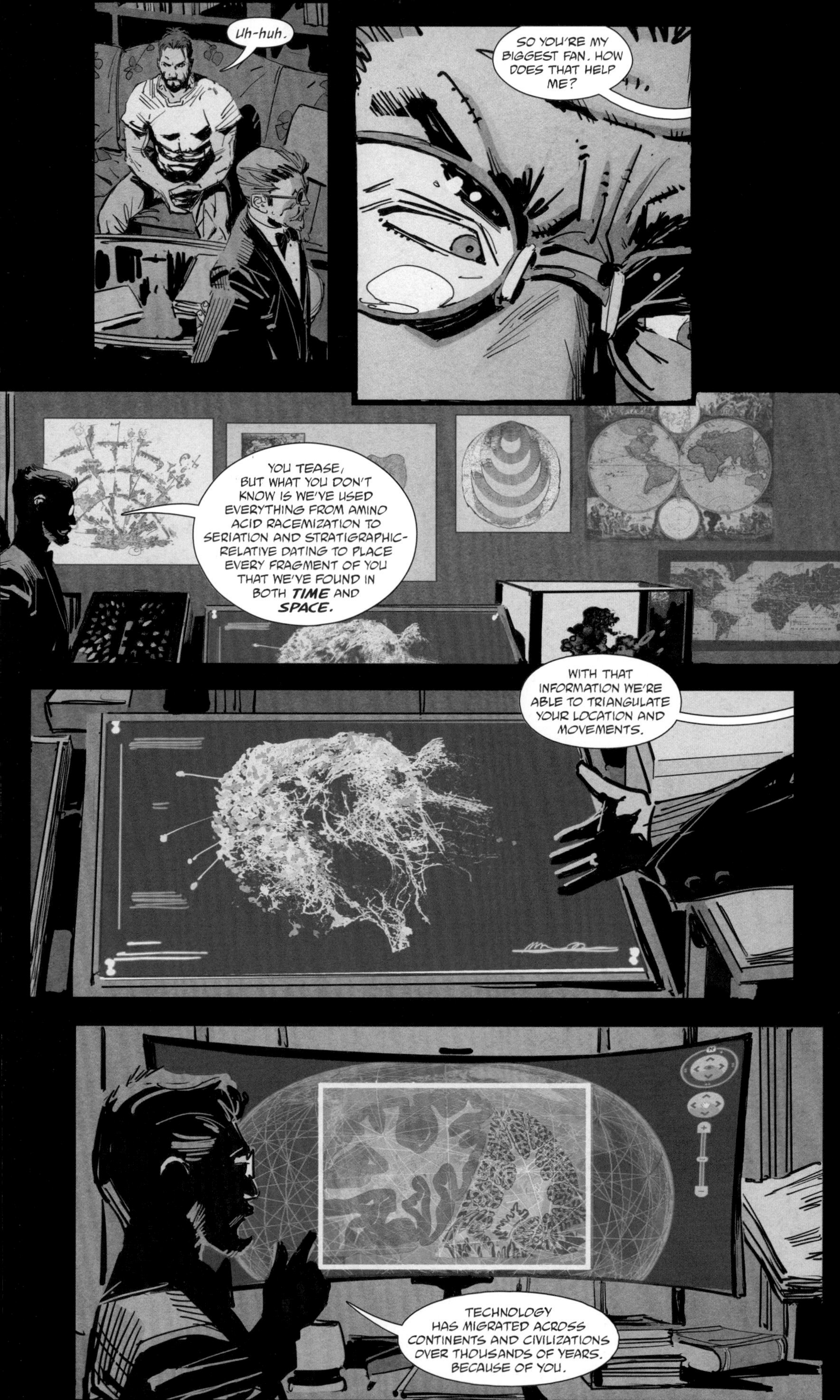
Uh-huh.
SO YOU'RE MY BIGGEST FAN. HOW DOES THAT HELP ME?
YOU TEASE, BUT WHAT YOU DON'T KNOW IS WE'VE USED EVERYTHING FROM AMINO ACID RACEMIZATION TO SERIATION AND STRATIGRAPHIC-RELATIVE DATING TO PLACE EVERY FRAGMENT OF YOU THAT WE'VE FOUND IN BOTH TIME AND SPACE.
WITH THAT INFORMATION WE'RE ABLE TO TRIANGULATE YOUR LOCATION AND MOVEMENTS.
TECHNOLOGY HAS MIGRATED ACROSS CONTINENTS AND CIVILIZATIONS OVER THOUSANDS OF YEARS. BECAUSE OF YOU.

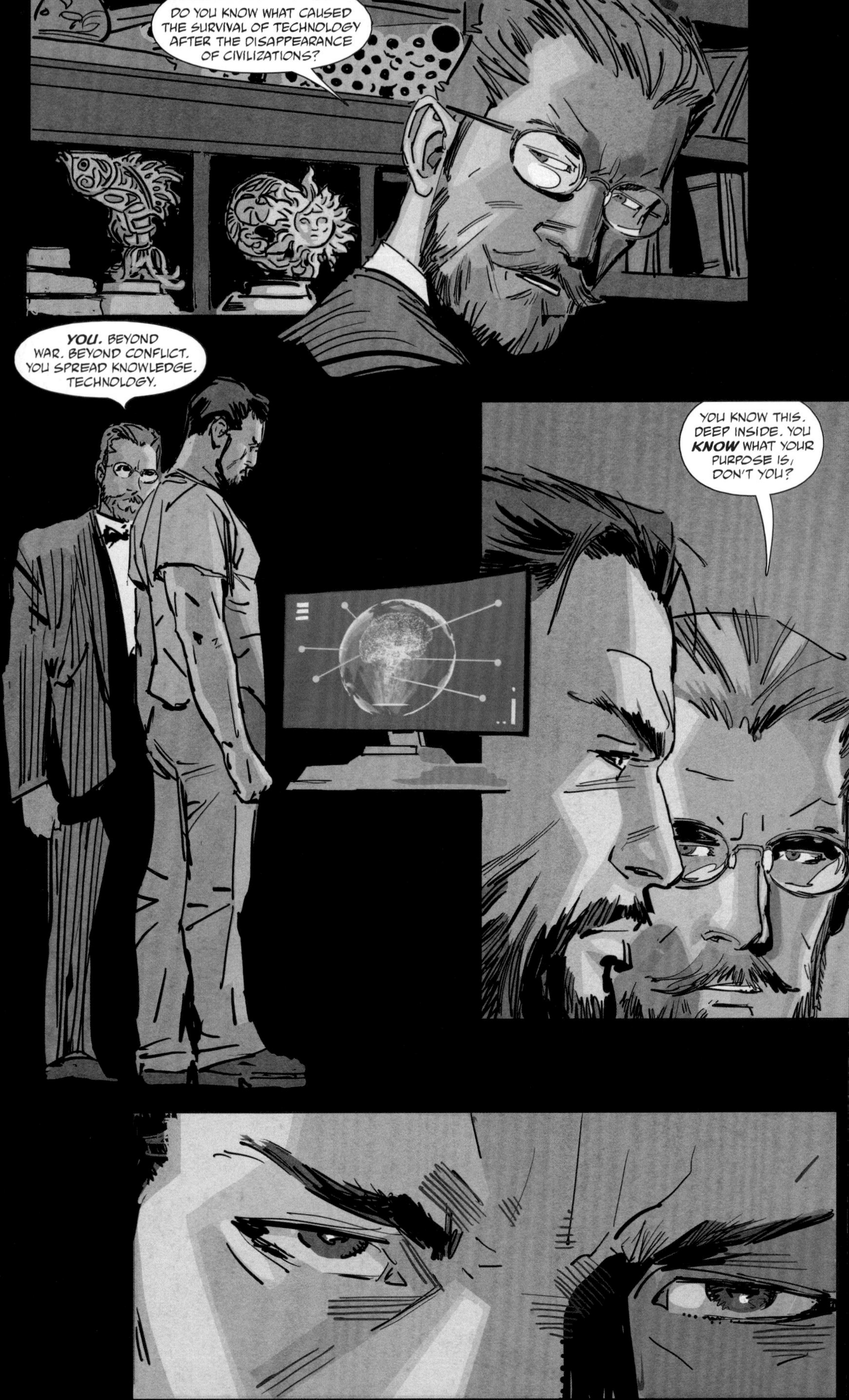
DO YOU KNOW WHAT CAUSED THE SURVIVAL OF TECHNOLOGY AFTER THE DISAPPEARANCE OF CIVILIZATIONS?
YOU. BEYOND WAR. BEYOND CONFLICT. YOU SPREAD KNOWLEDGE. TECHNOLOGY.
YOU KNOW THIS. DEEP INSIDE. YOU *KNOW* WHAT YOUR PURPOSE IS, DON'T YOU?

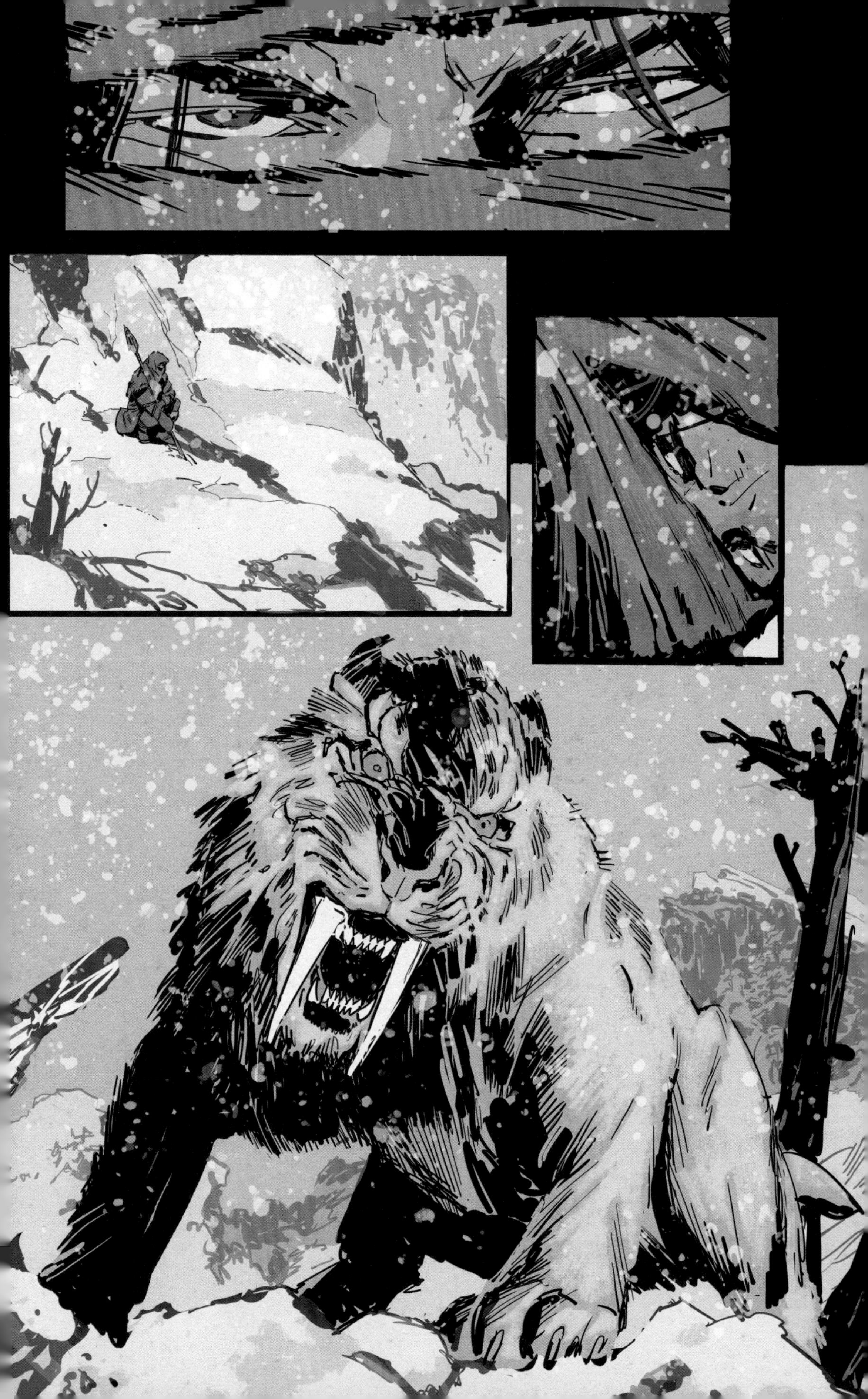

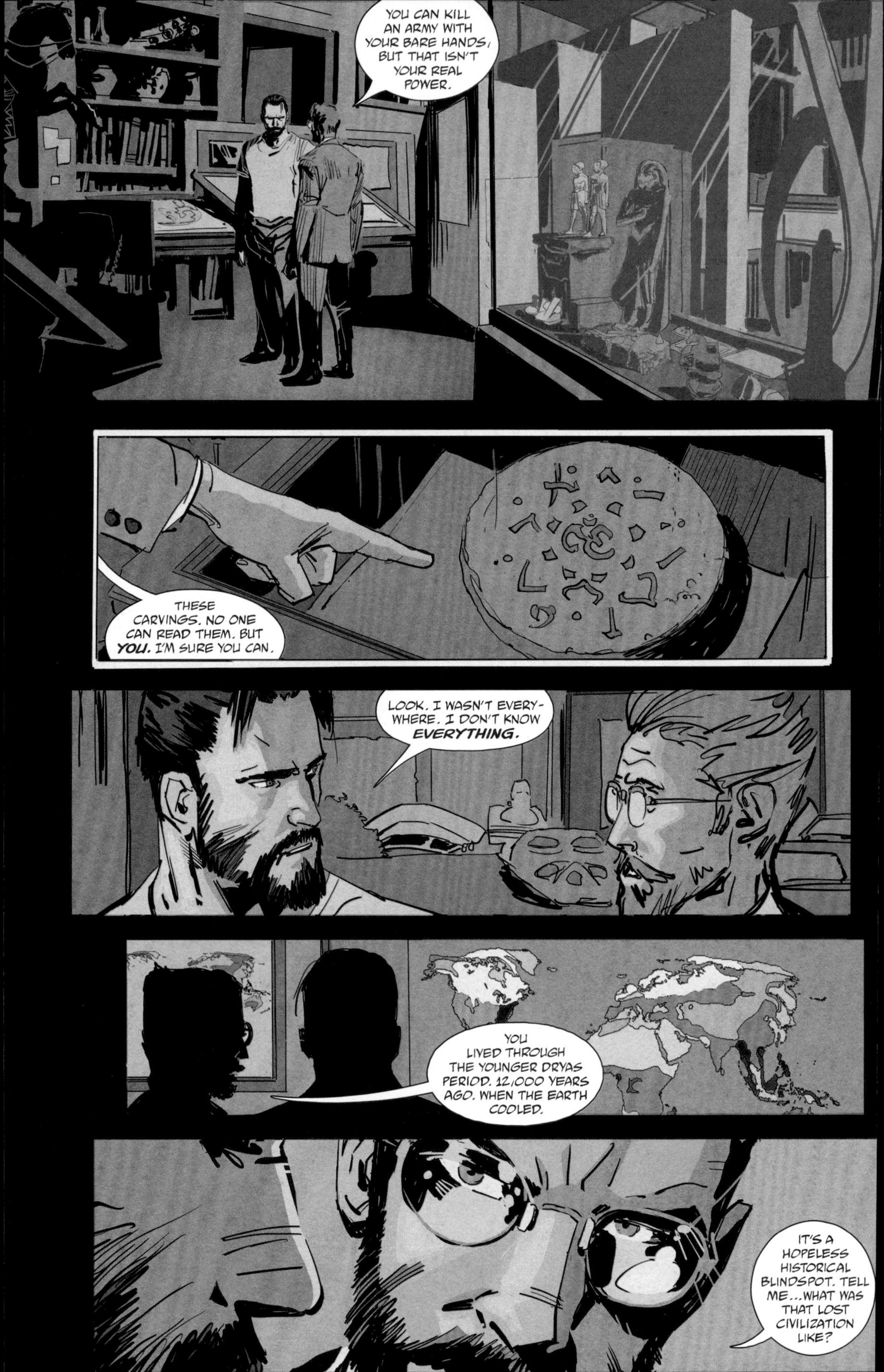
YOU CAN KILL AN ARMY WITH YOUR BARE HANDS, BUT THAT ISN'T YOUR REAL POWER.
THESE CARVINGS. NO ONE CAN READ THEM. BUT **YOU.** I'M SURE YOU CAN.
LOOK. I WASN'T EVERY-WHERE. I DON'T KNOW **EVERYTHING.**
YOU LIVED THROUGH THE YOUNGER DRYAS PERIOD. 12,000 YEARS AGO. WHEN THE EARTH COOLED.
IT'S A HOPELESS HISTORICAL BLINDSPOT. TELL ME...WHAT WAS THAT LOST CIVILIZATION LIKE?

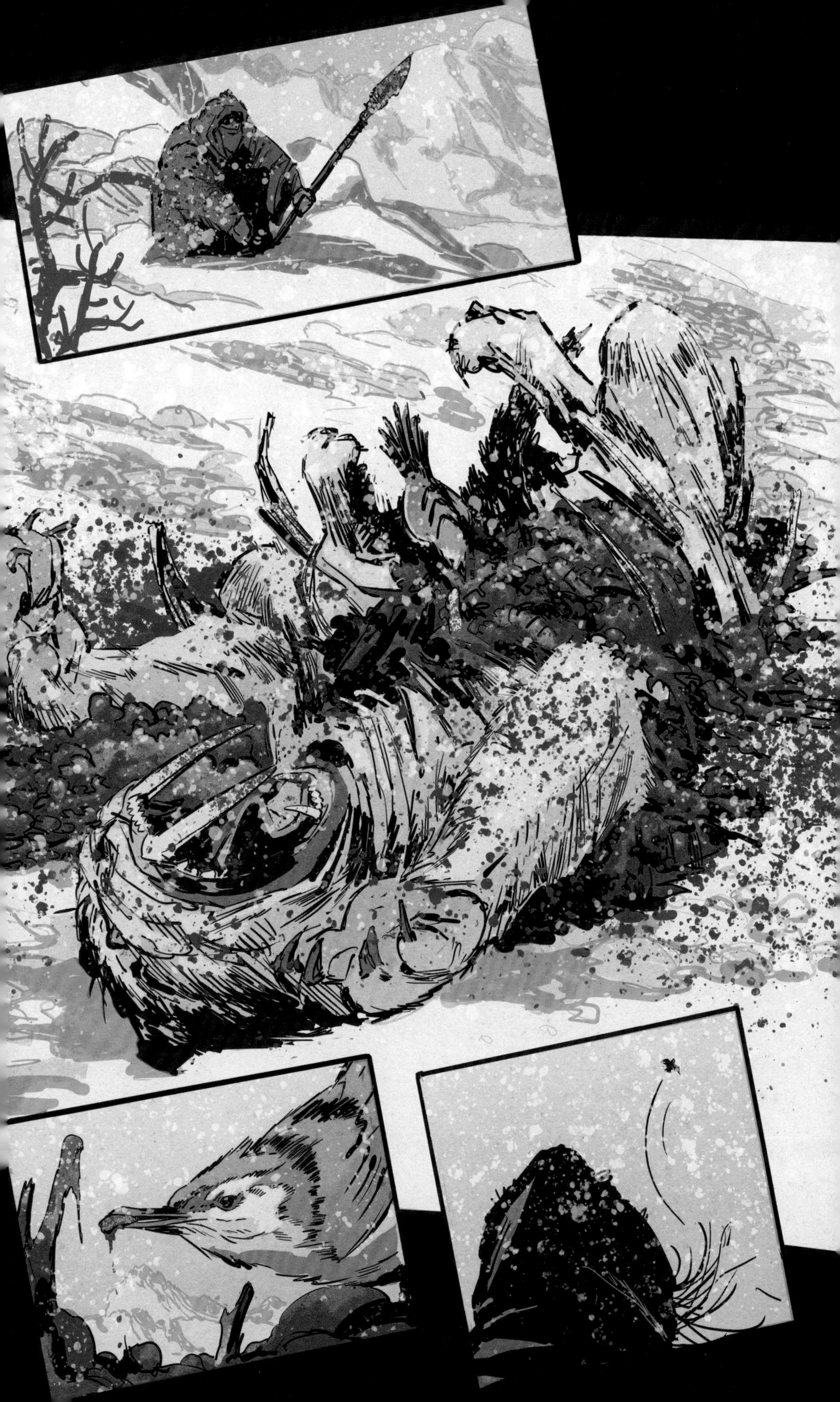

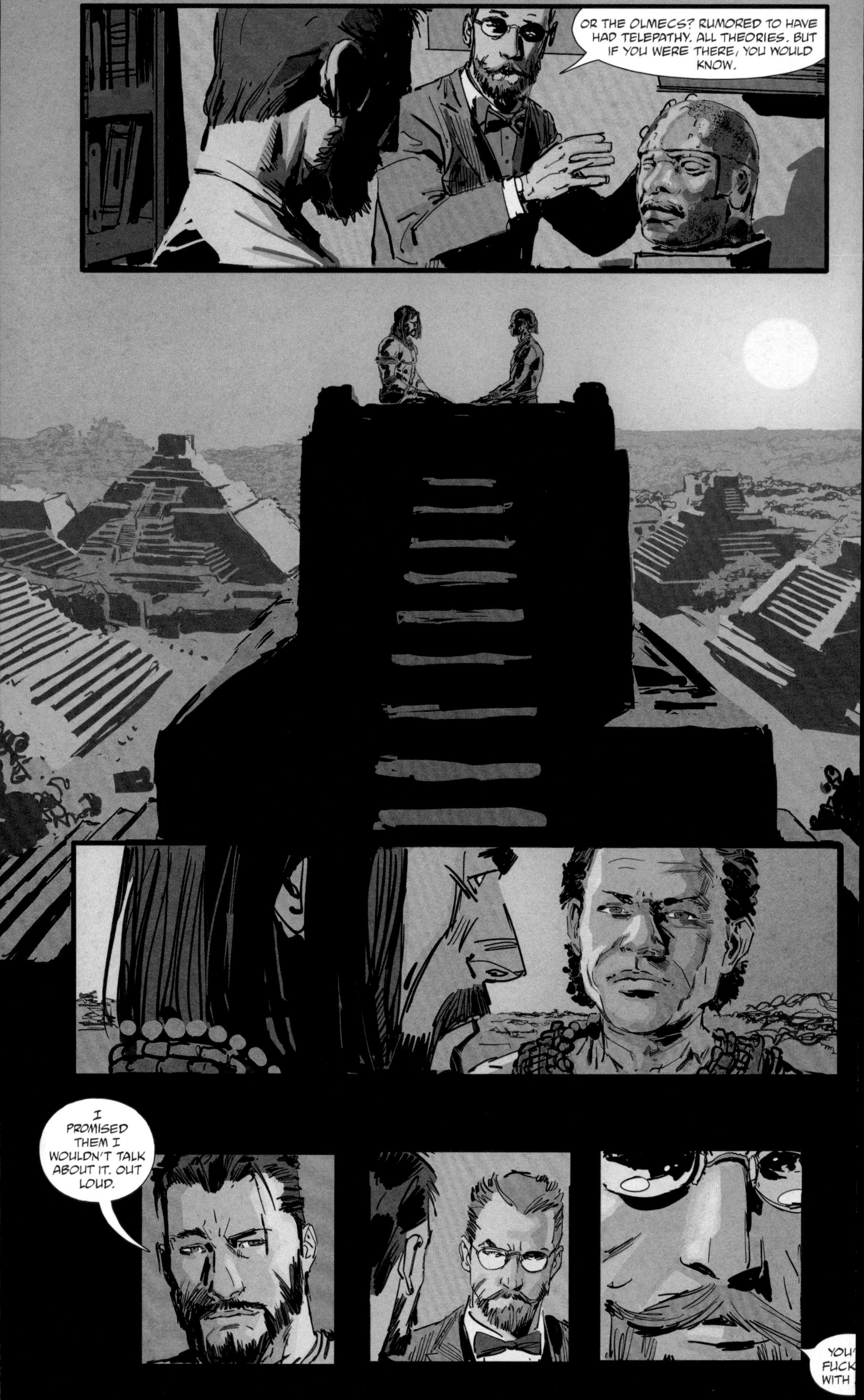
OR THE OLMECS? RUMORED TO HAVE HAD TELEPATHY. ALL THEORIES. BUT IF YOU WERE THERE, YOU WOULD KNOW.
I PROMISED THEM I WOULDN'T TALK ABOUT IT. OUT LOUD.
YOU' FUCK WITH

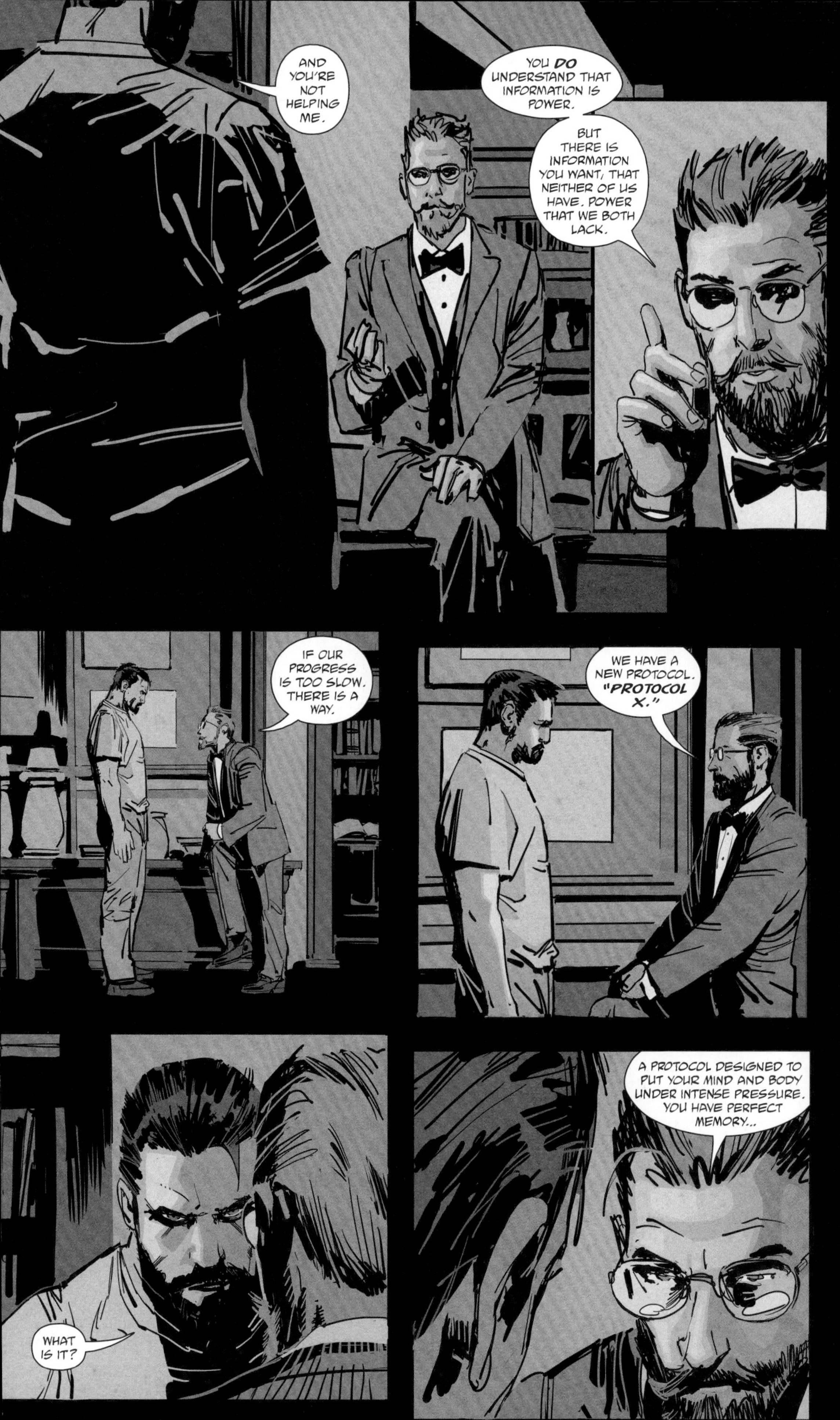
AND YOU'RE NOT HELPING ME.
YOU DO UNDERSTAND THAT INFORMATION IS POWER.
BUT THERE IS INFORMATION YOU WANT, THAT NEITHER OF US HAVE. POWER THAT WE BOTH LACK.
IF OUR PROGRESS IS TOO SLOW. THERE IS A WAY.
WE HAVE A NEW PROTOCOL. "PROTOCOL X."
WHAT IS IT?
A PROTOCOL DESIGNED TO PUT YOUR MIND AND BODY UNDER INTENSE PRESSURE. YOU HAVE PERFECT MEMORY...

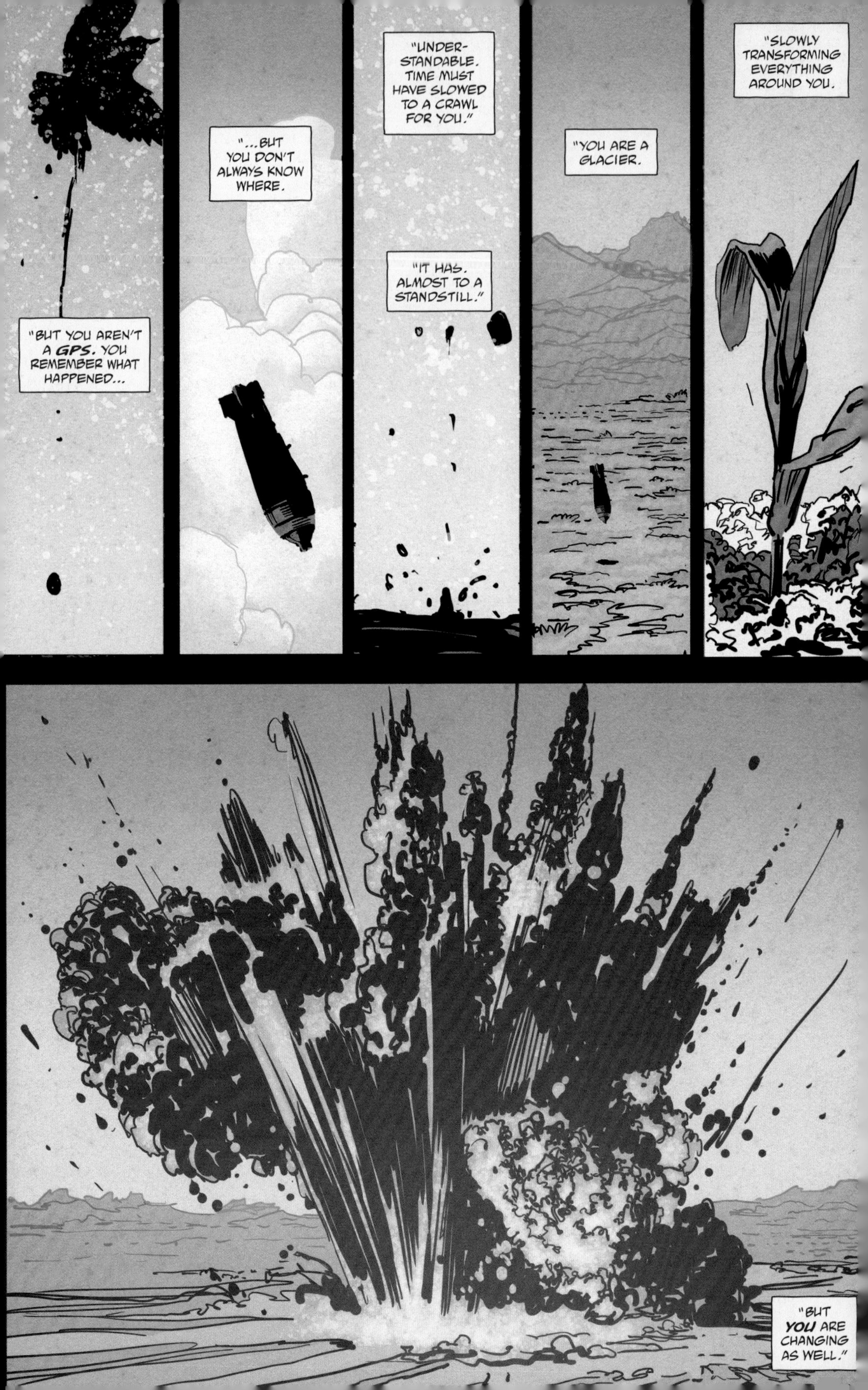
"BUT YOU AREN'T A GPS. YOU REMEMBER WHAT HAPPENED...
"...BUT YOU DON'T ALWAYS KNOW WHERE.
"UNDER-STANDABLE. TIME MUST HAVE SLOWED TO A CRAWL FOR YOU."
"IT HAS. ALMOST TO A STANDSTILL."
"YOU ARE A GLACIER.
"SLOWLY TRANSFORMING EVERYTHING AROUND YOU.
"BUT YOU ARE CHANGING AS WELL."

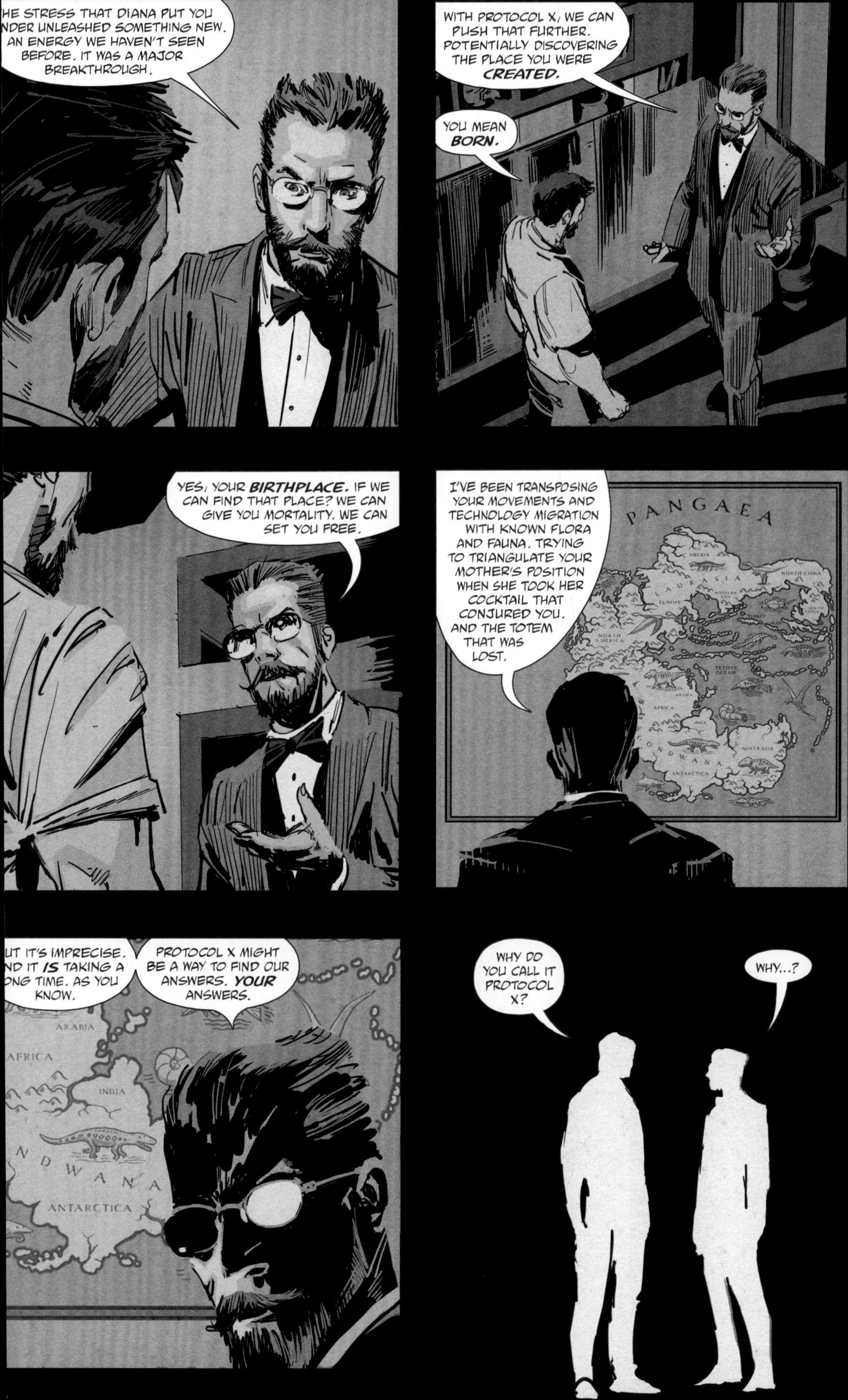
HE STRESS THAT DIANA PUT YOU NDER UNLEASHED SOMETHING NEW. AN ENERGY WE HAVEN'T SEEN BEFORE. IT WAS A MAJOR BREAKTHROUGH.
WITH PROTOCOL X, WE CAN PUSH THAT FURTHER. POTENTIALLY DISCOVERING THE PLACE YOU WERE **CREATED.**
YOU MEAN **BORN.**
YES, YOUR **BIRTHPLACE.** IF WE CAN FIND THAT PLACE? WE CAN GIVE YOU MORTALITY. WE CAN SET YOU FREE.
I'VE BEEN TRANSPOSING YOUR MOVEMENTS AND TECHNOLOGY MIGRATION WITH KNOWN FLORA AND FAUNA. TRYING TO TRIANGULATE YOUR MOTHER'S POSITION WHEN SHE TOOK HER COCKTAIL THAT CONJURED YOU. AND THE TOTEM THAT WAS LOST.
PANGAEA
UT IT'S IMPRECISE. ND IT *IS* TAKING A ONG TIME. AS YOU KNOW.
PROTOCOL X MIGHT BE A WAY TO FIND OUR ANSWERS. *YOUR* ANSWERS.
ARABIA
AFRICA
INDIA
ANTARCTICA
WHY DO YOU CALL IT PROTOCOL X?
WHY...?

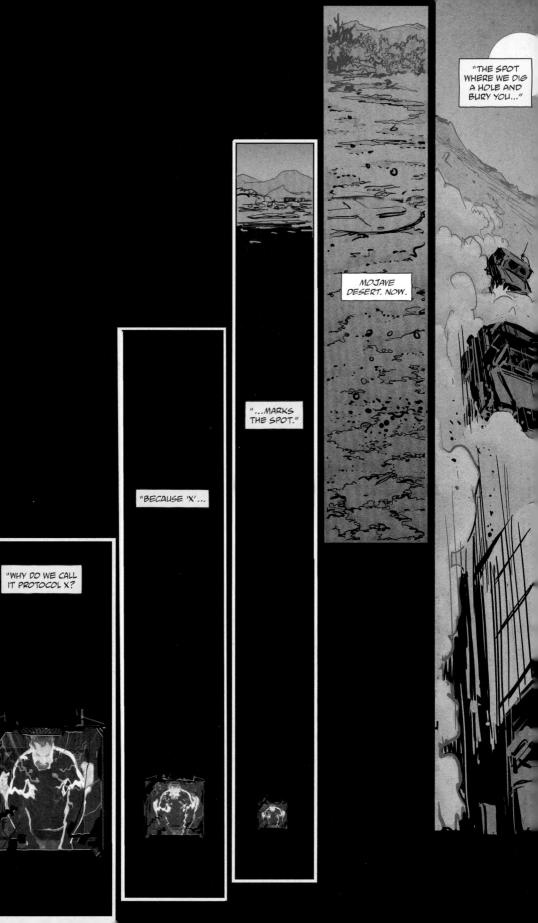

"THE SPOT WHERE WE DIG A HOLE AND BURY YOU..."

MOJAVE DESERT. NOW.

"...MARKS THE SPOT."

"BECAUSE 'X'...

"WHY DO WE CALL IT PROTOCOL X?

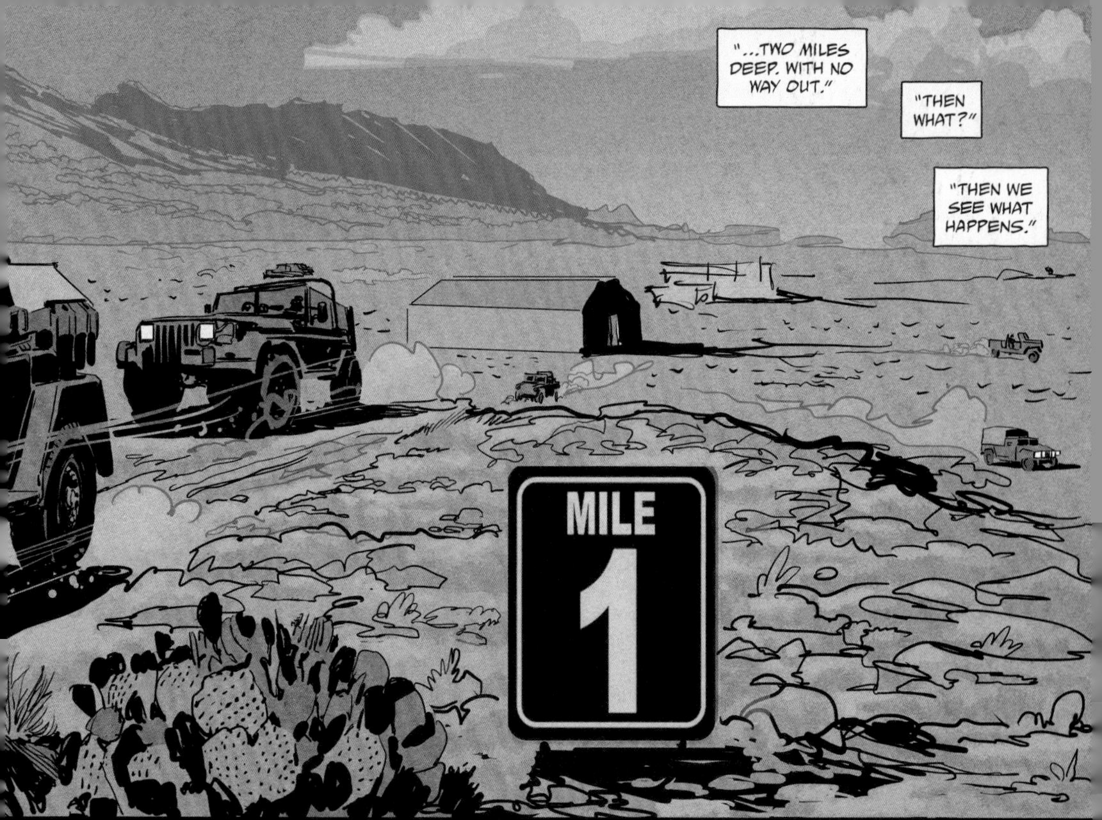
"...TWO MILES DEEP. WITH NO WAY OUT."
"THEN WHAT?"
"THEN WE SEE WHAT HAPPENS."
MILE
1

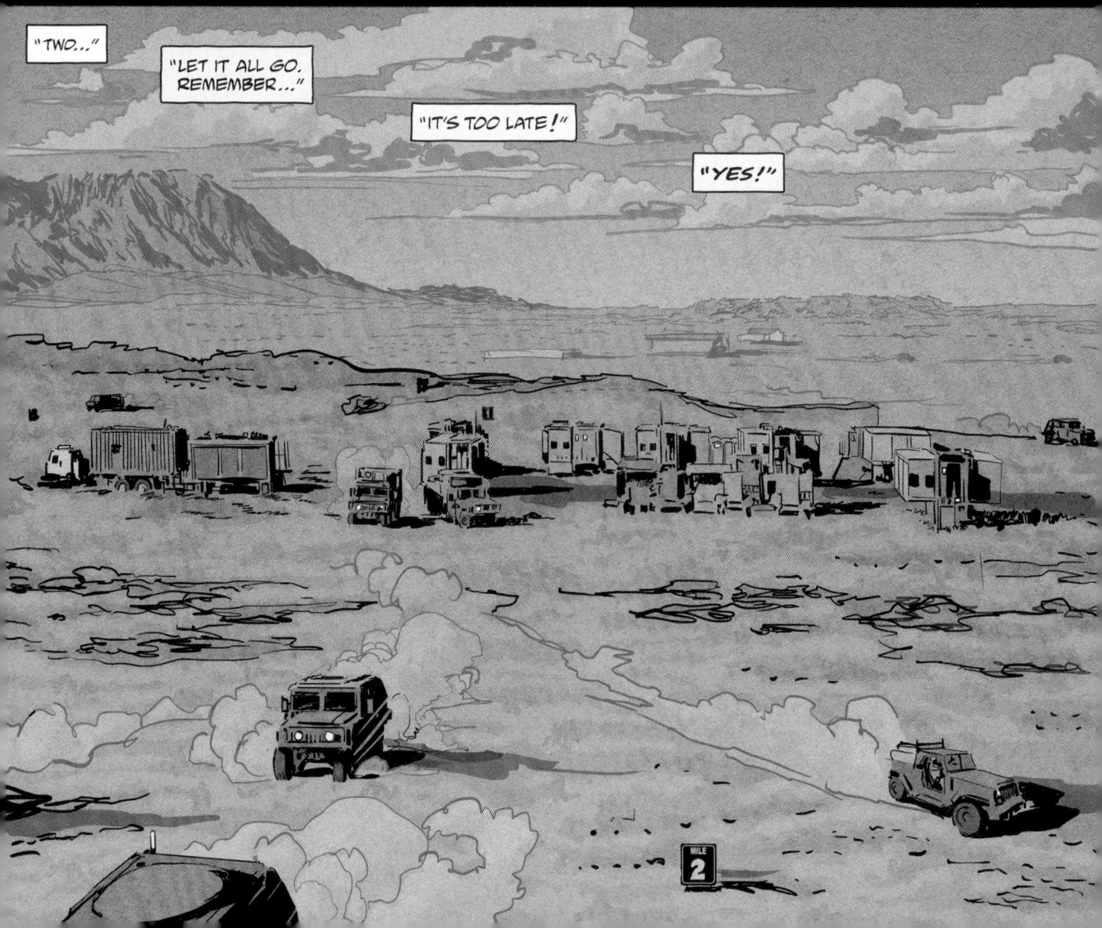
"TWO..."
"LET IT ALL GO. REMEMBER..."
"IT'S TOO LATE!"
"YES!"

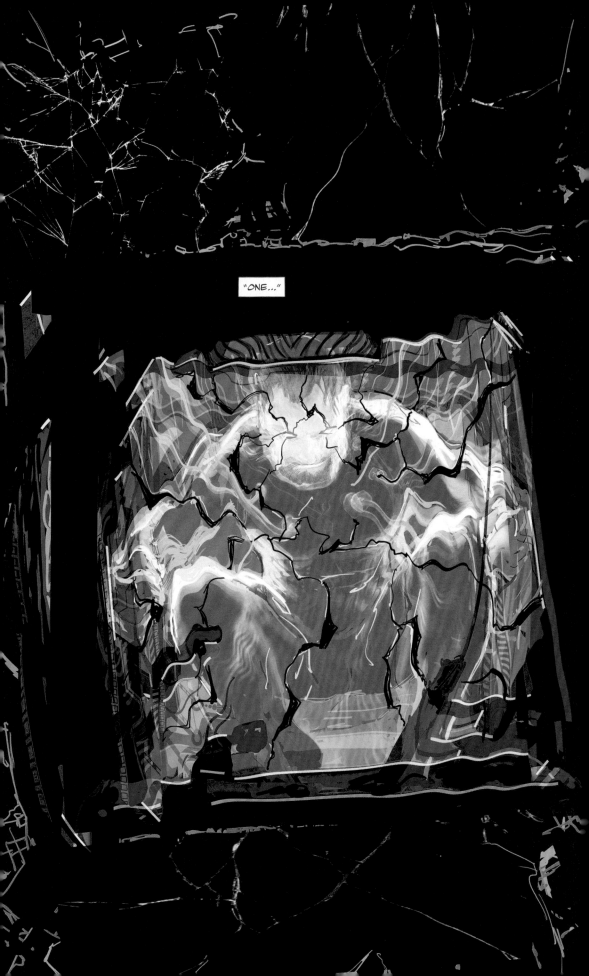

"ONE..."

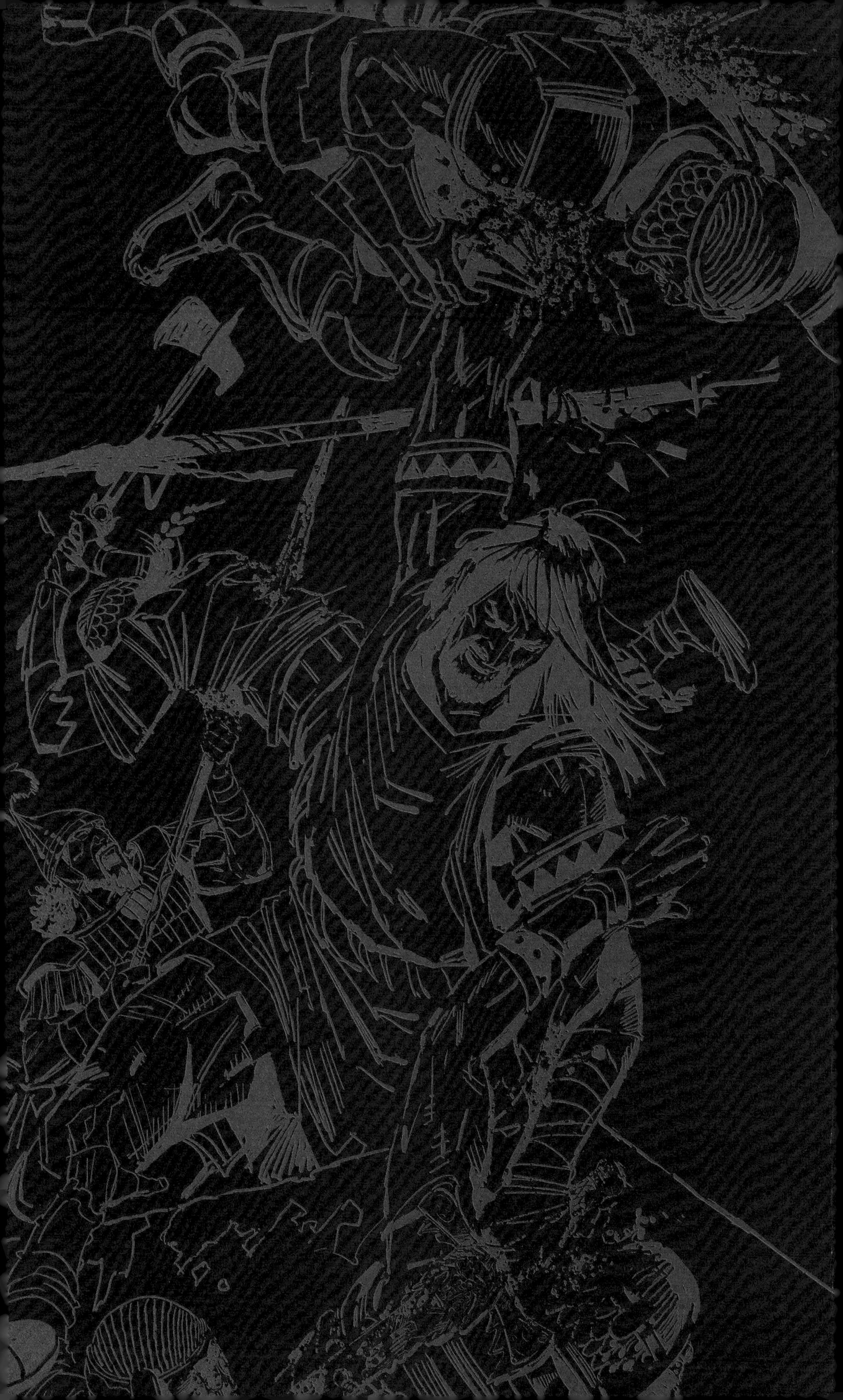

CHAPTER
EIGHT

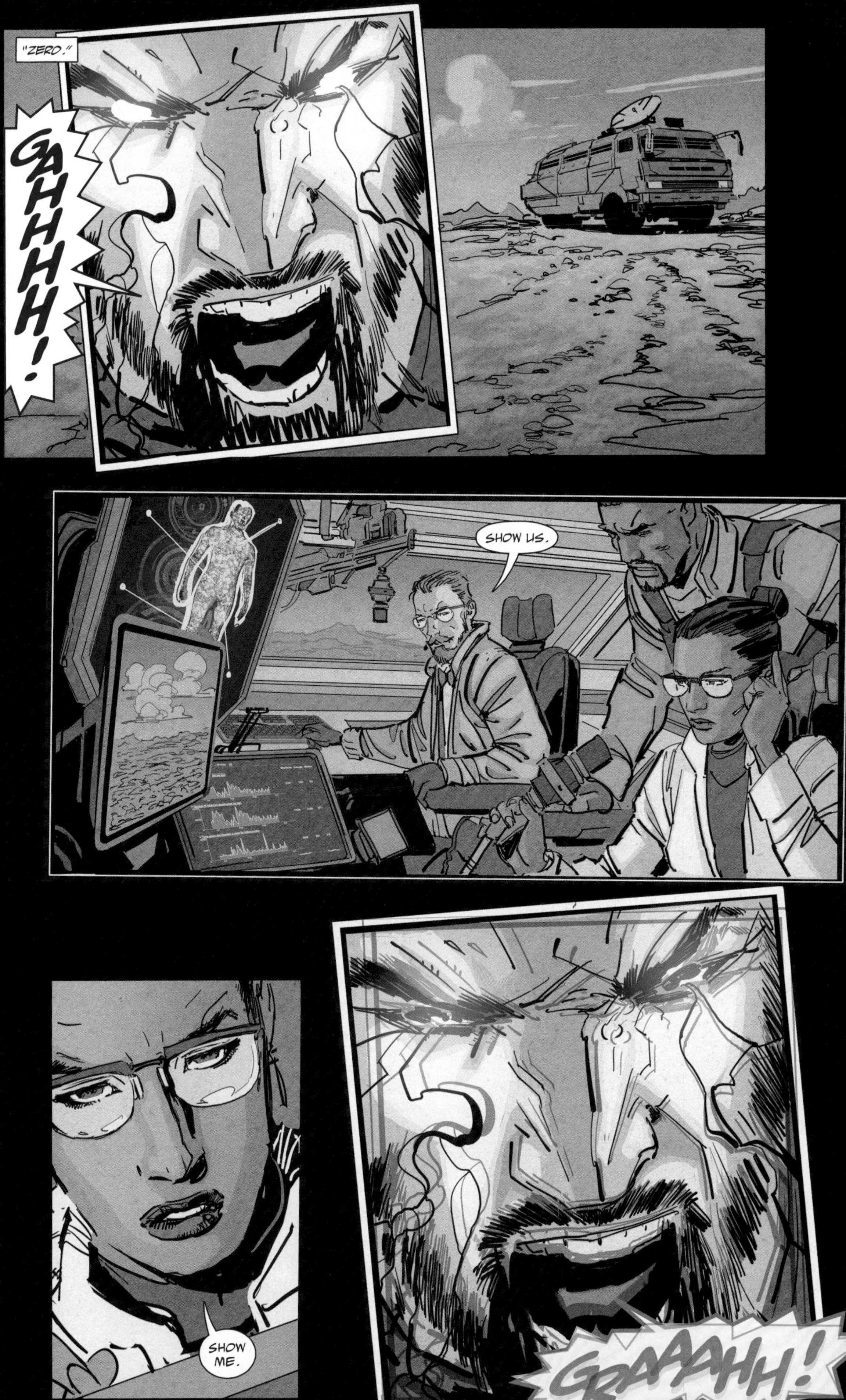
"ZERO."
GAHHHHH!
SHOW US.
SHOW ME.
GRAAAHH!

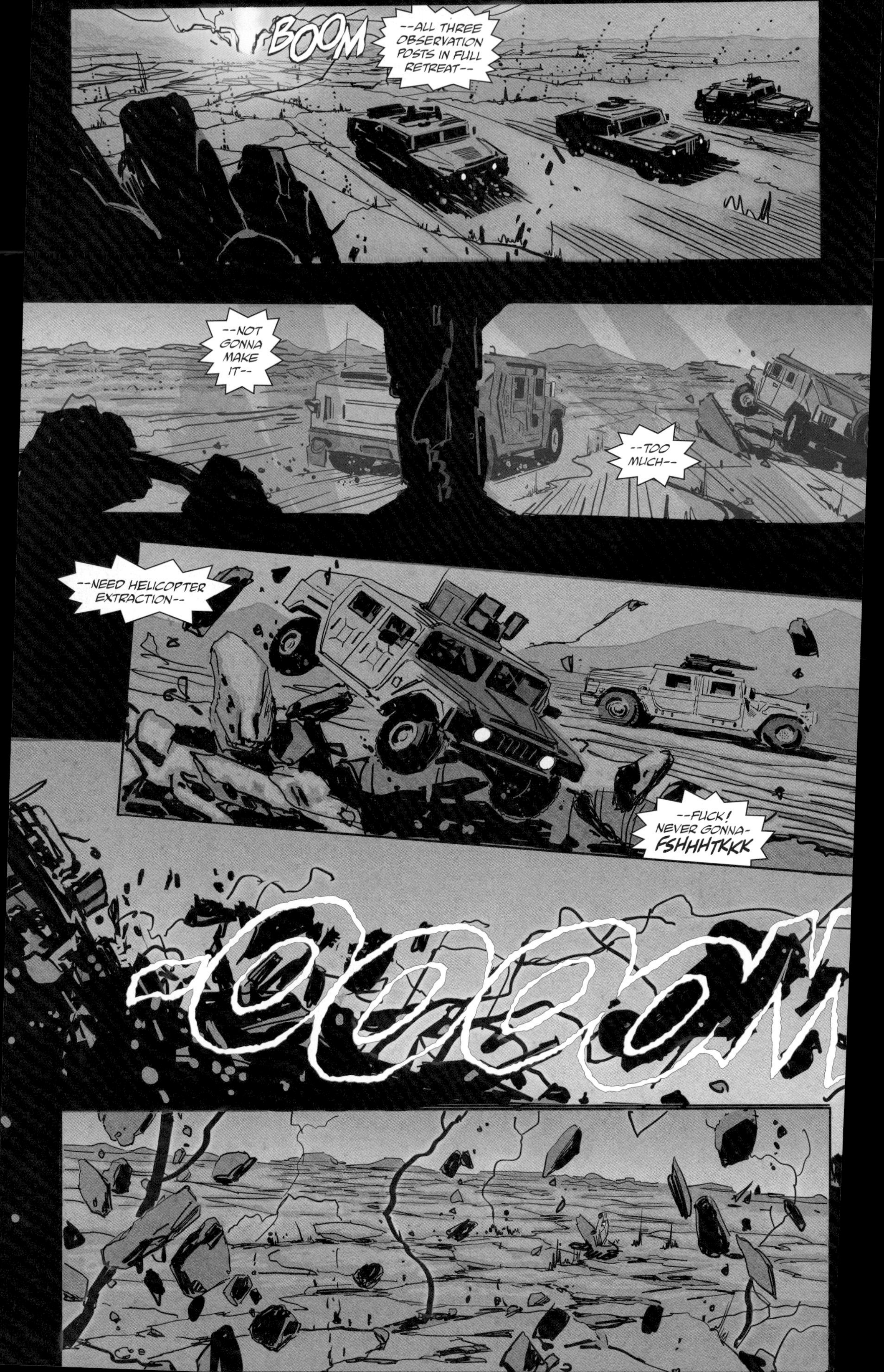
BOOM
--ALL THREE OBSERVATION POSTS IN FULL RETREAT--
--NOT GONNA MAKE IT--
--TOO MUCH--
--NEED HELICOPTER EXTRACTION--
--FUCK! NEVER GONNA- FSHHHTKKK

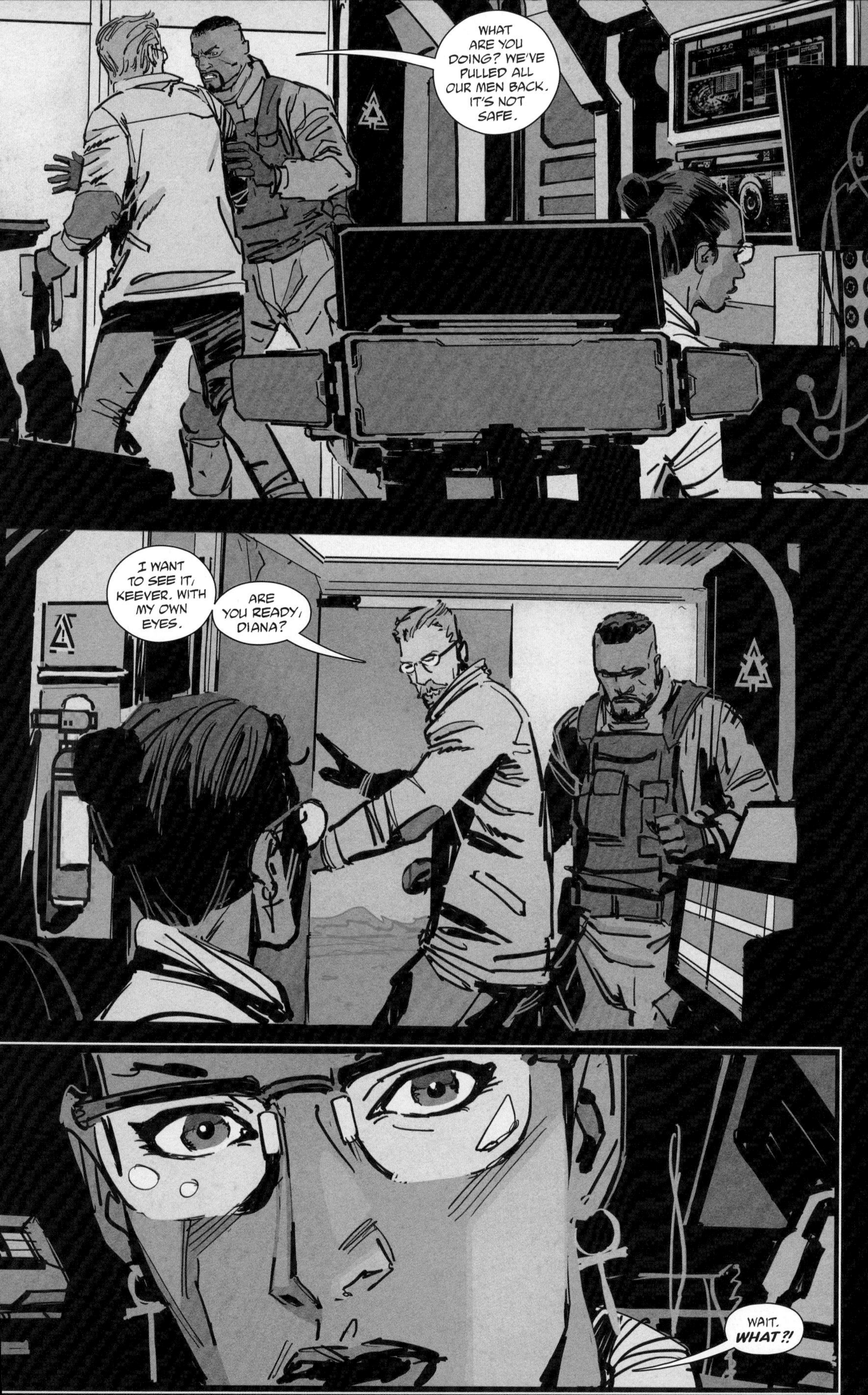
WHAT ARE YOU DOING? WE'VE PULLED ALL OUR MEN BACK. IT'S NOT SAFE.
I WANT TO SEE IT, KEEVER. WITH MY OWN EYES.
ARE YOU READY, DIANA?
WAIT. **WHAT?!**

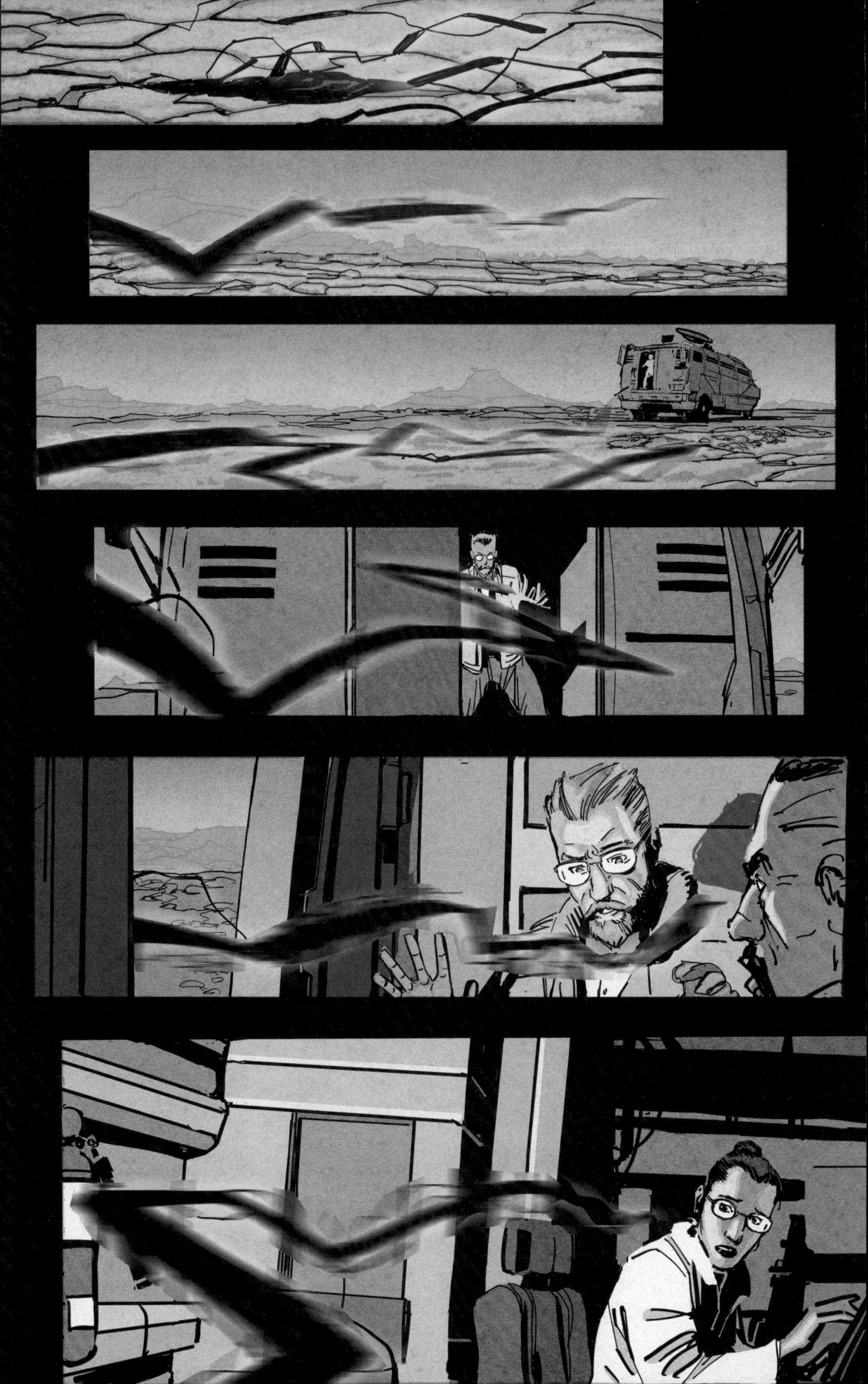

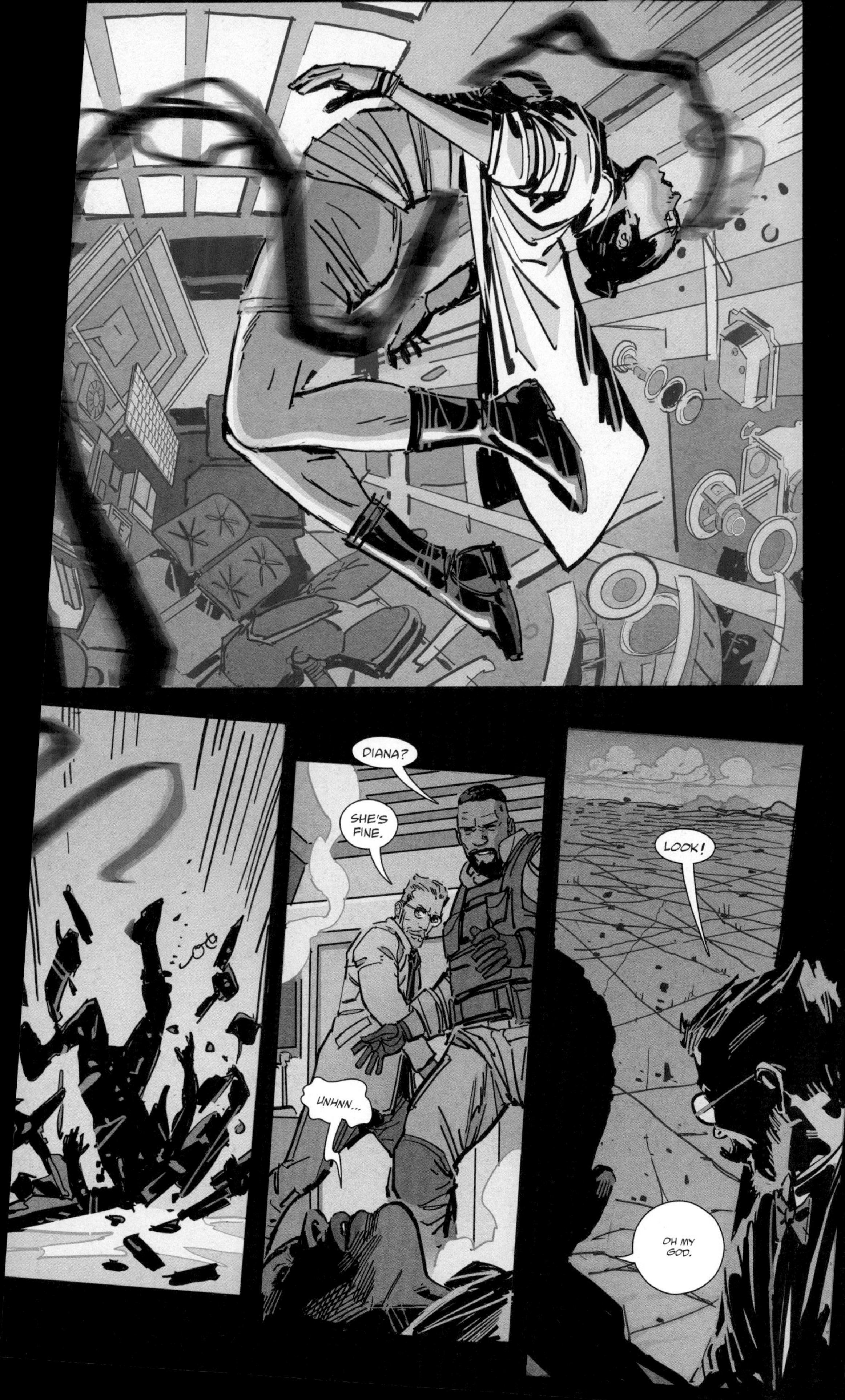
DIANA?
SHE'S FINE.
UNHNN...
LOOK!
OH MY GOD.

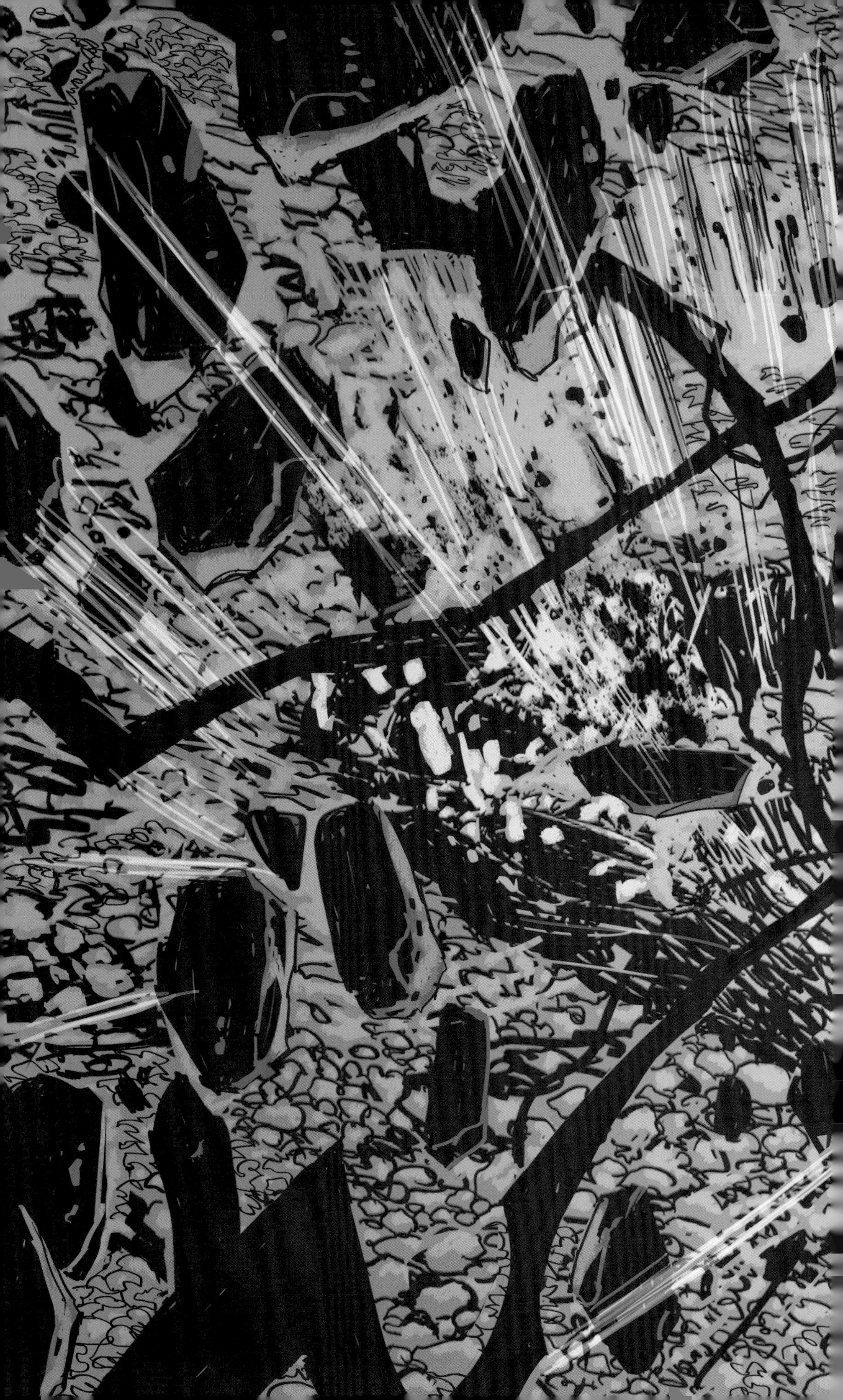

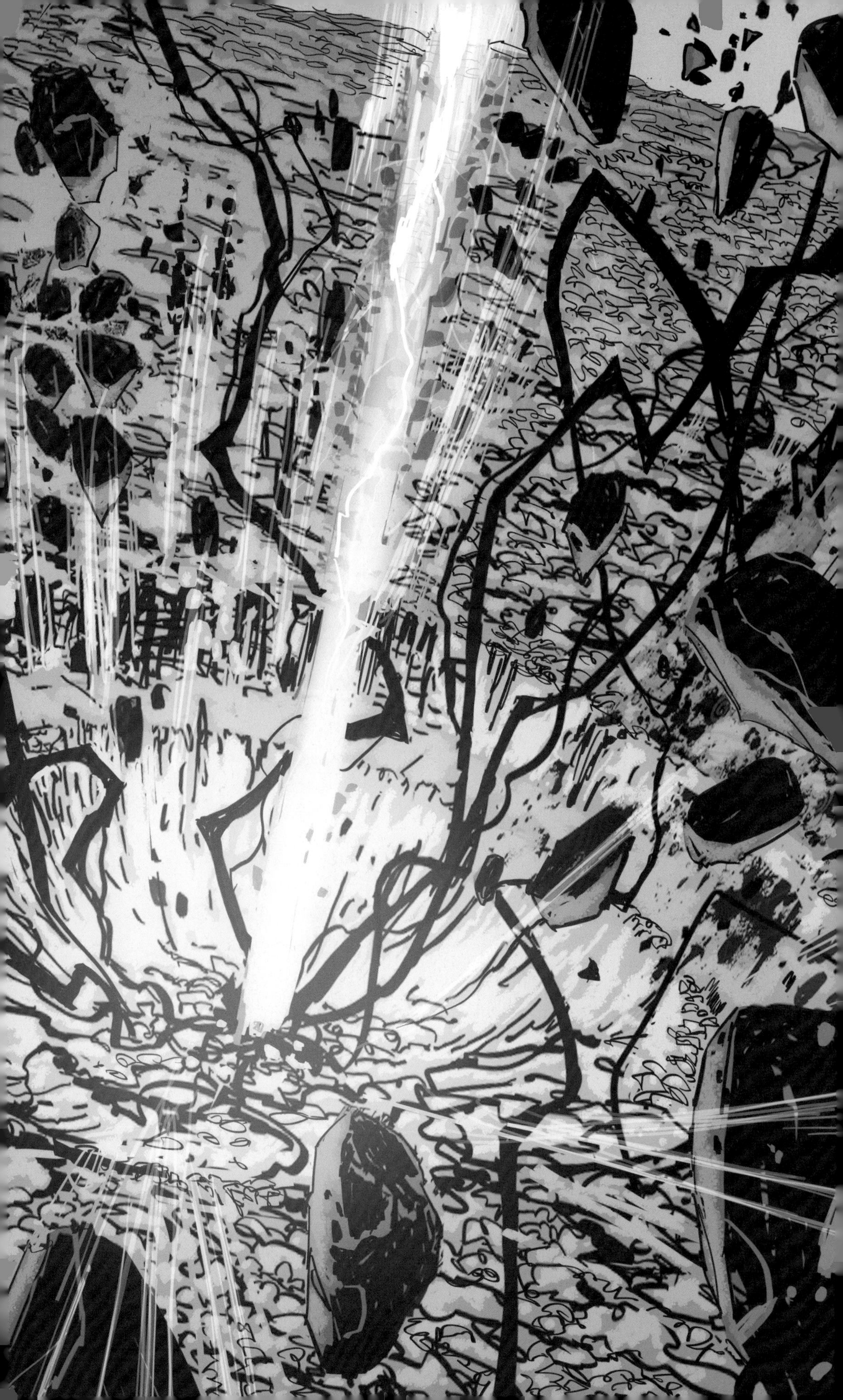

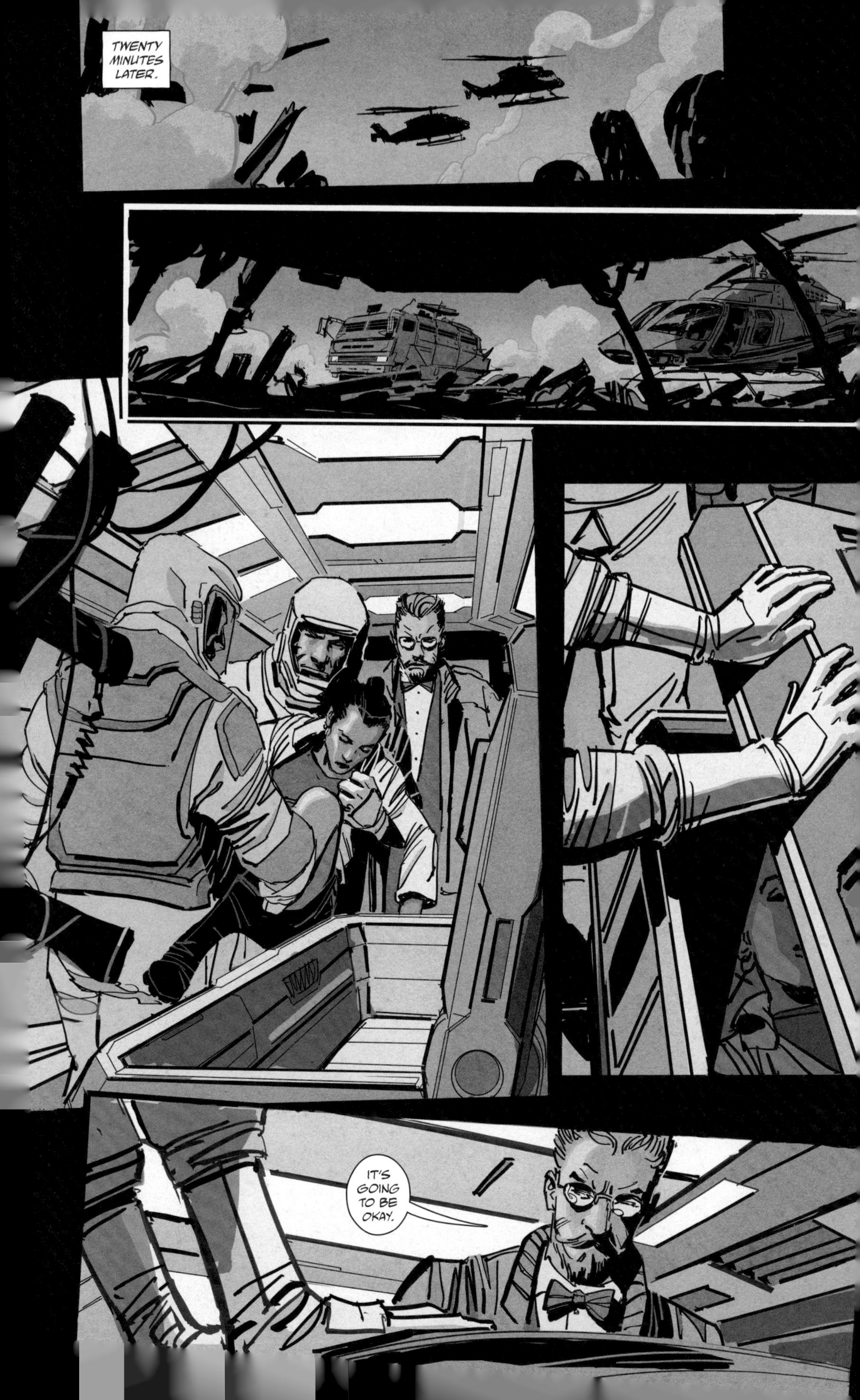
TWENTY MINUTES LATER.
IT'S GOING TO BE OKAY.

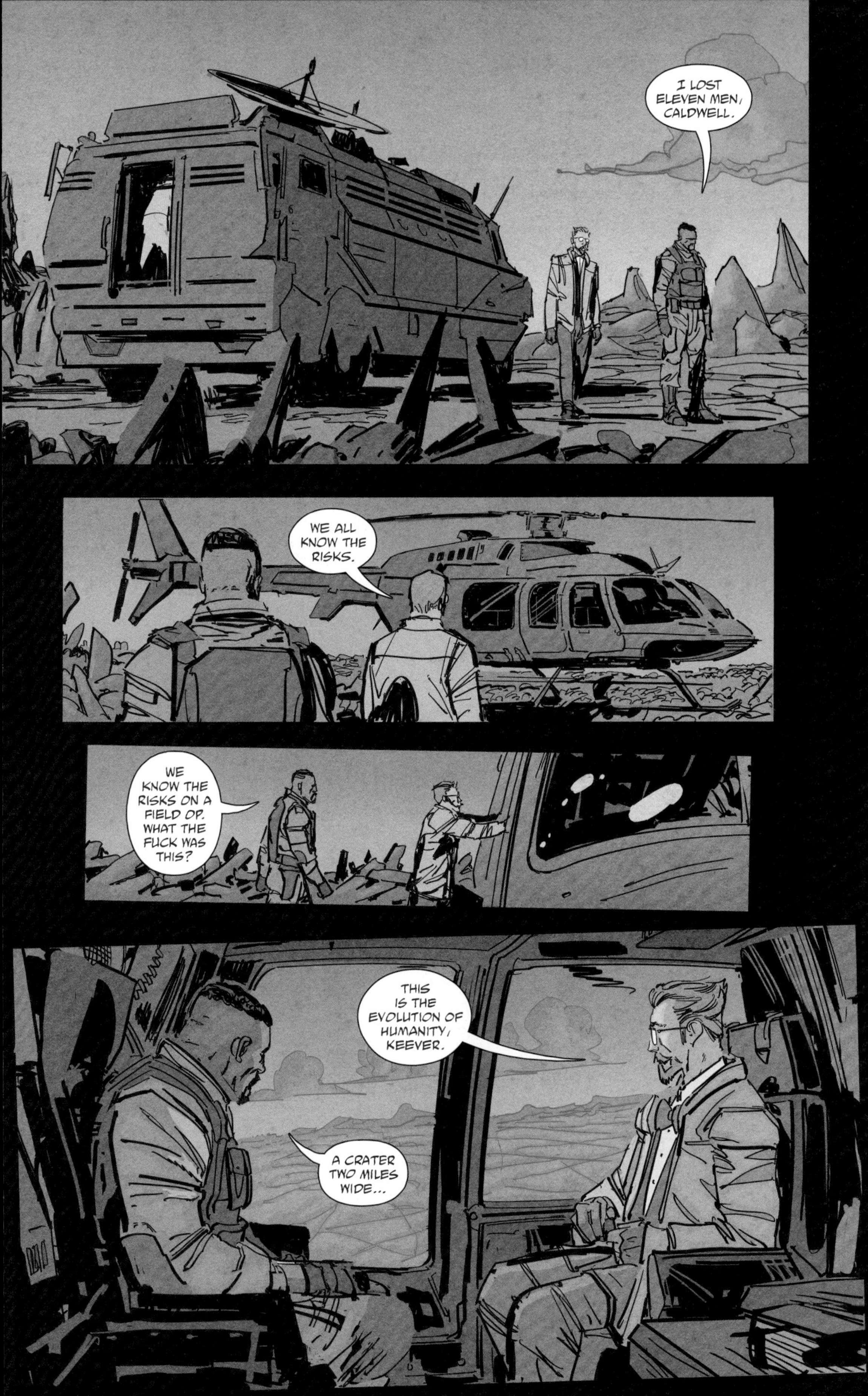
I LOST ELEVEN MEN, CALDWELL.
WE ALL KNOW THE RISKS.
WE KNOW THE RISKS ON A FIELD OP. WHAT THE FUCK WAS THIS?
THIS IS THE EVOLUTION OF HUMANITY, KEEVER.
A CRATER TWO MILES WIDE...

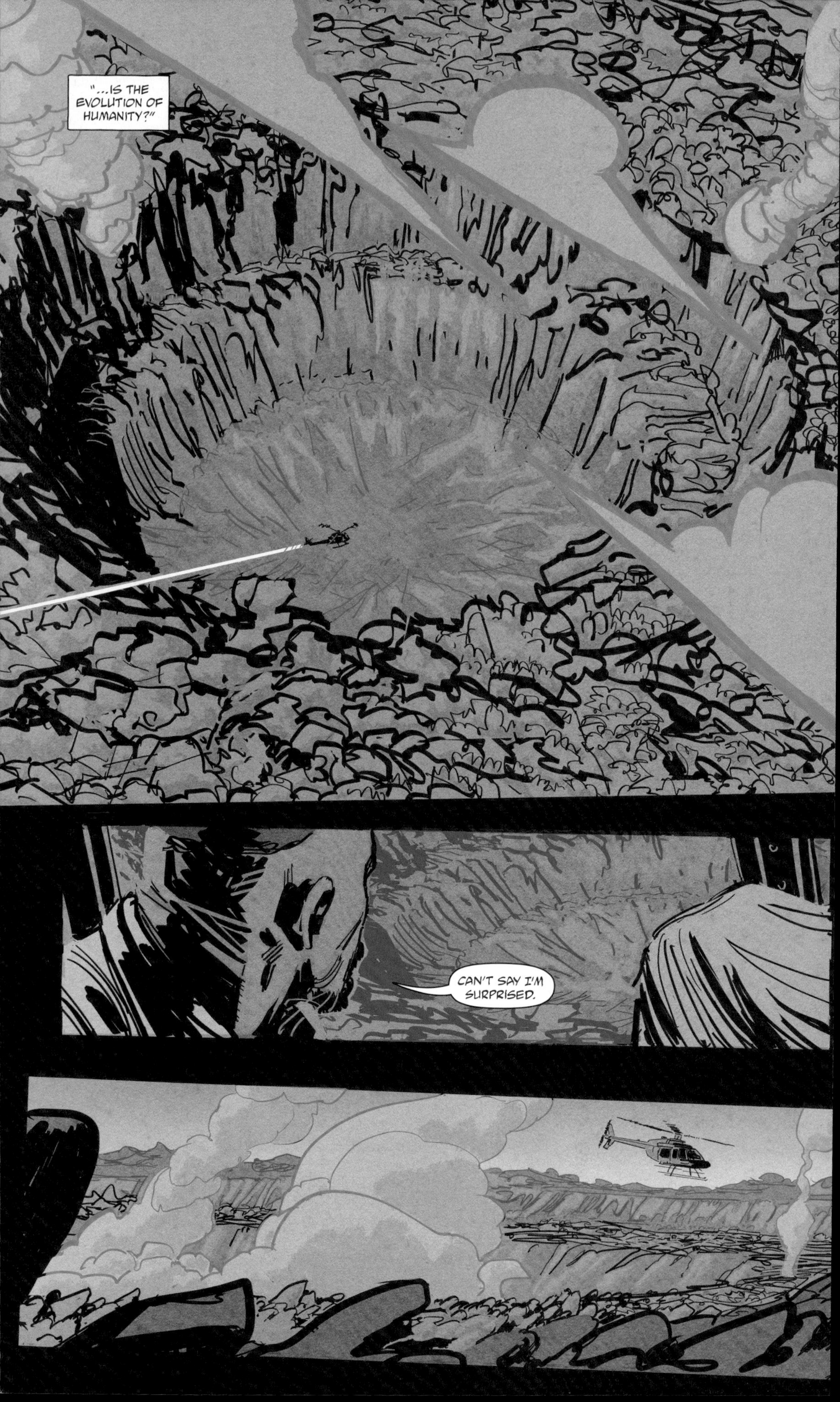
"...IS THE EVOLUTION OF HUMANITY?"
CAN'T SAY I'M SURPRISED.

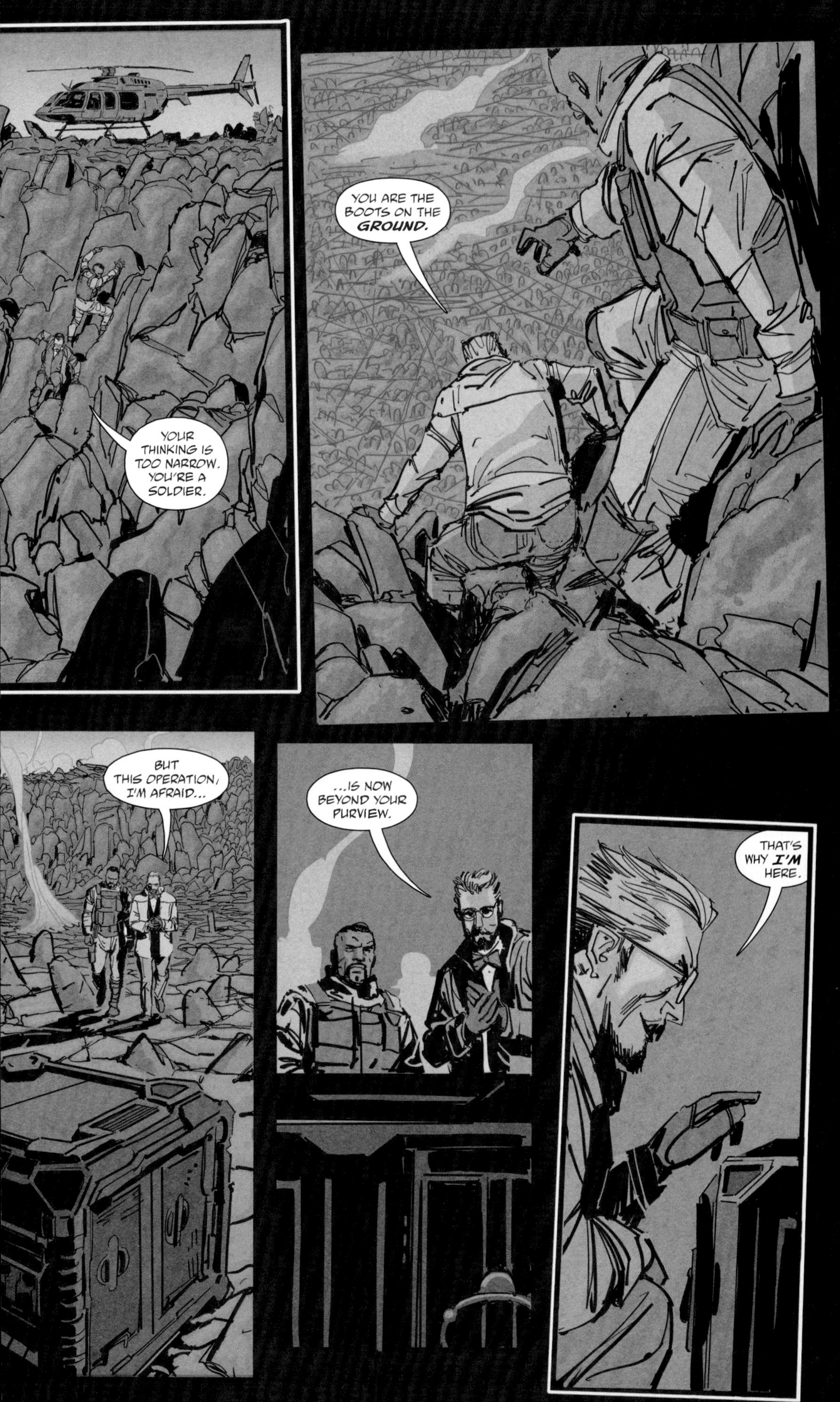

YOUR THINKING IS TOO NARROW. YOU'RE A SOLDIER.
YOU ARE THE BOOTS ON THE **GROUND.**
BUT THIS OPERATION, I'M AFRAID...
...IS NOW BEYOND YOUR PURVIEW.
THAT'S WHY ***I'M*** HERE.

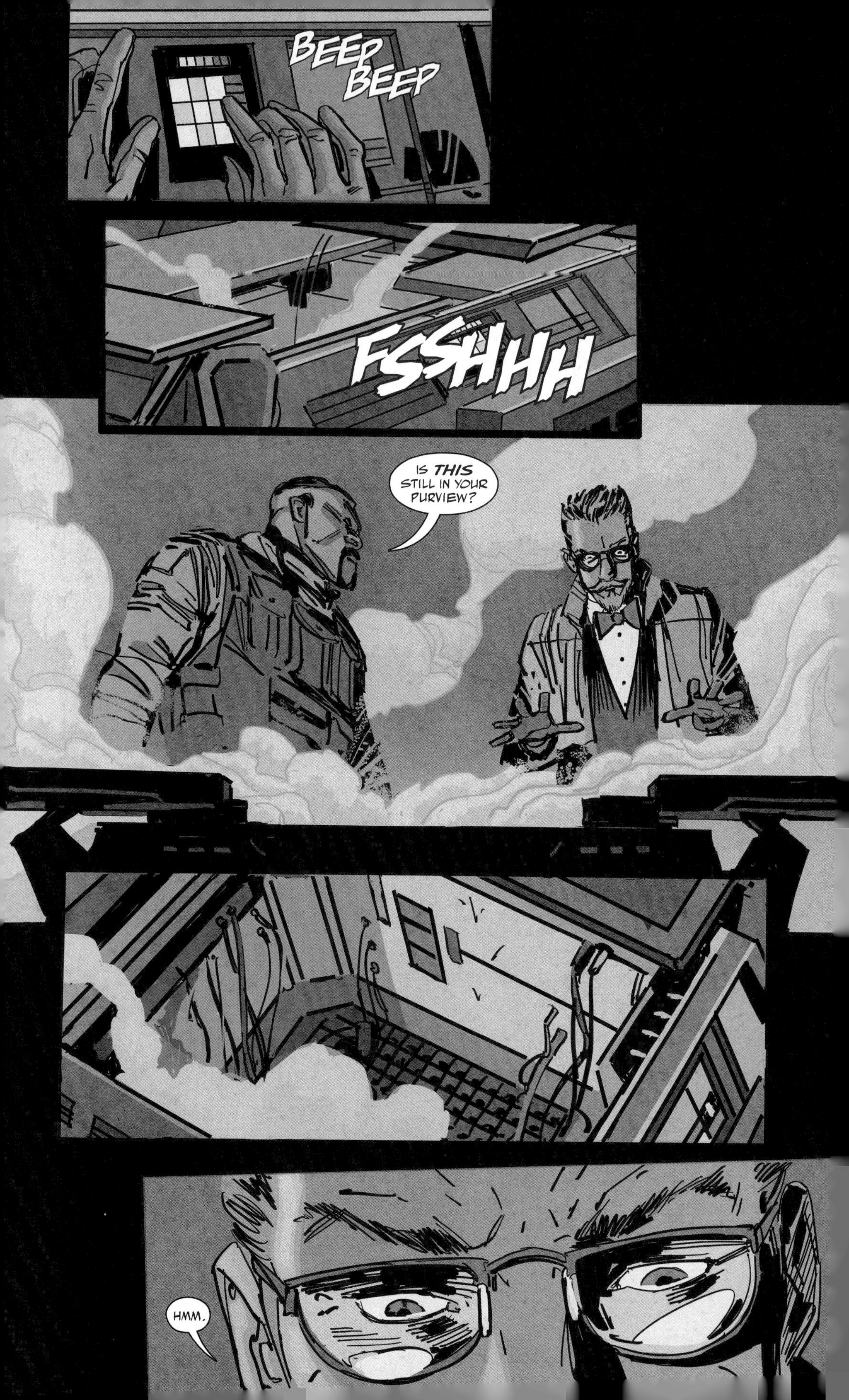
BEEP BEEP
FSSHHH
IS THIS STILL IN YOUR PURVIEW?
HMM.

5,000
YEARS AGO.

10,000
YEARS AGO.

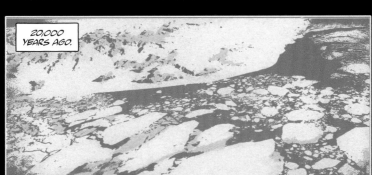

20,000
YEARS AGO.

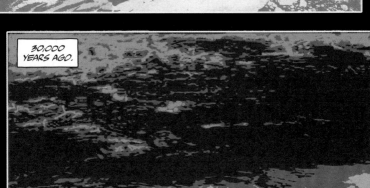

30,000
YEARS AGO.

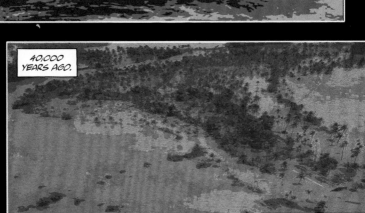

40,000
YEARS AGO.

50,000
YEARS AGO.

60,000
YEARS AGO.

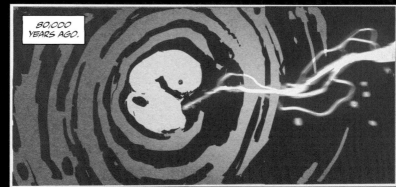

80,000
YEARS AGO.

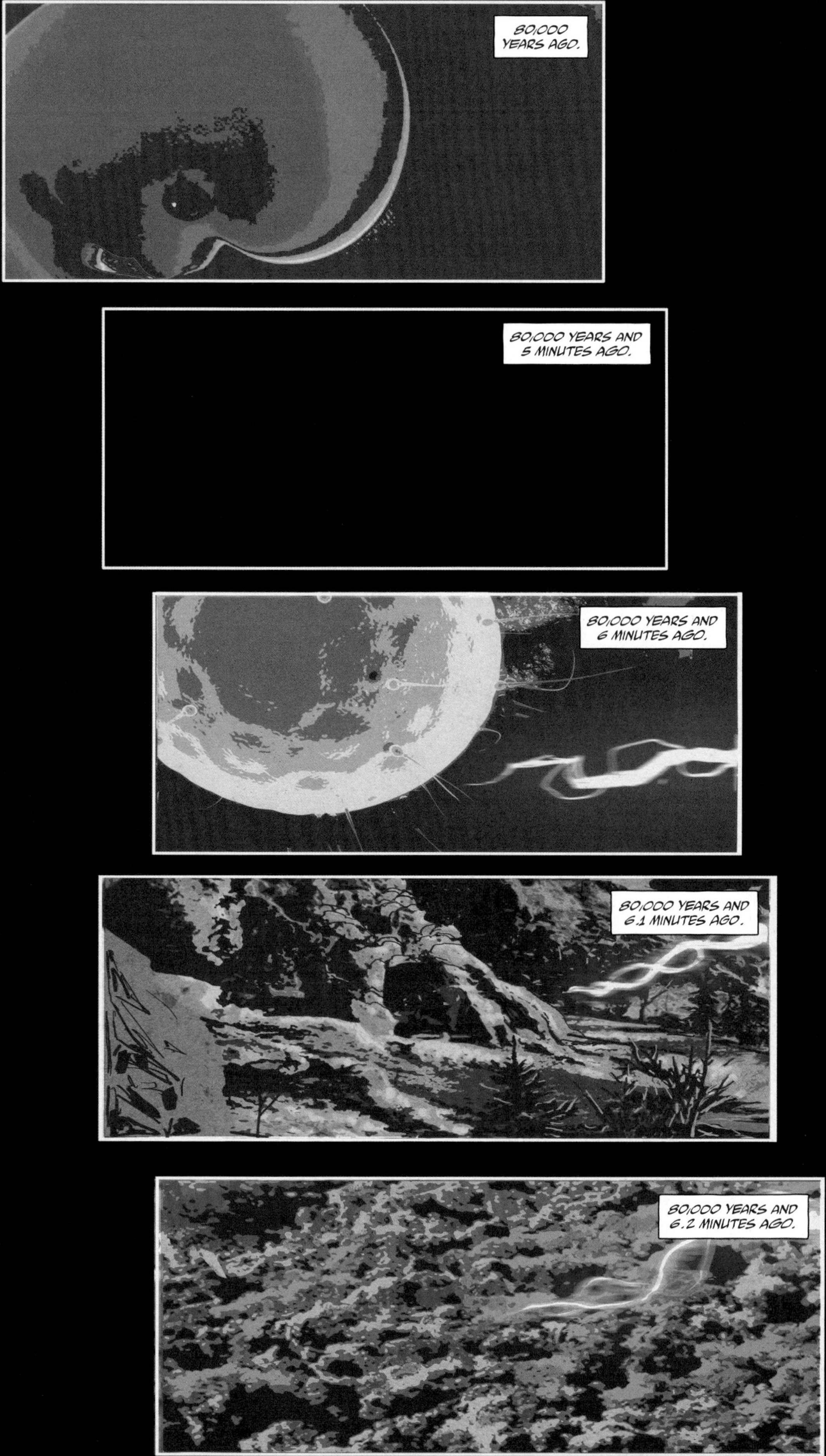
80,000 YEARS AGO.
80,000 YEARS AND 5 MINUTES AGO.
80,000 YEARS AND 6 MINUTES AGO.
80,000 YEARS AND 6.1 MINUTES AGO.
80,000 YEARS AND 6.2 MINUTES AGO.

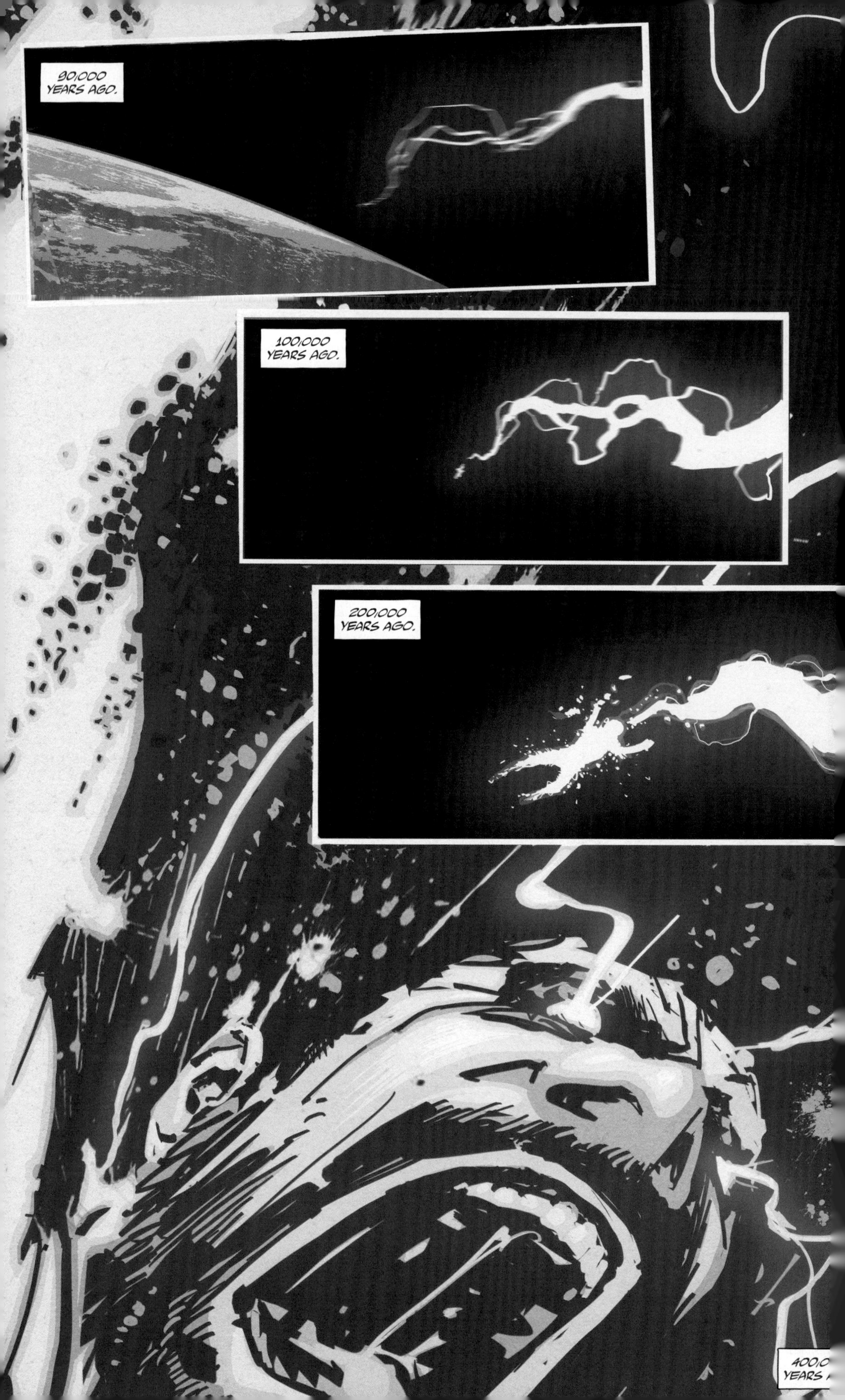
90,000 YEARS AGO.
100,000 YEARS AGO.
200,000 YEARS AGO.
400,0
YEARS

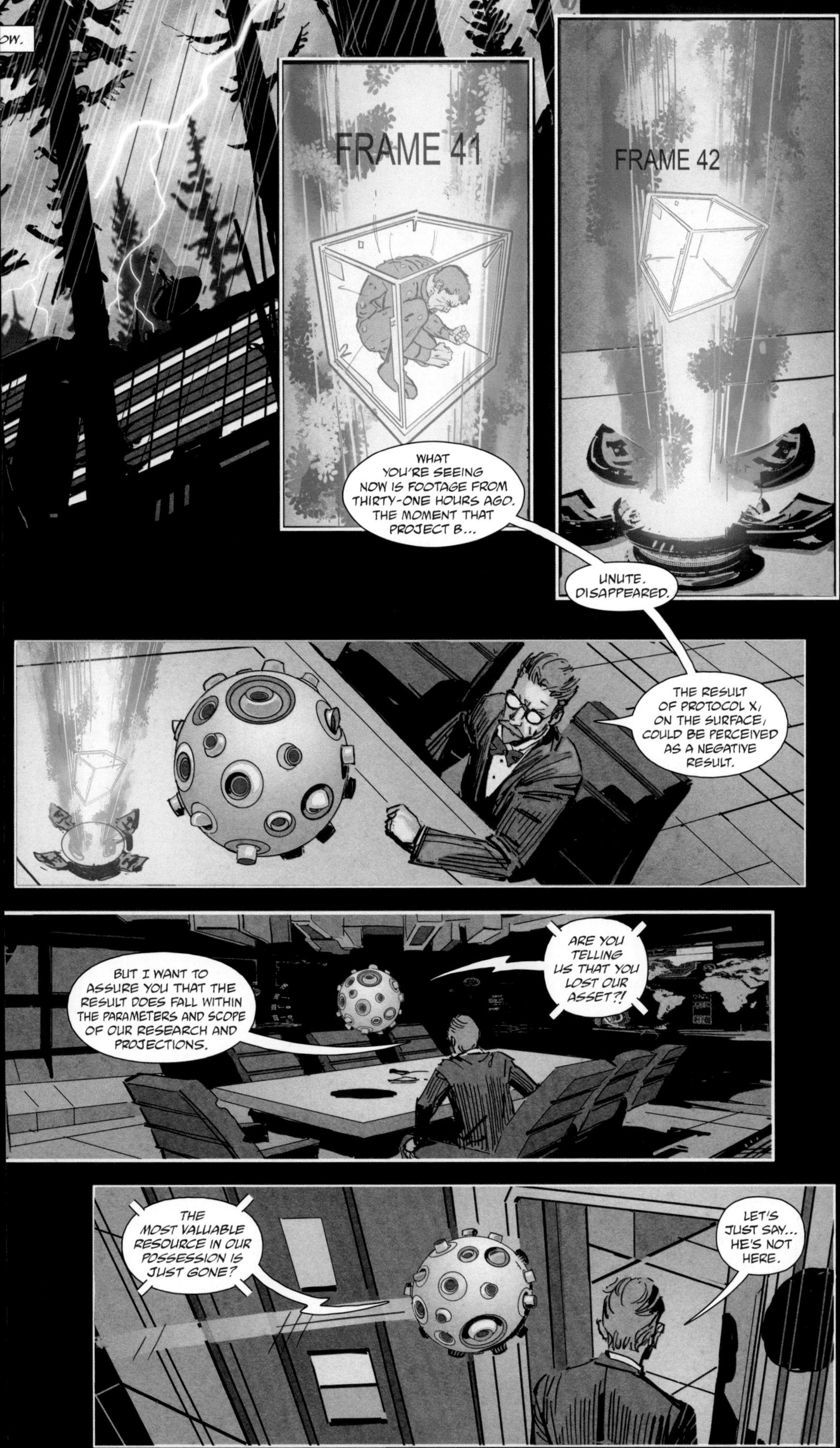
OW.
FRAME 41
FRAME 42
WHAT YOU'RE SEEING NOW IS FOOTAGE FROM THIRTY-ONE HOURS AGO. THE MOMENT THAT PROJECT B...
UNUTE. DISAPPEARED.
THE RESULT OF PROTOCOL X, ON THE SURFACE, COULD BE PERCEIVED AS A NEGATIVE RESULT.
BUT I WANT TO ASSURE YOU THAT THE RESULT DOES FALL WITHIN THE PARAMETERS AND SCOPE OF OUR RESEARCH AND PROJECTIONS.
ARE YOU TELLING US THAT YOU LOST OUR ASSET?!
THE MOST VALUABLE RESOURCE IN OUR POSSESSION IS JUST GONE?
LET'S JUST SAY... HE'S NOT HERE.

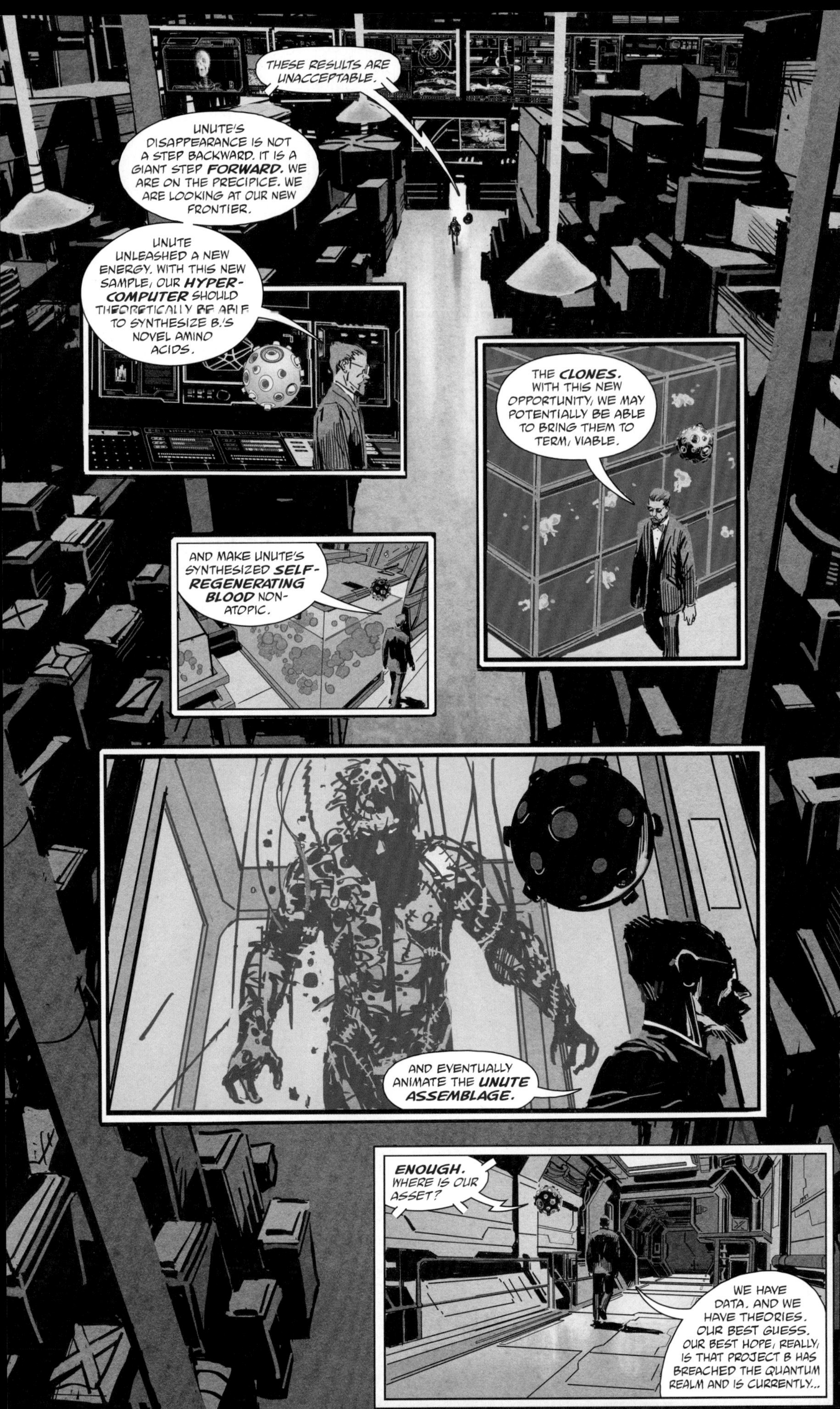
THESE RESULTS ARE UNACCEPTABLE.
UNUTE'S DISAPPEARANCE IS NOT A STEP BACKWARD. IT IS A GIANT STEP FORWARD. WE ARE ON THE PRECIPICE. WE ARE LOOKING AT OUR NEW FRONTIER.
UNUTE UNLEASHED A NEW ENERGY. WITH THIS NEW SAMPLE, OUR HYPER-COMPUTER SHOULD THEORETICALLY BE ABLE TO SYNTHESIZE B.'S NOVEL AMINO ACIDS.
THE CLONES. WITH THIS NEW OPPORTUNITY, WE MAY POTENTIALLY BE ABLE TO BRING THEM TO TERM, VIABLE.
AND MAKE UNUTE'S SYNTHESIZED SELF-REGENERATING BLOOD NON-ATOPIC.
AND EVENTUALLY ANIMATE THE UNUTE ASSEMBLAGE.
ENOUGH. WHERE IS OUR ASSET?
WE HAVE DATA. AND WE HAVE THEORIES. OUR BEST GUESS. OUR BEST HOPE, REALLY, IS THAT PROJECT B HAS BREACHED THE QUANTUM REALM AND IS CURRENTLY...

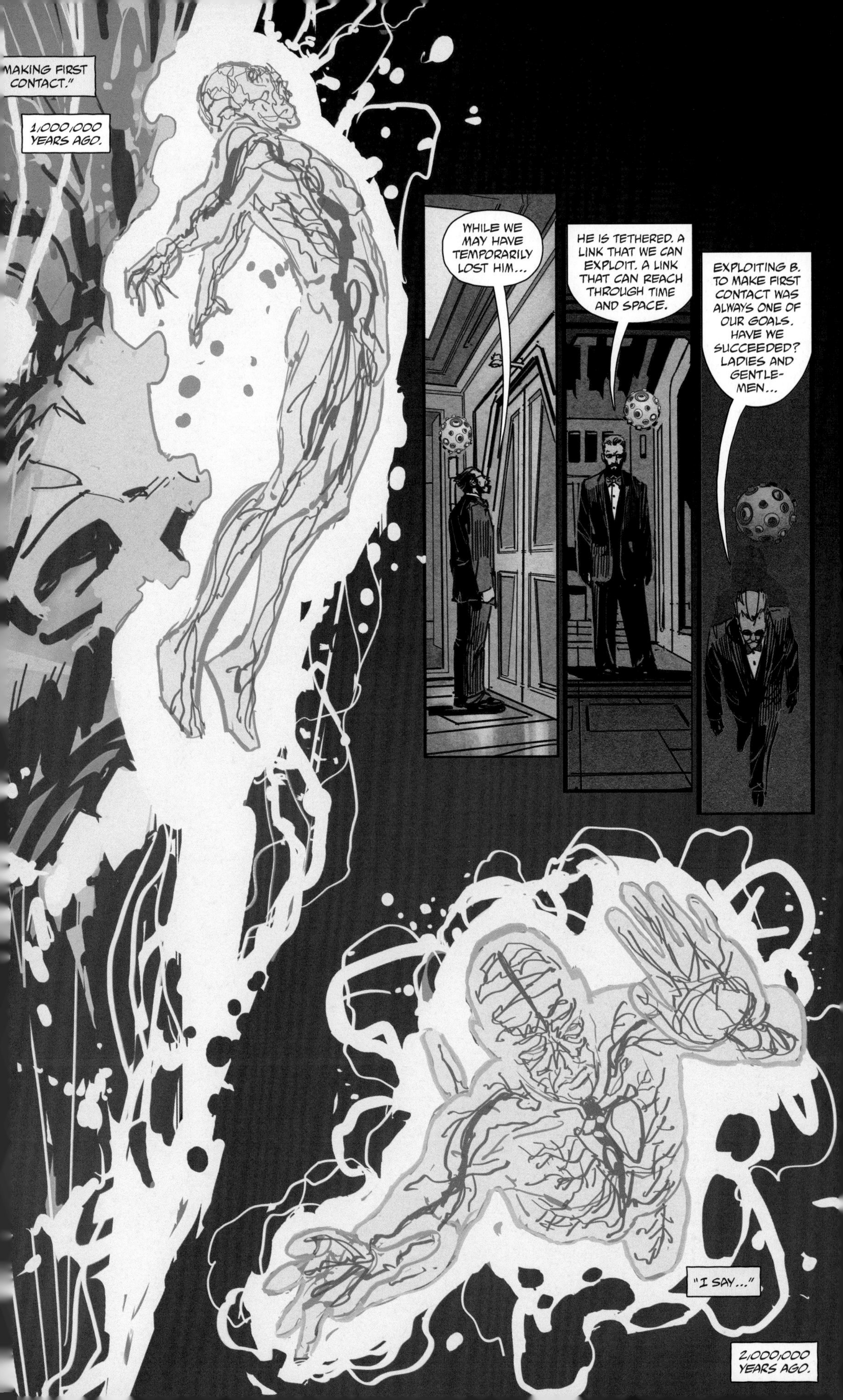
MAKING FIRST CONTACT."
1,000,000 YEARS AGO.
WHILE WE MAY HAVE TEMPORARILY LOST HIM...
HE IS TETHERED. A LINK THAT WE CAN EXPLOIT. A LINK THAT CAN REACH THROUGH TIME AND SPACE.
EXPLOITING B. TO MAKE FIRST CONTACT WAS ALWAYS ONE OF OUR GOALS. HAVE WE SUCCEEDED? LADIES AND GENTLE-MEN...
"I SAY..."
2,000,000 YEARS AGO.

"YES."
PRESENT DAY.
FATHER?

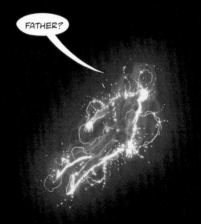

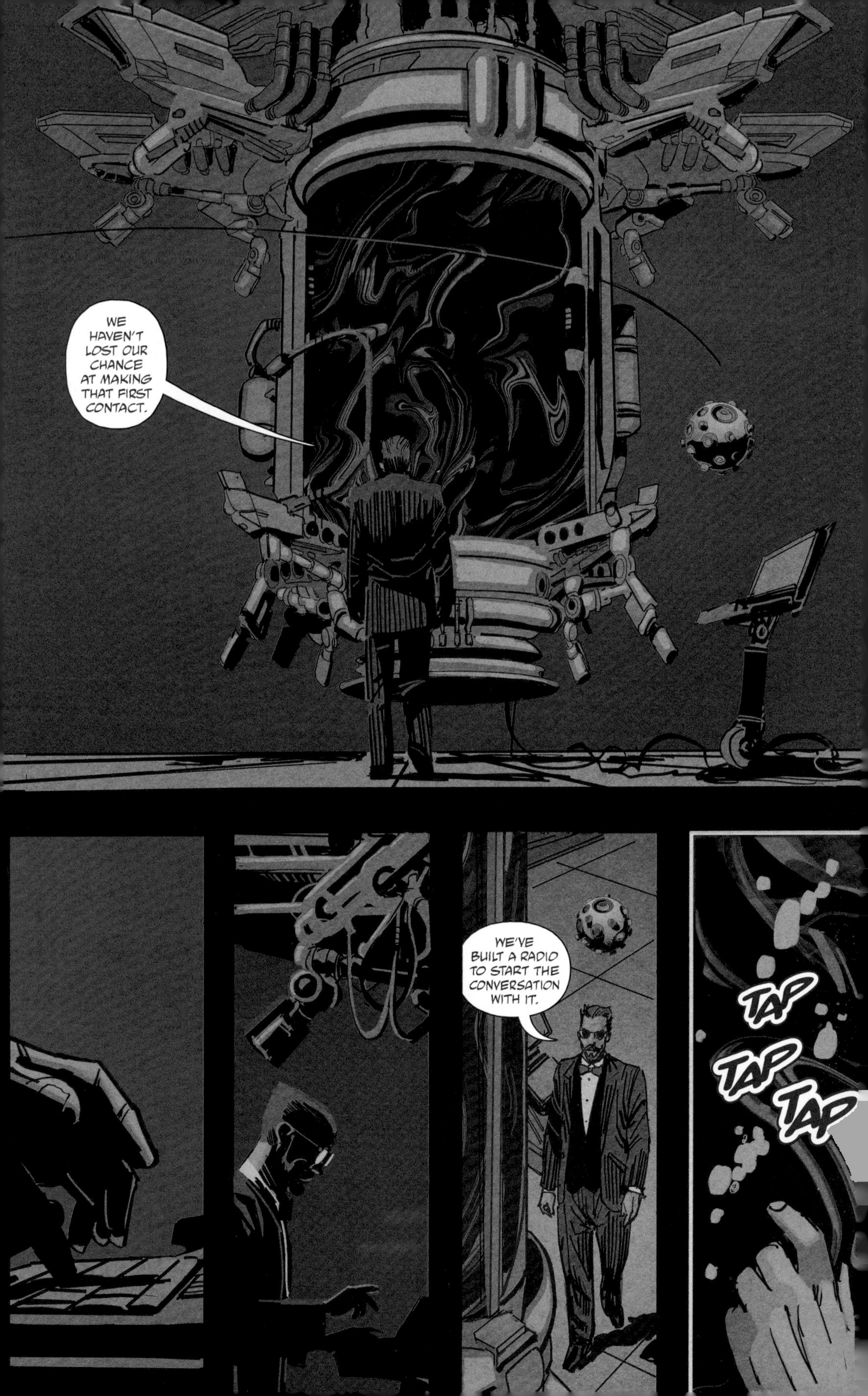
WE HAVEN'T LOST OUR CHANCE AT MAKING THAT FIRST CONTACT.
WE'VE BUILT A RADIO TO START THE CONVERSATION WITH IT.
TAP
TAP
TAP

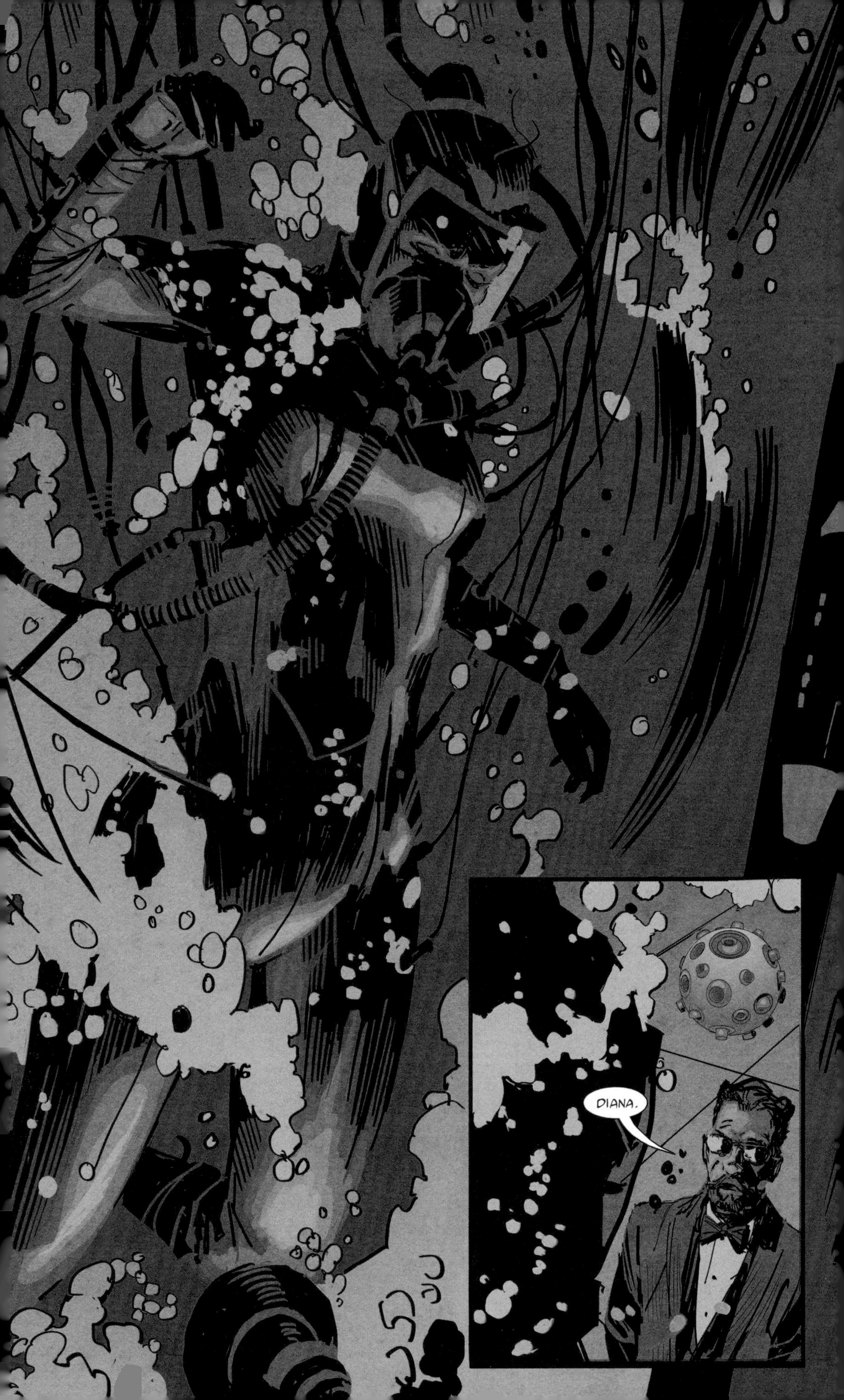
DIANA.

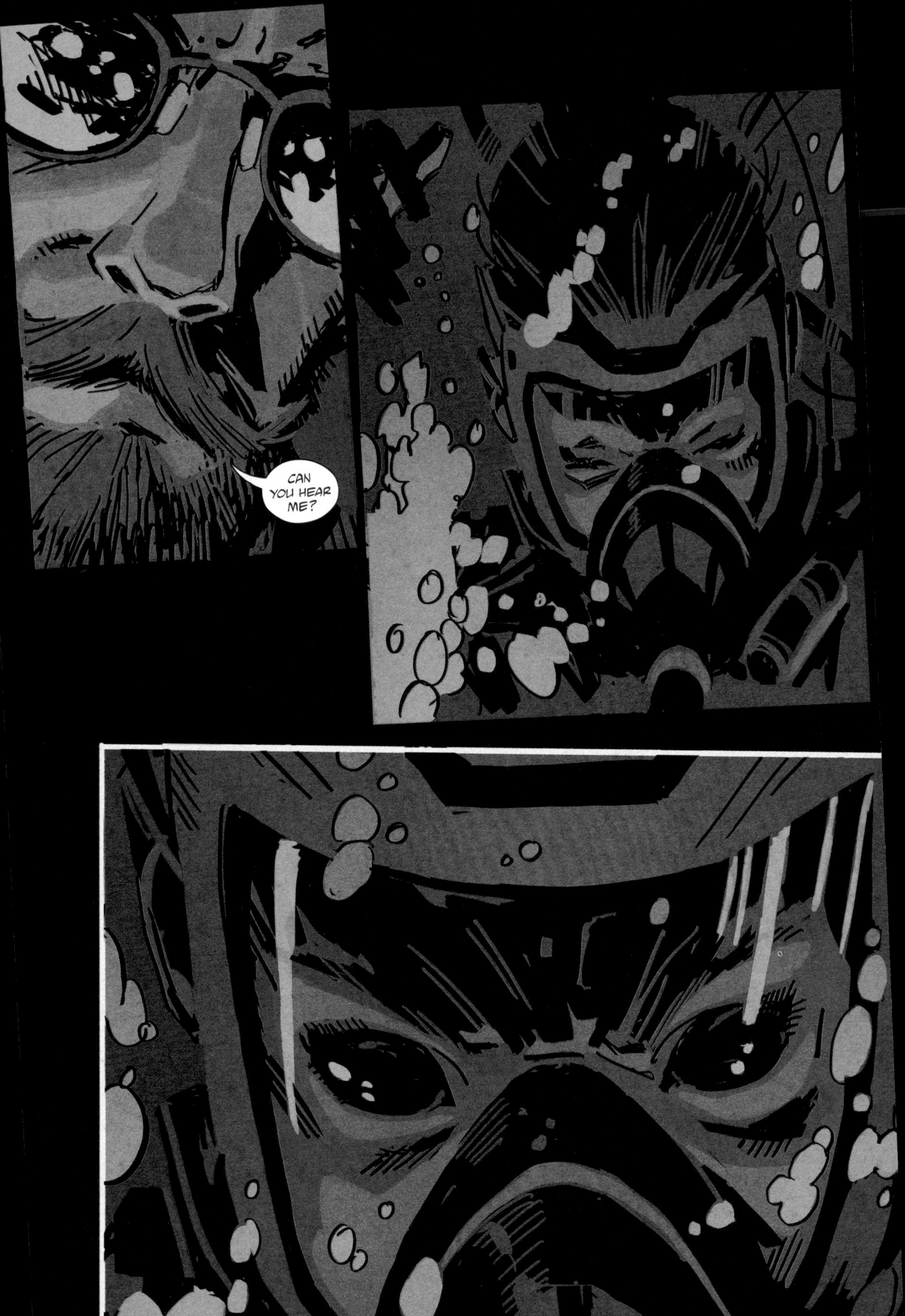
CAN YOU HEAR ME?

TO BE CONTINUED...

COVER GALLERY

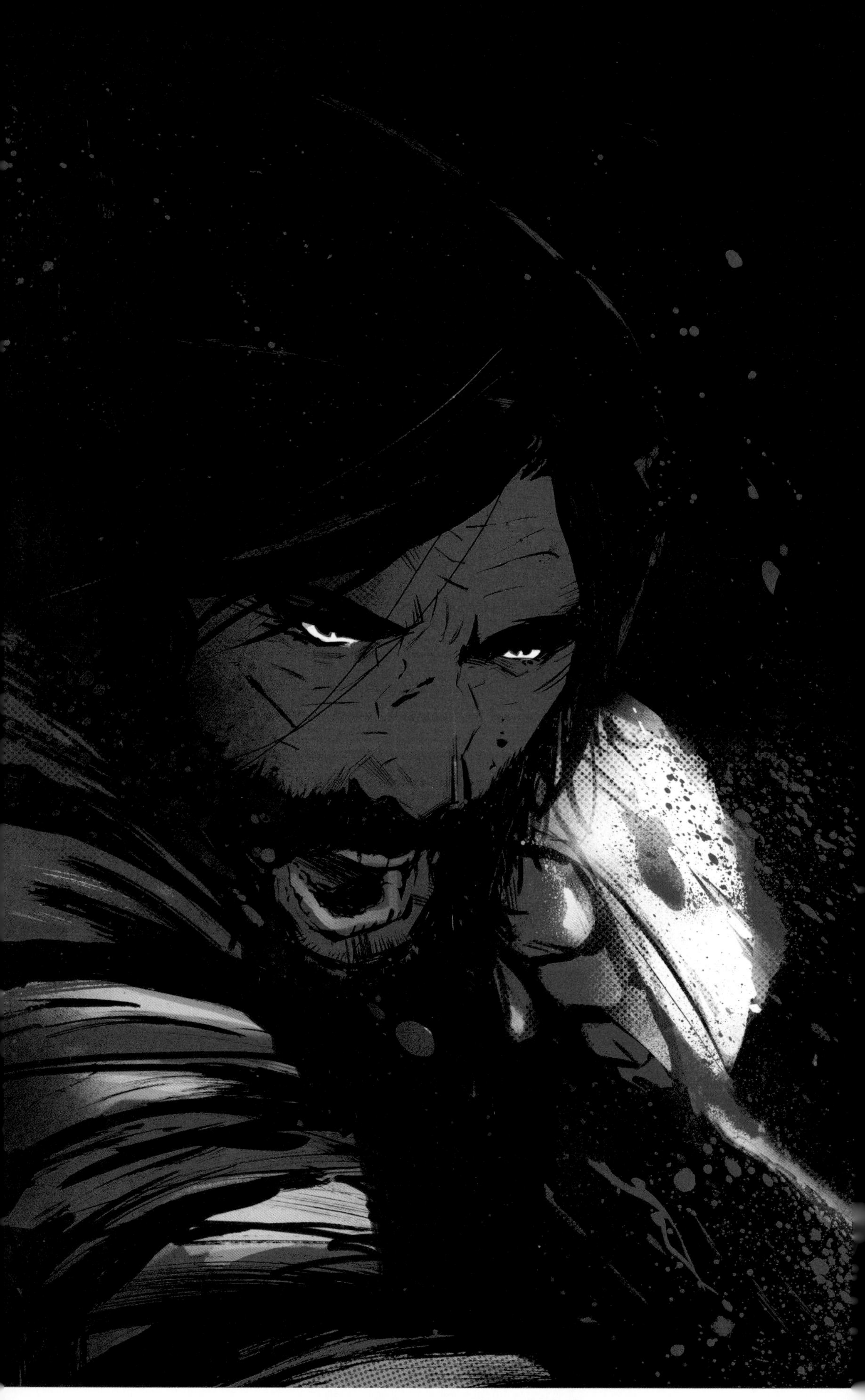

Issue #5 Cover by **LEE GARBETT**

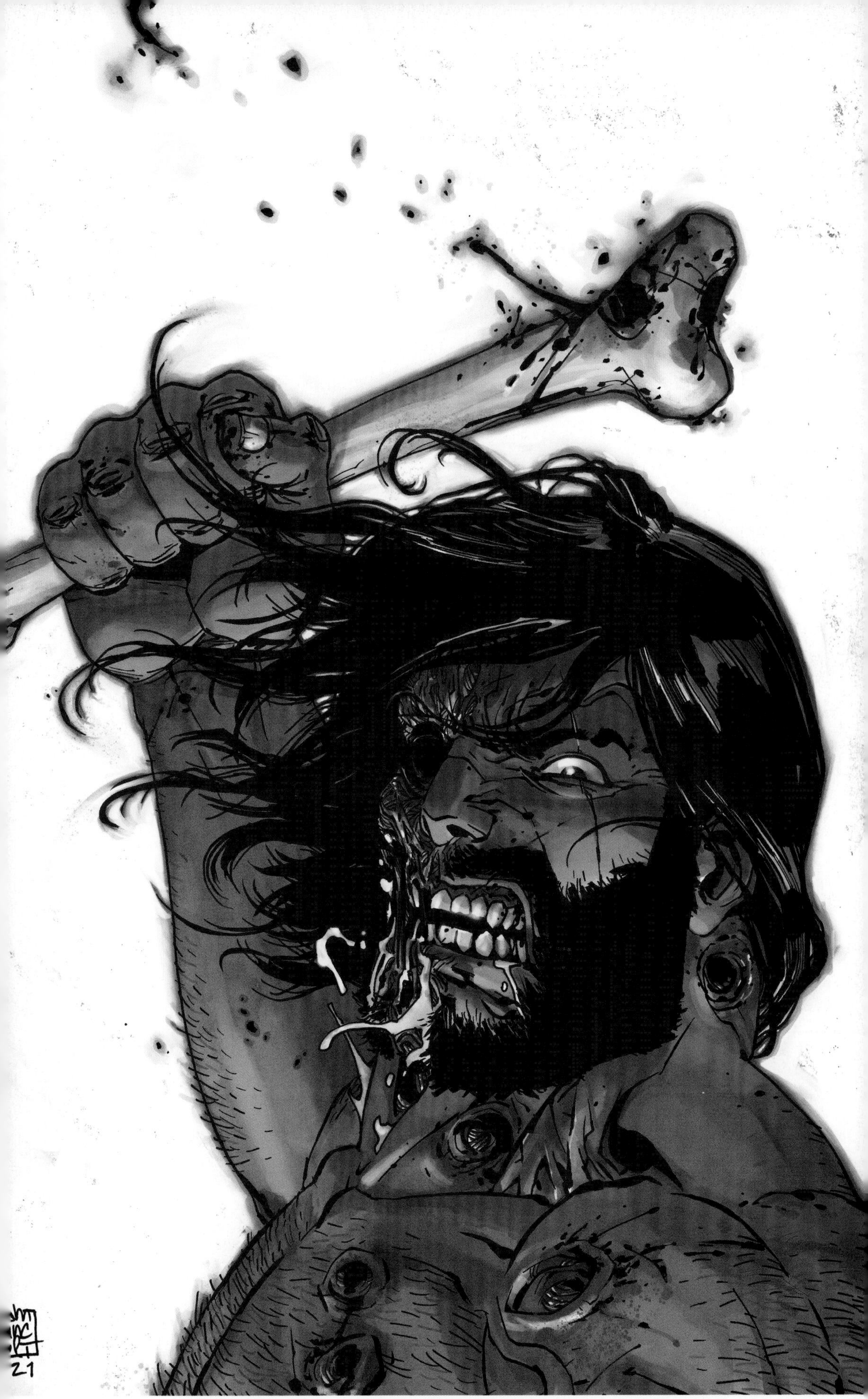
21
Issue #5 Cover by **GIUSEPPE CAMUNCOLI**

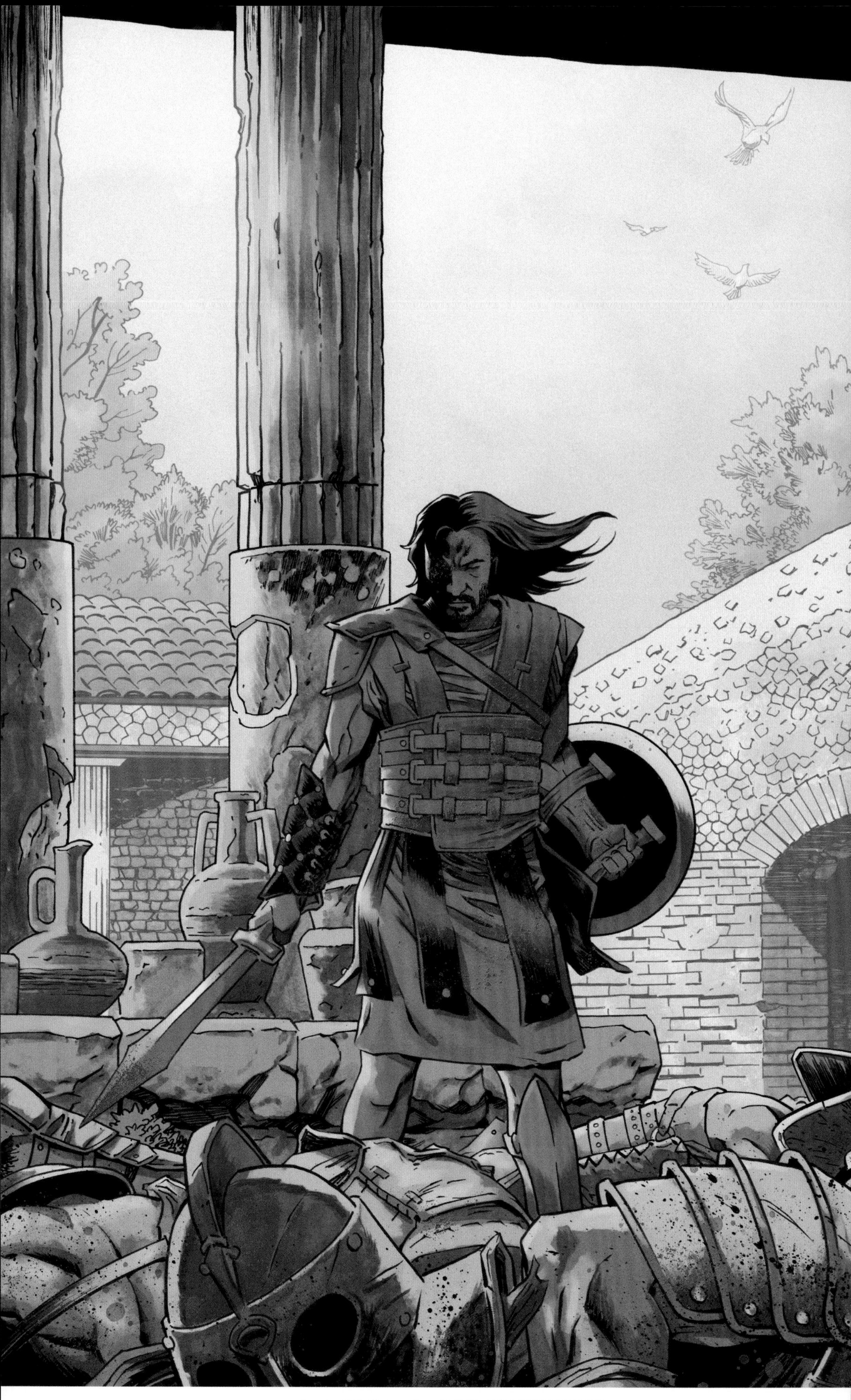

Issue #5 Cover by **DECLAN SHALVEY**

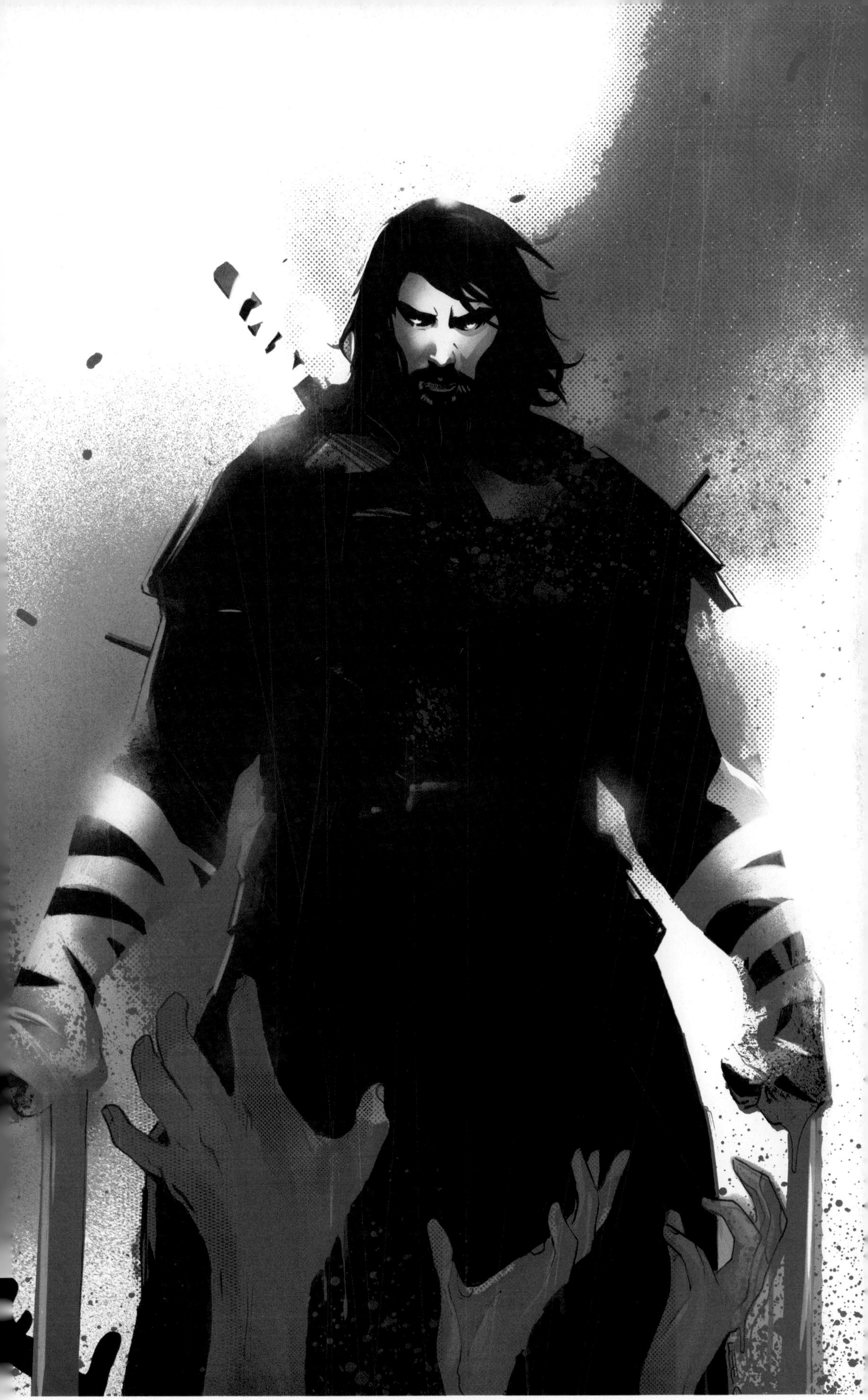

Issue #6 Cover by **LEE GARBETT**

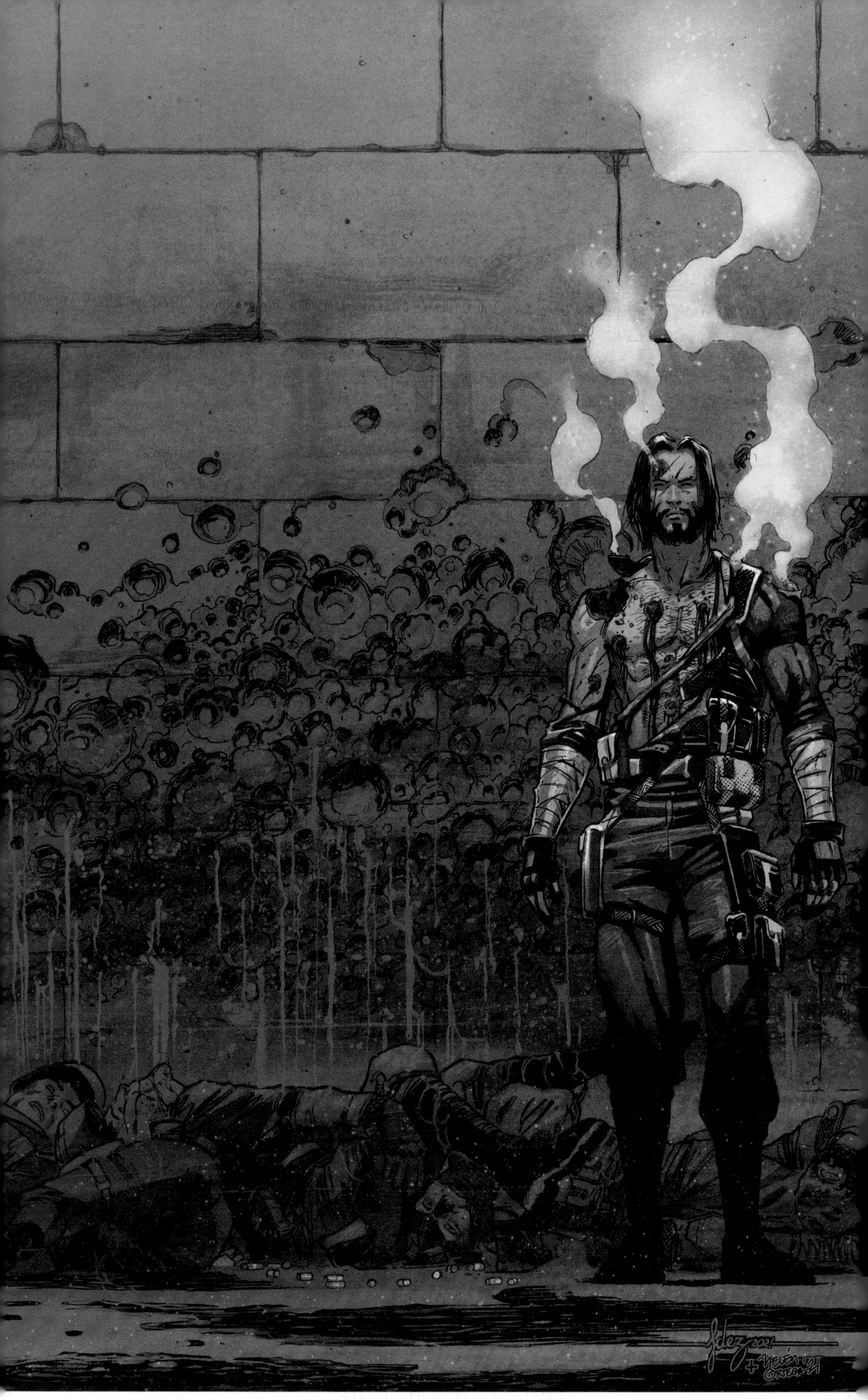

Issue #6 Cover by **JAVIER FERNANDEZ** with colors by **BELÉN ORTEGA**

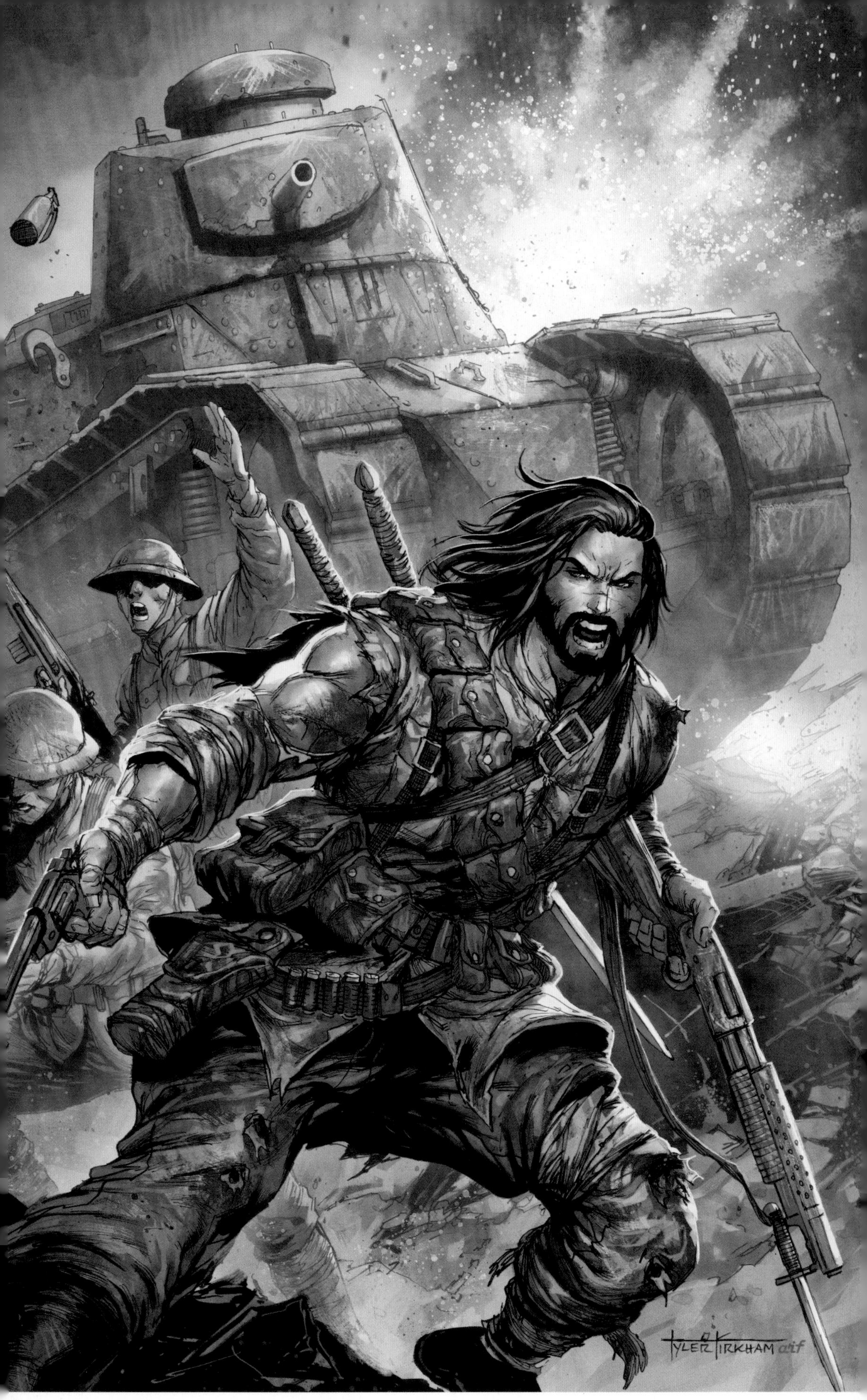
TYLER KIRKHAM arif

Issue #6 Cover by **TYLER KIRKHAM** with colors by **ARIF PRIANTO**

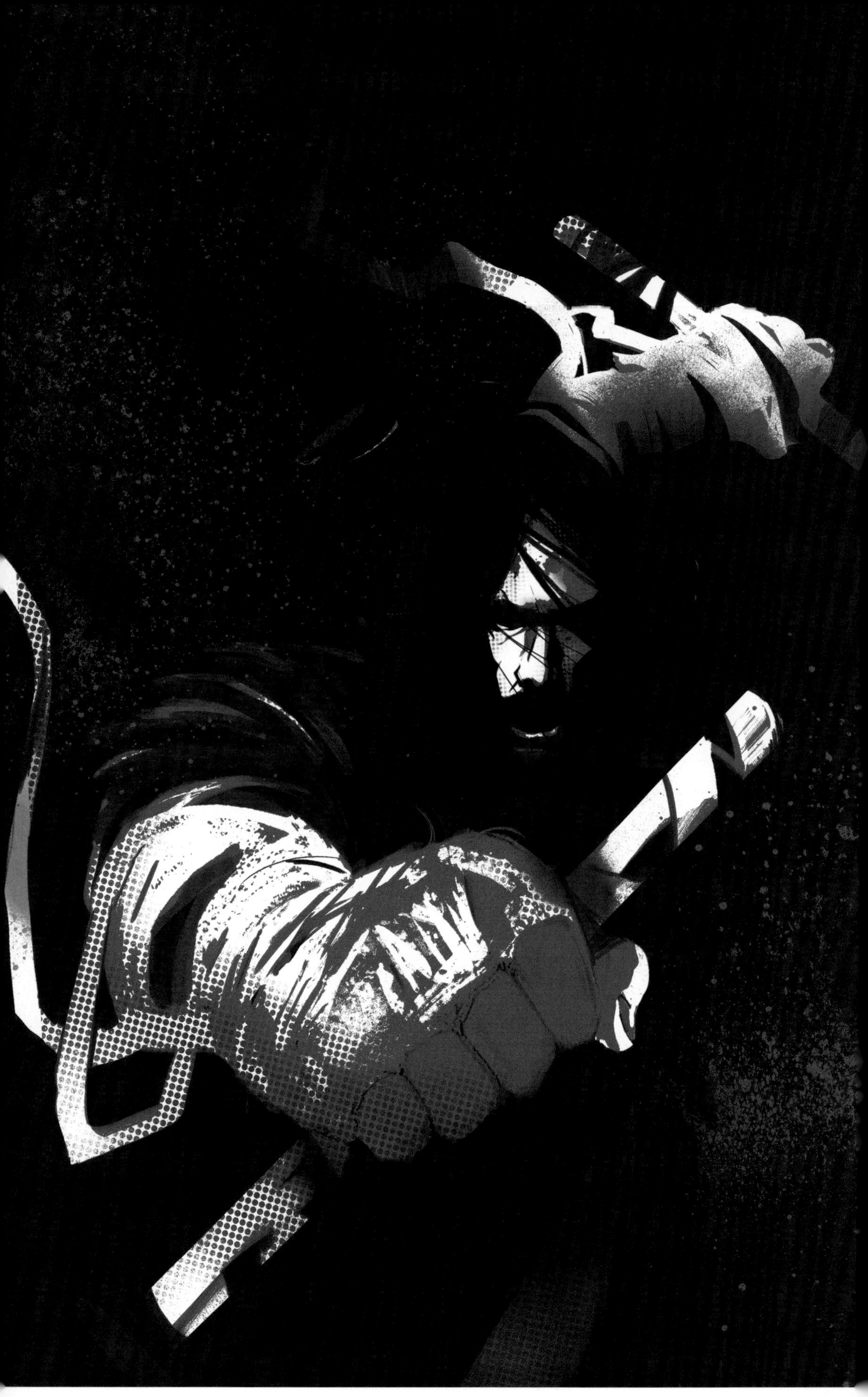

Issue #7 Cover by **LEE GARBETT**

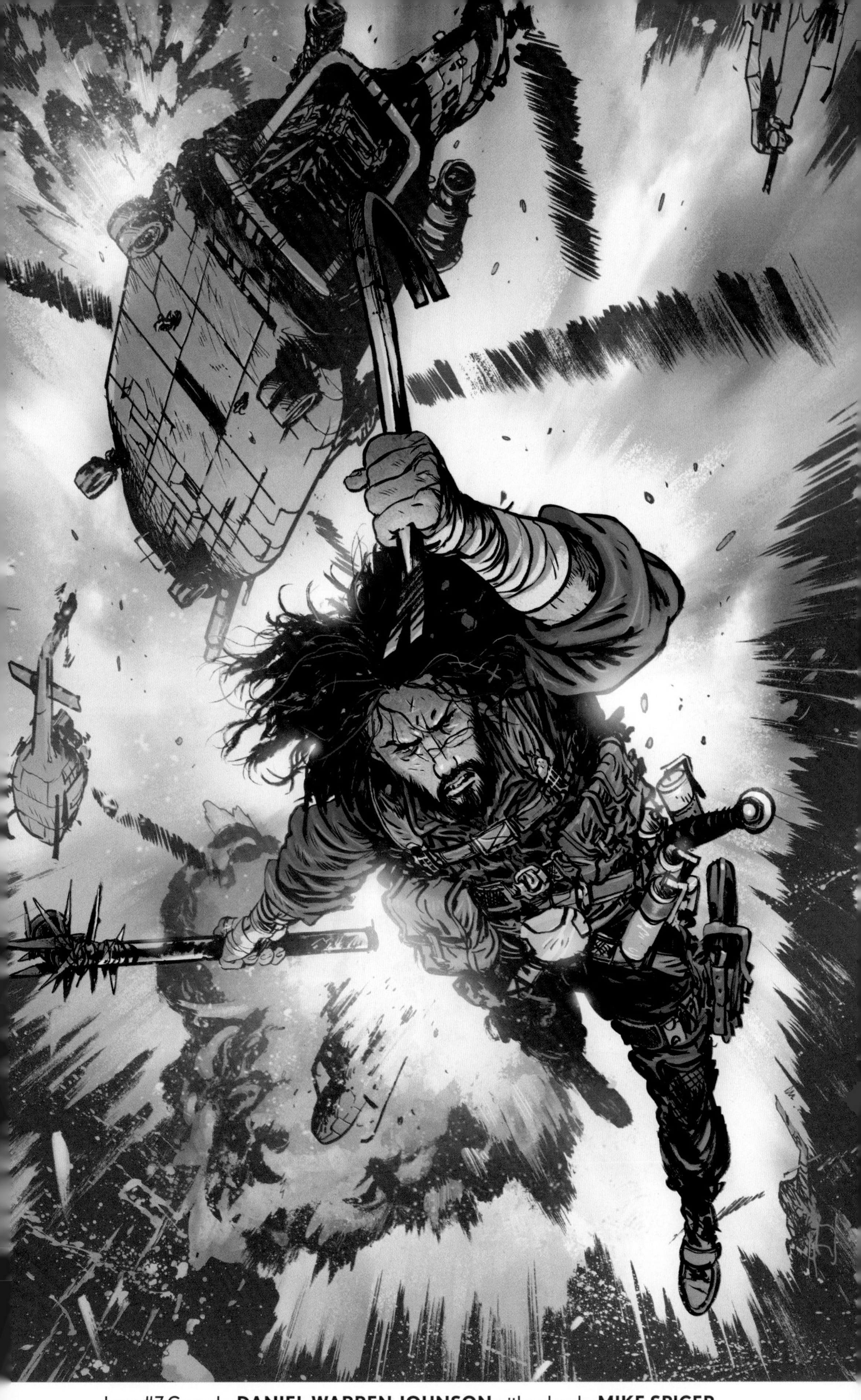

Issue #7 Cover by **DANIEL WARREN JOHNSON** with colors by **MIKE SPICER**

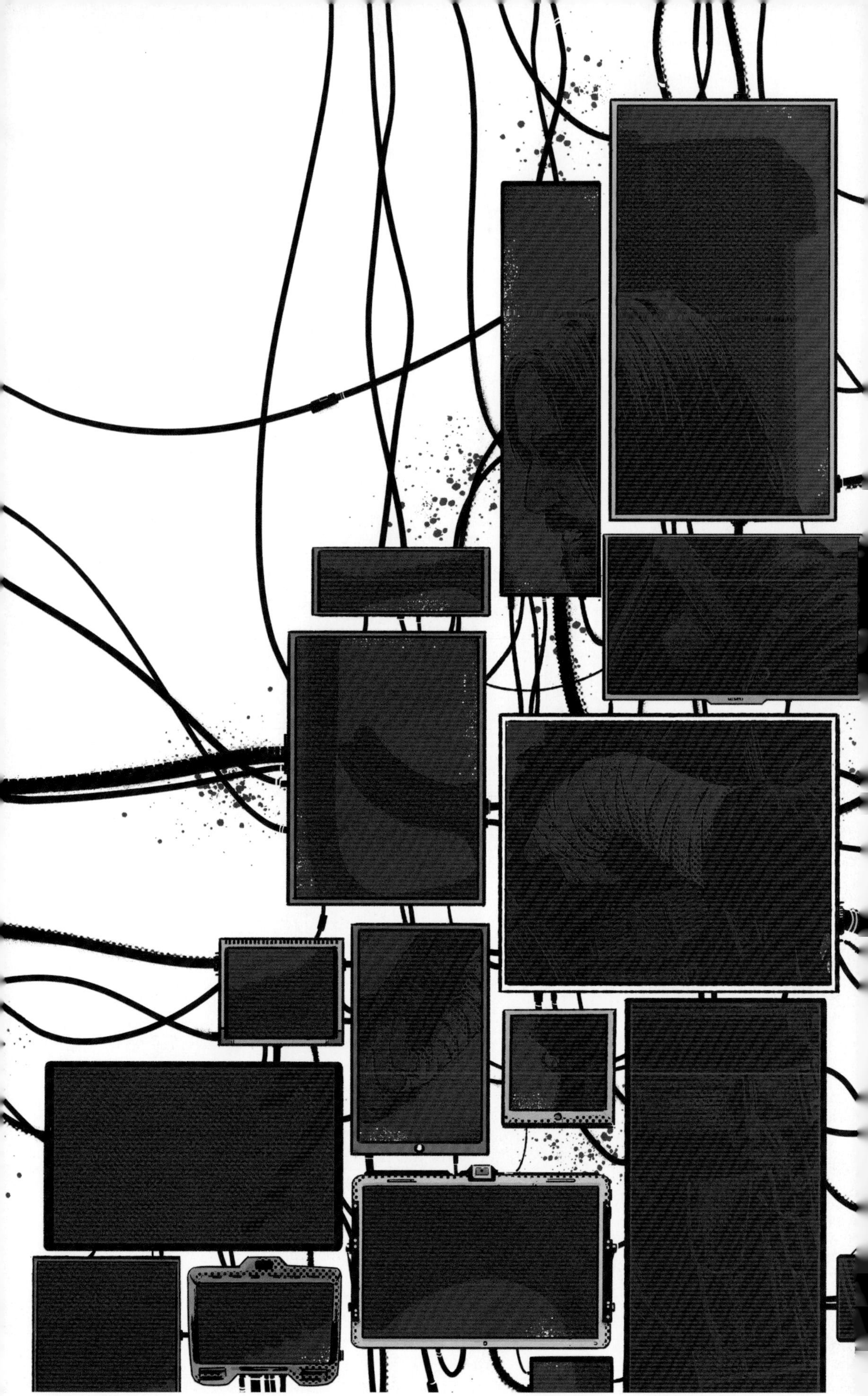

Issue #7 Cover by **JORGE FORNÉS**

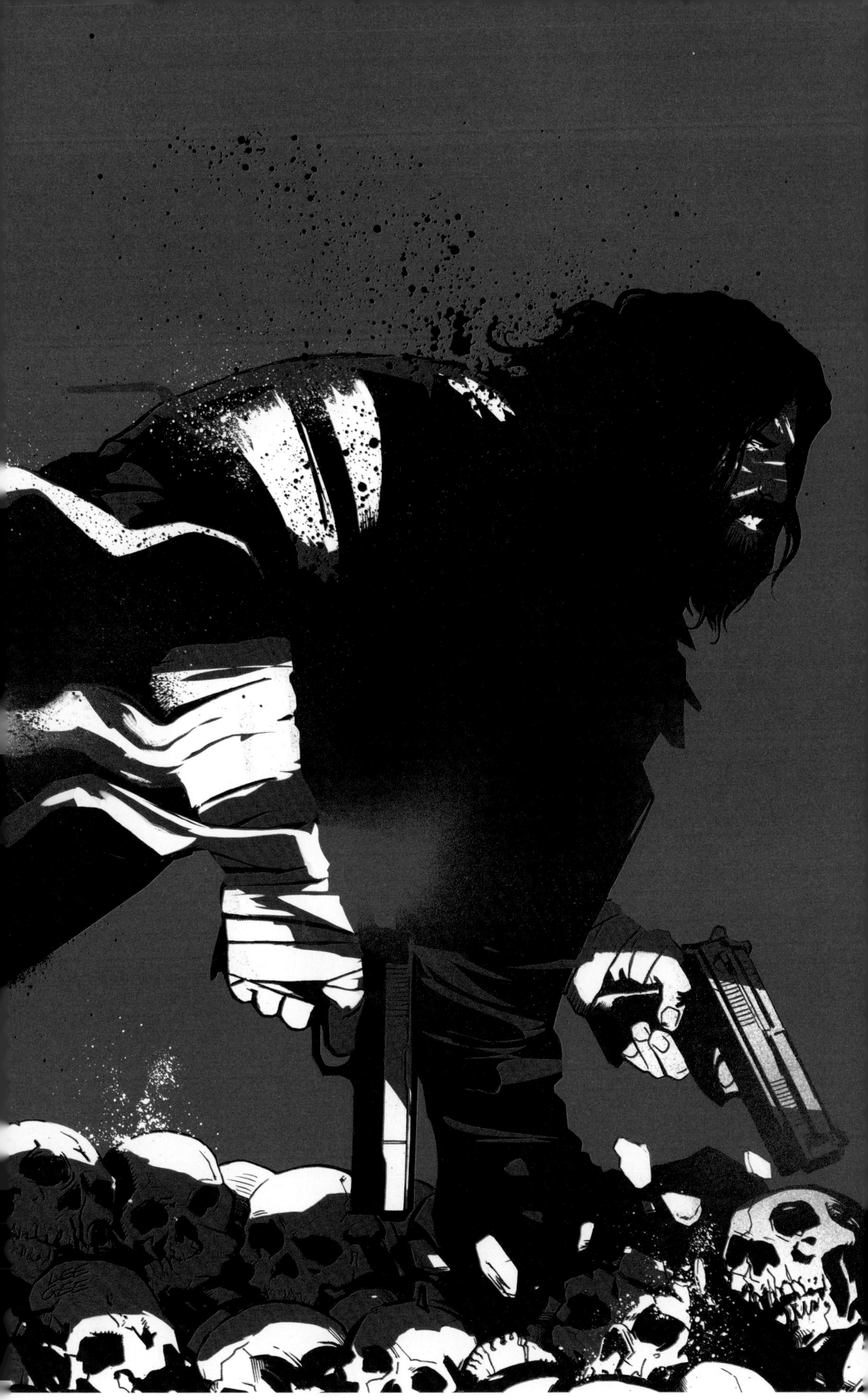

Issue #8 Cover by **LEE GARBETT**

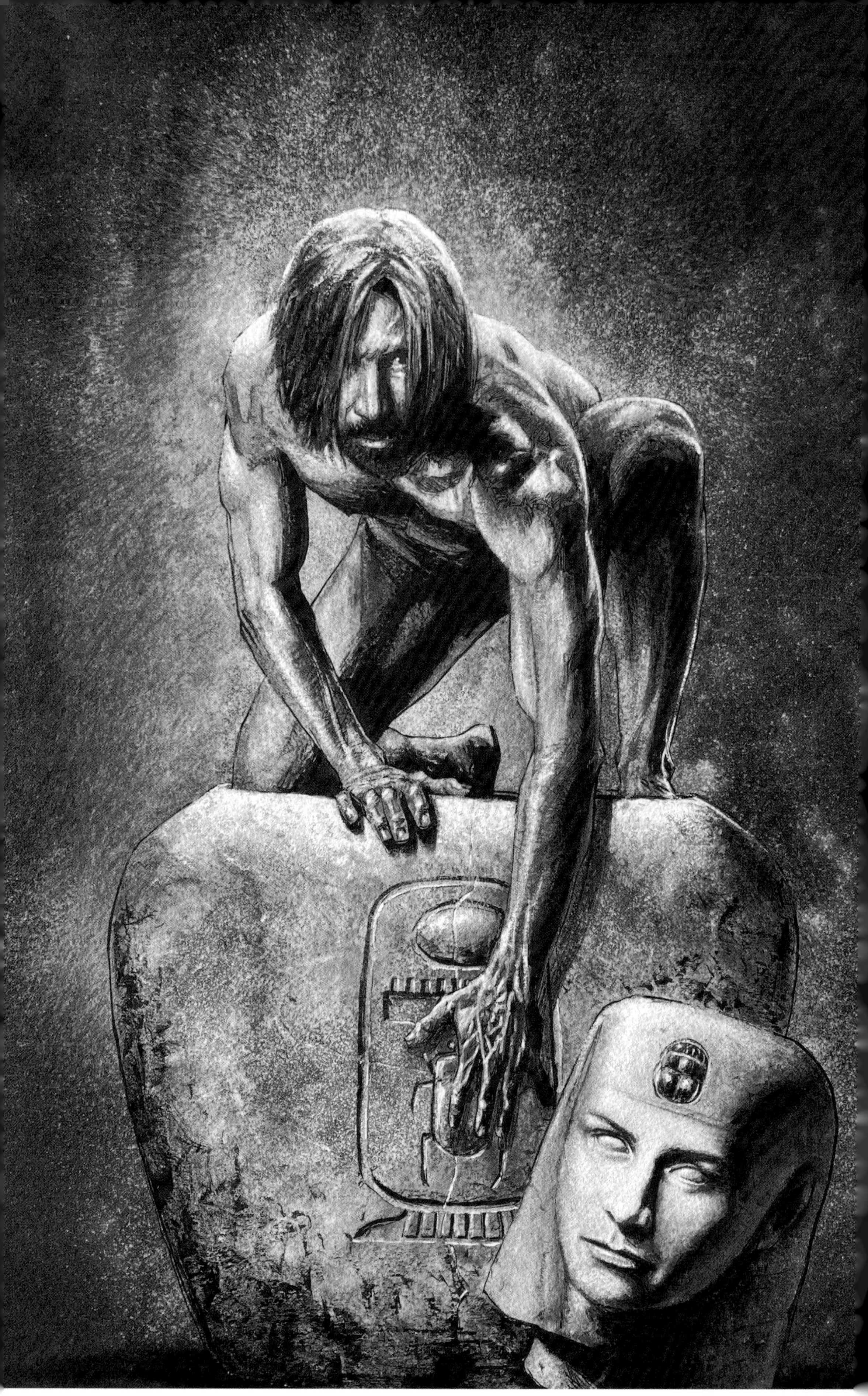

Issue #8 Cover by **AARON CAMPBELL**

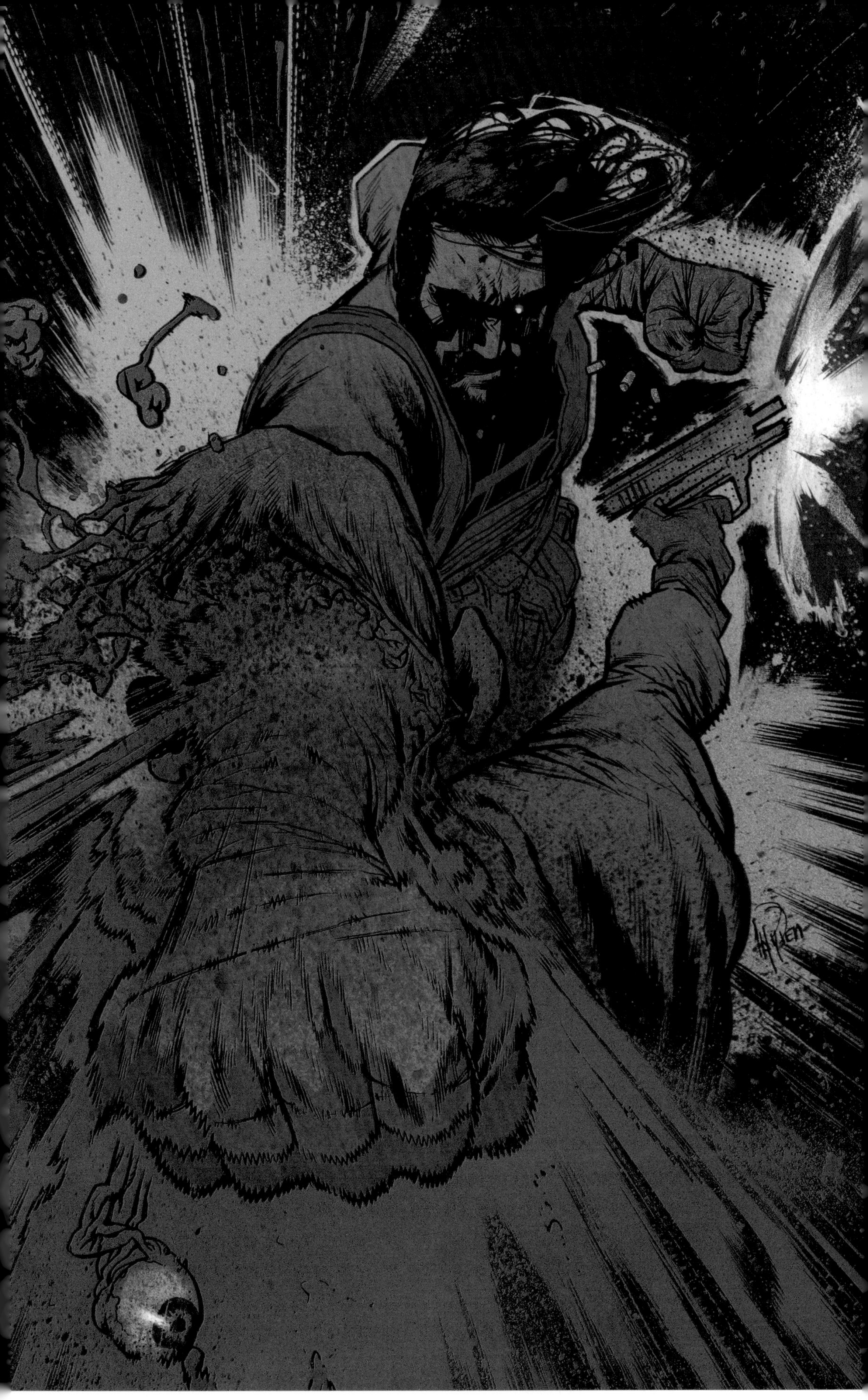

Issue #8 Cover by **JAMES HARREN**

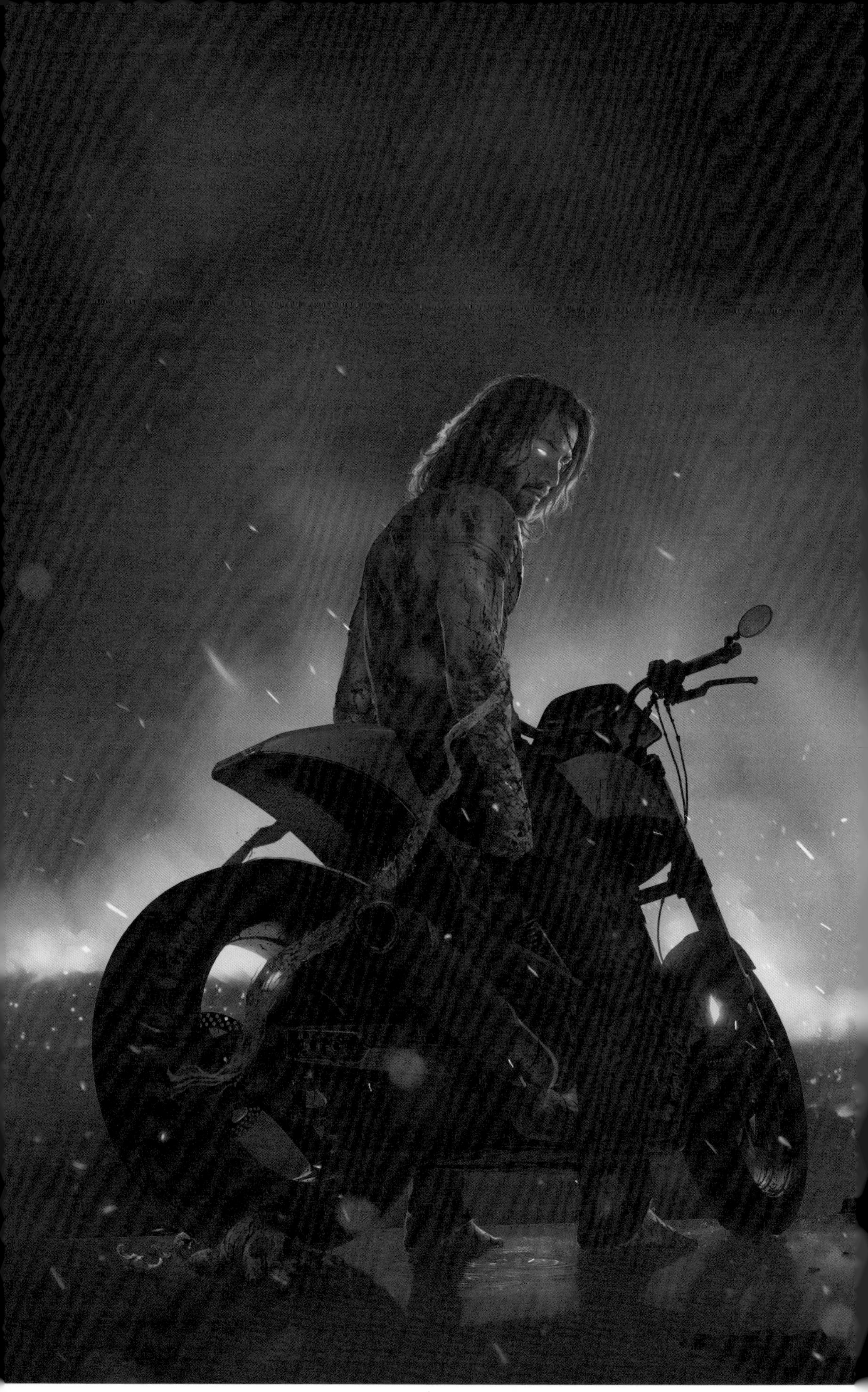

Additional Artwork by **RAHZZAH**

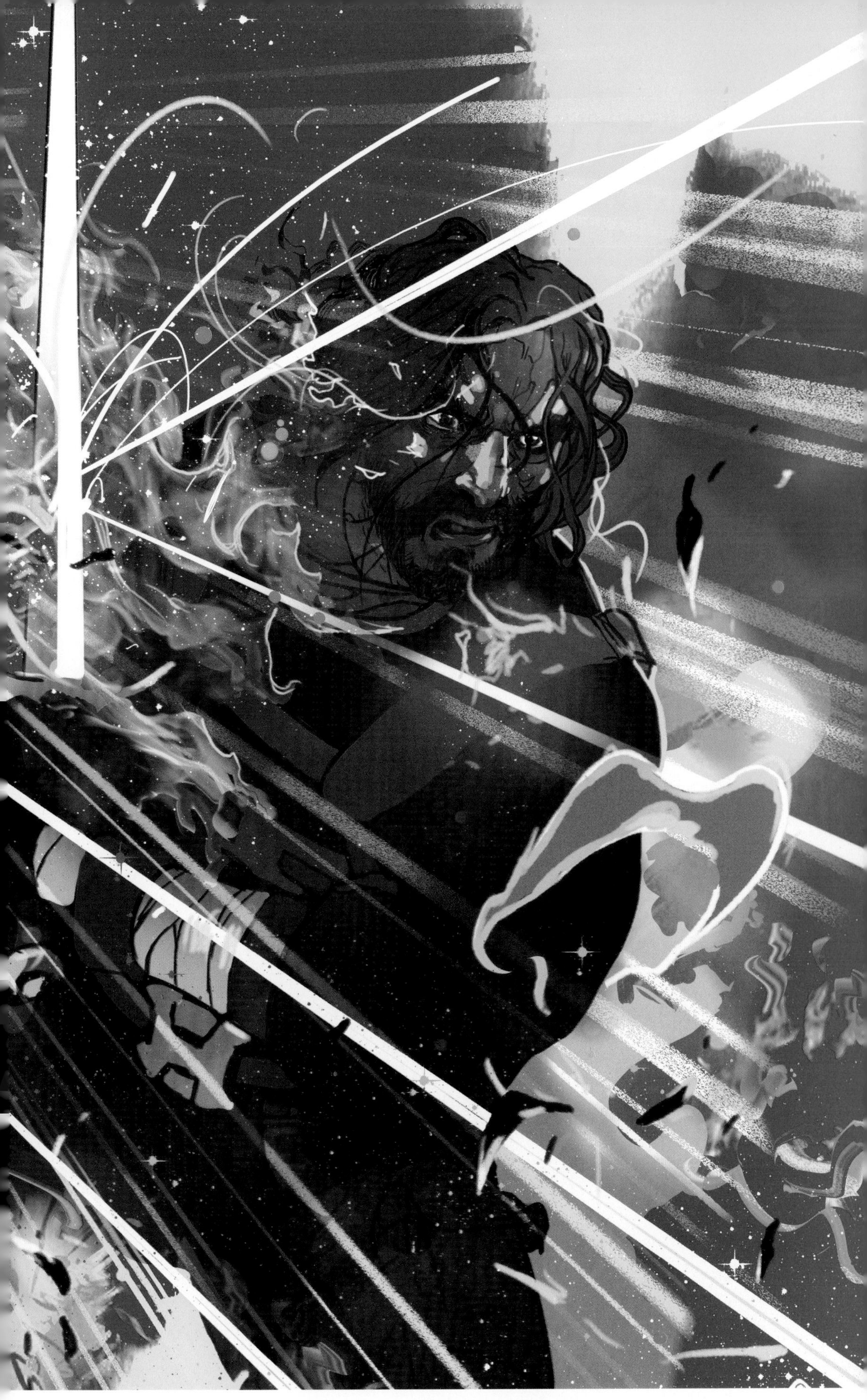

Additional Artwork by **CHRISTIAN WARD**

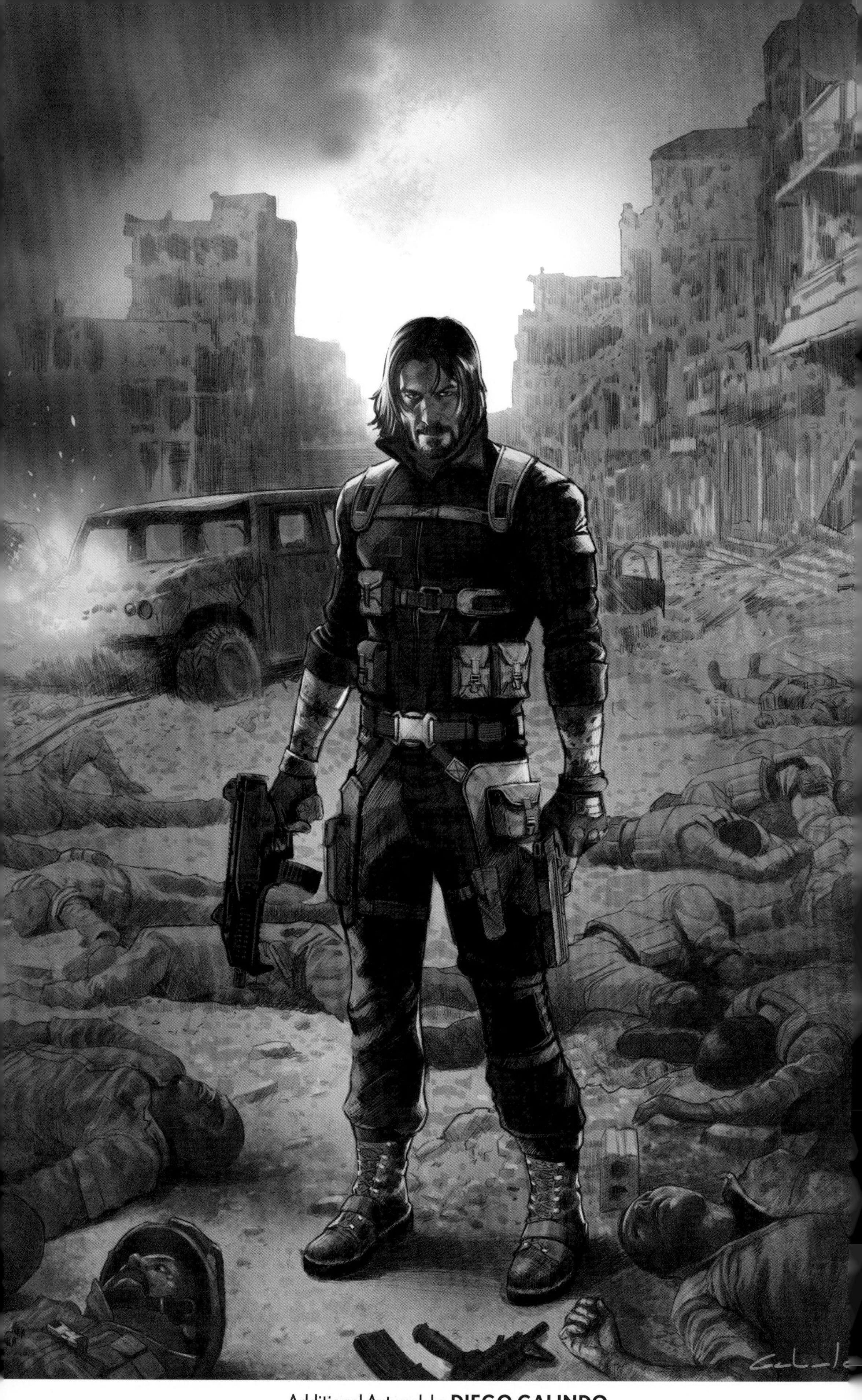

Additional Artwork by **DIEGO GALINDO**

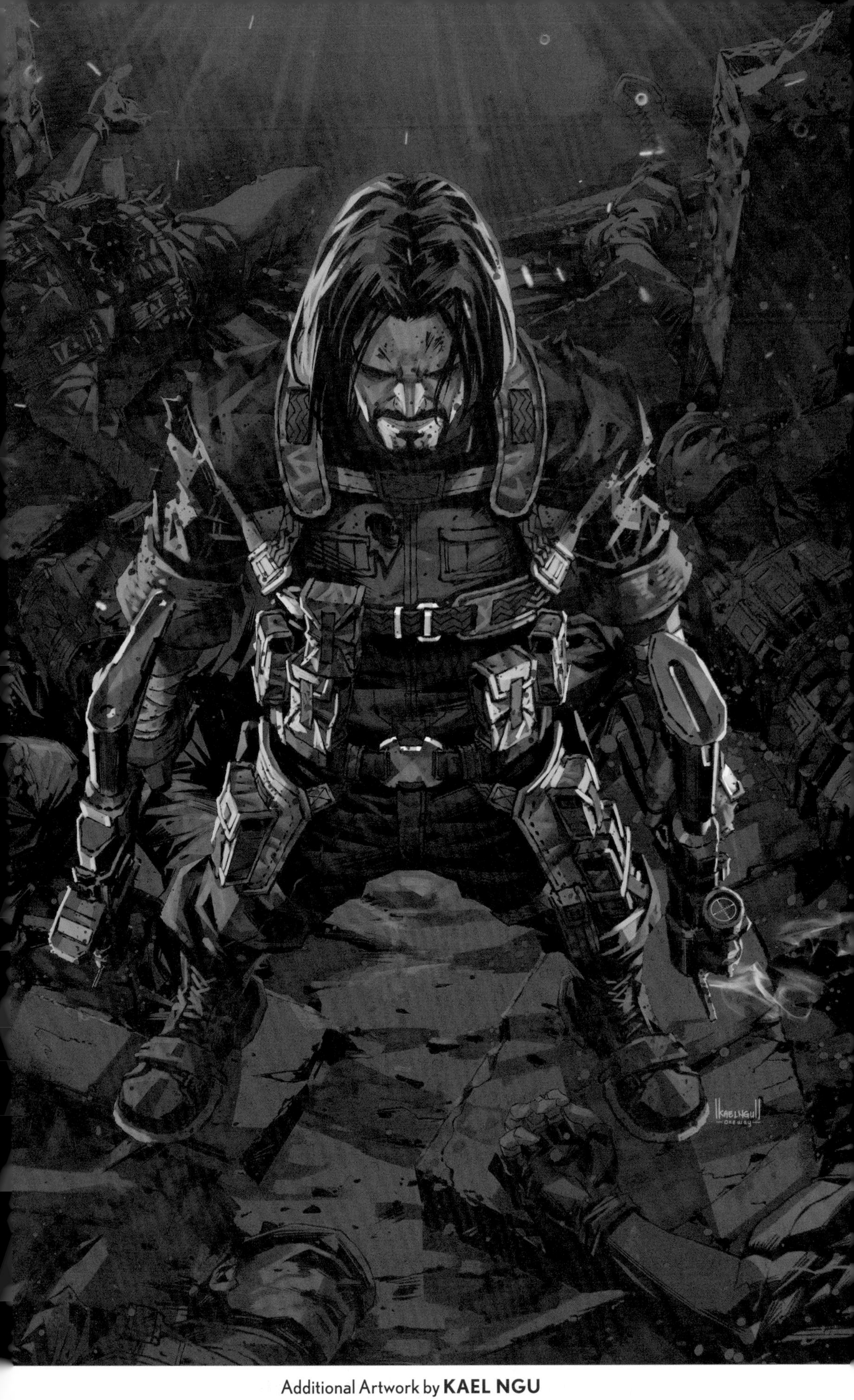

Additional Artwork by **KAEL NGU**

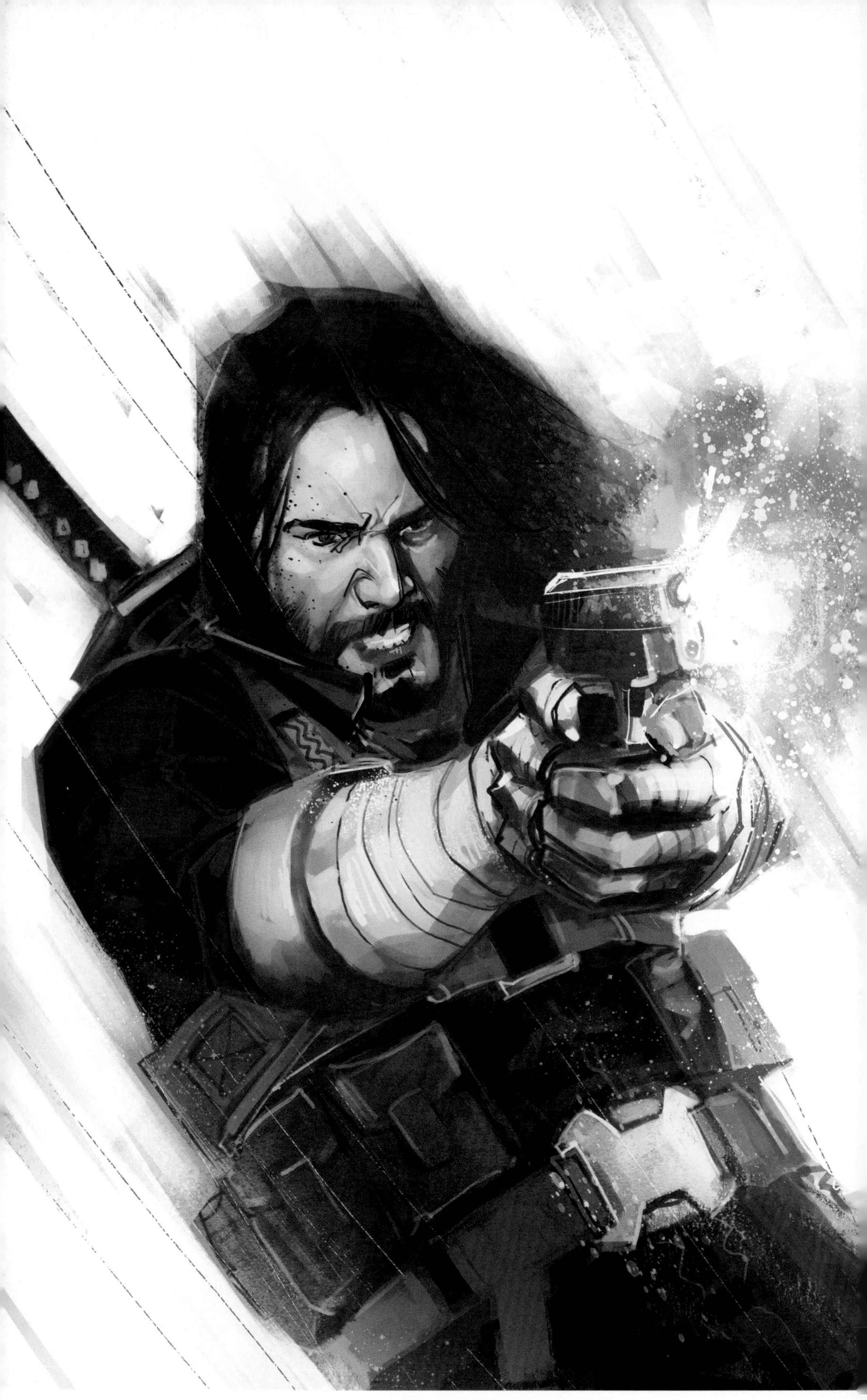

Additional Artwork by **ROD REIS**

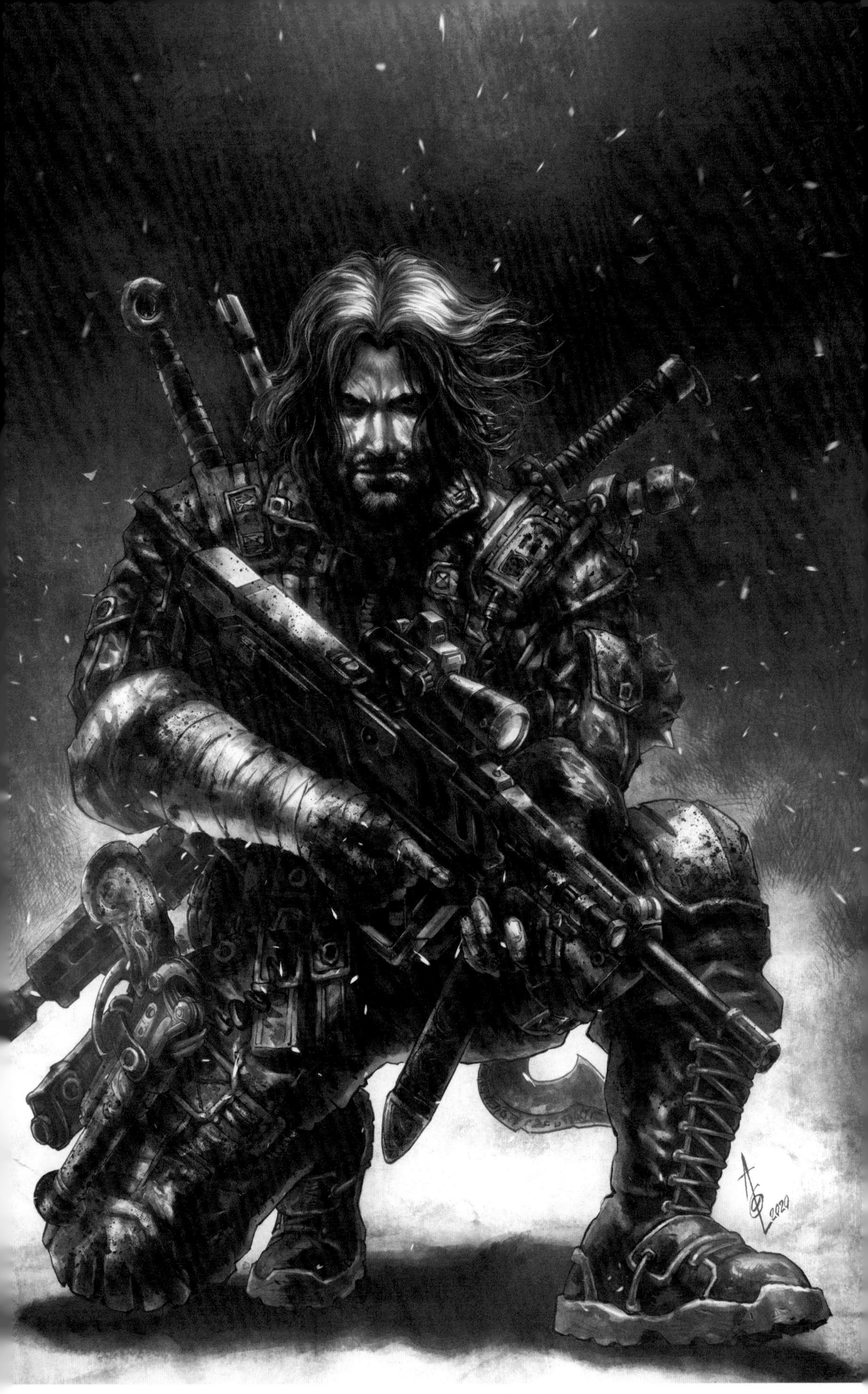

Additional Artwork by **ALAN QUAH**

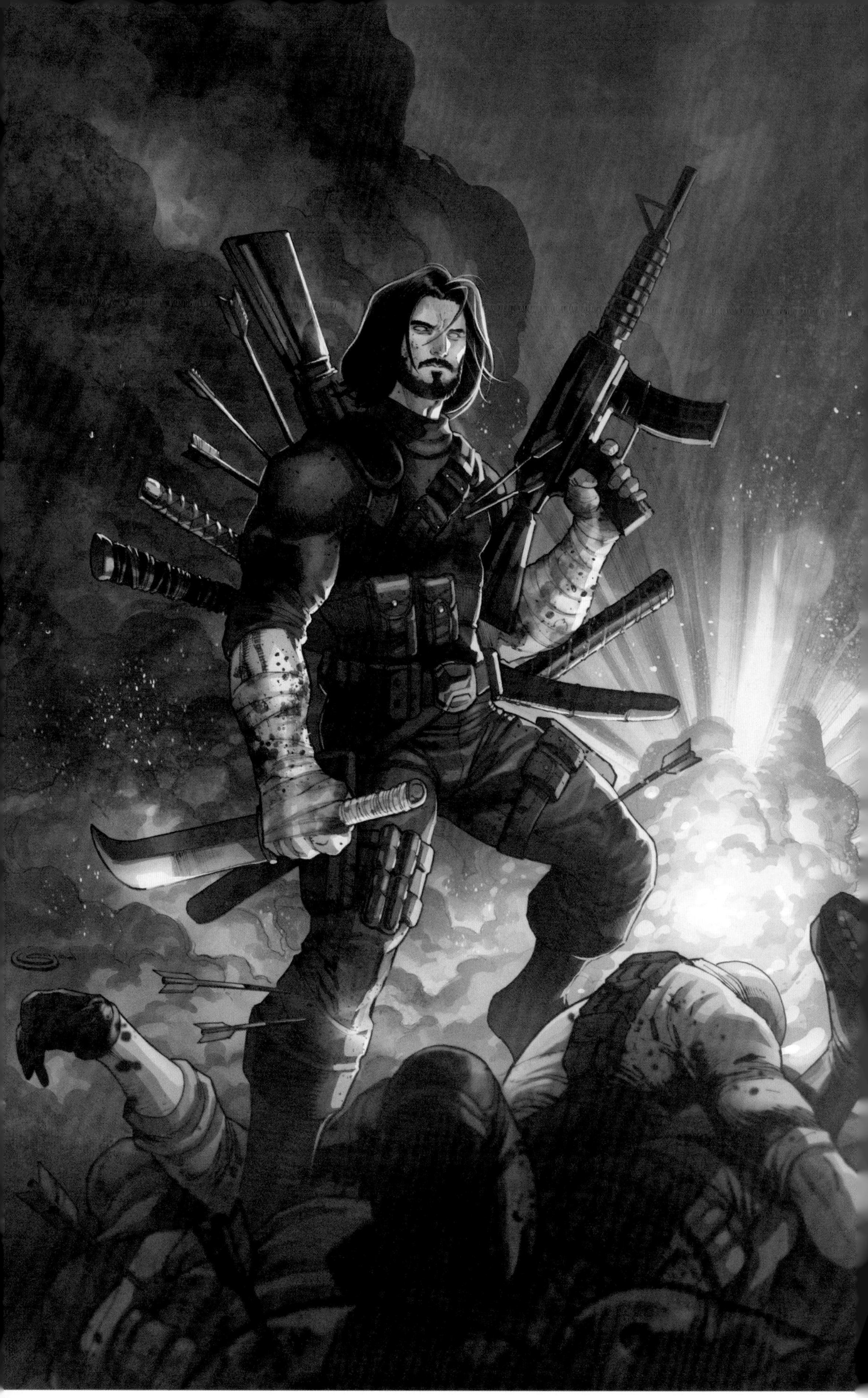

Additional Artwork by **SAJAD SHAH**

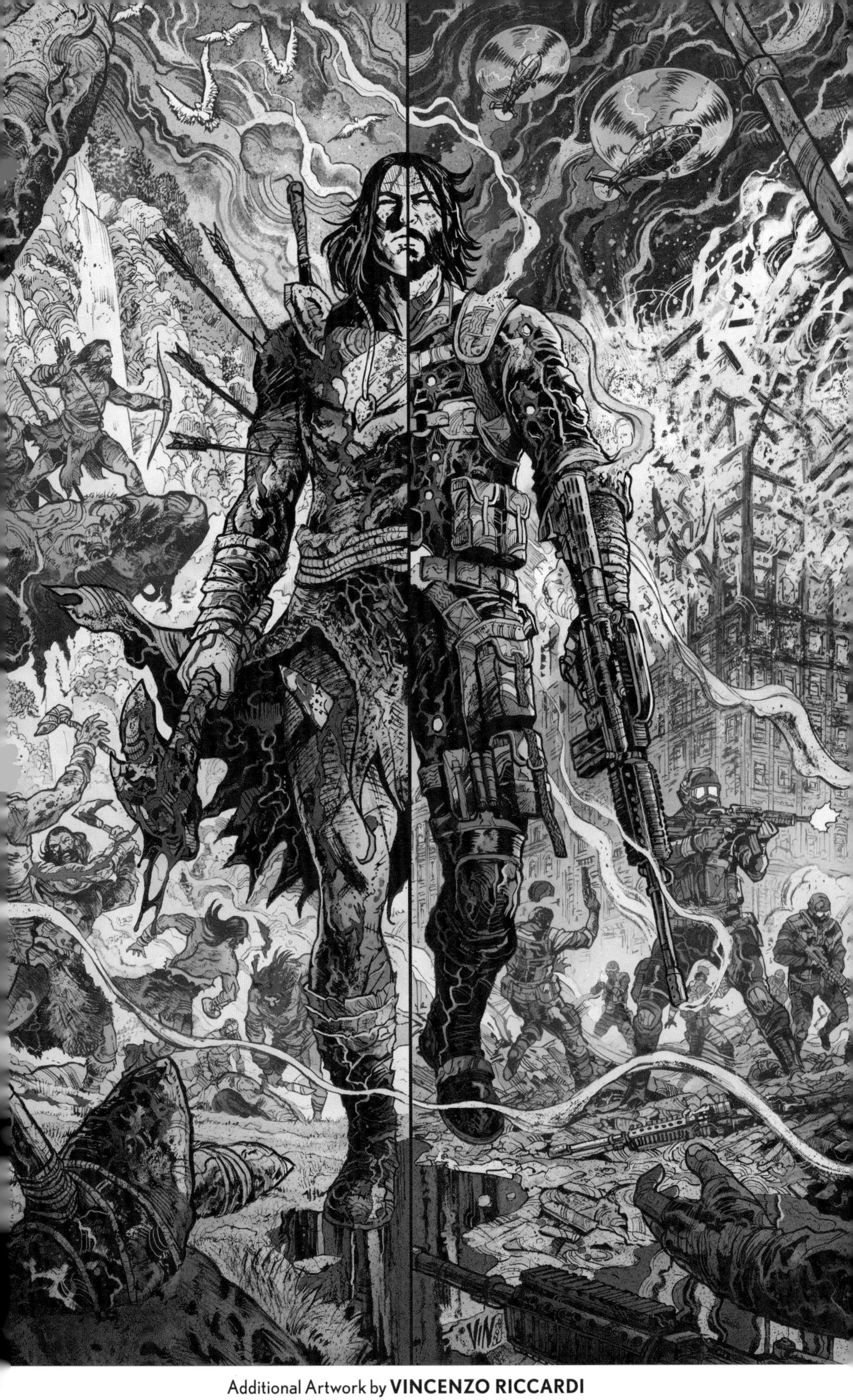

Additional Artwork by **VINCENZO RICCARDI**

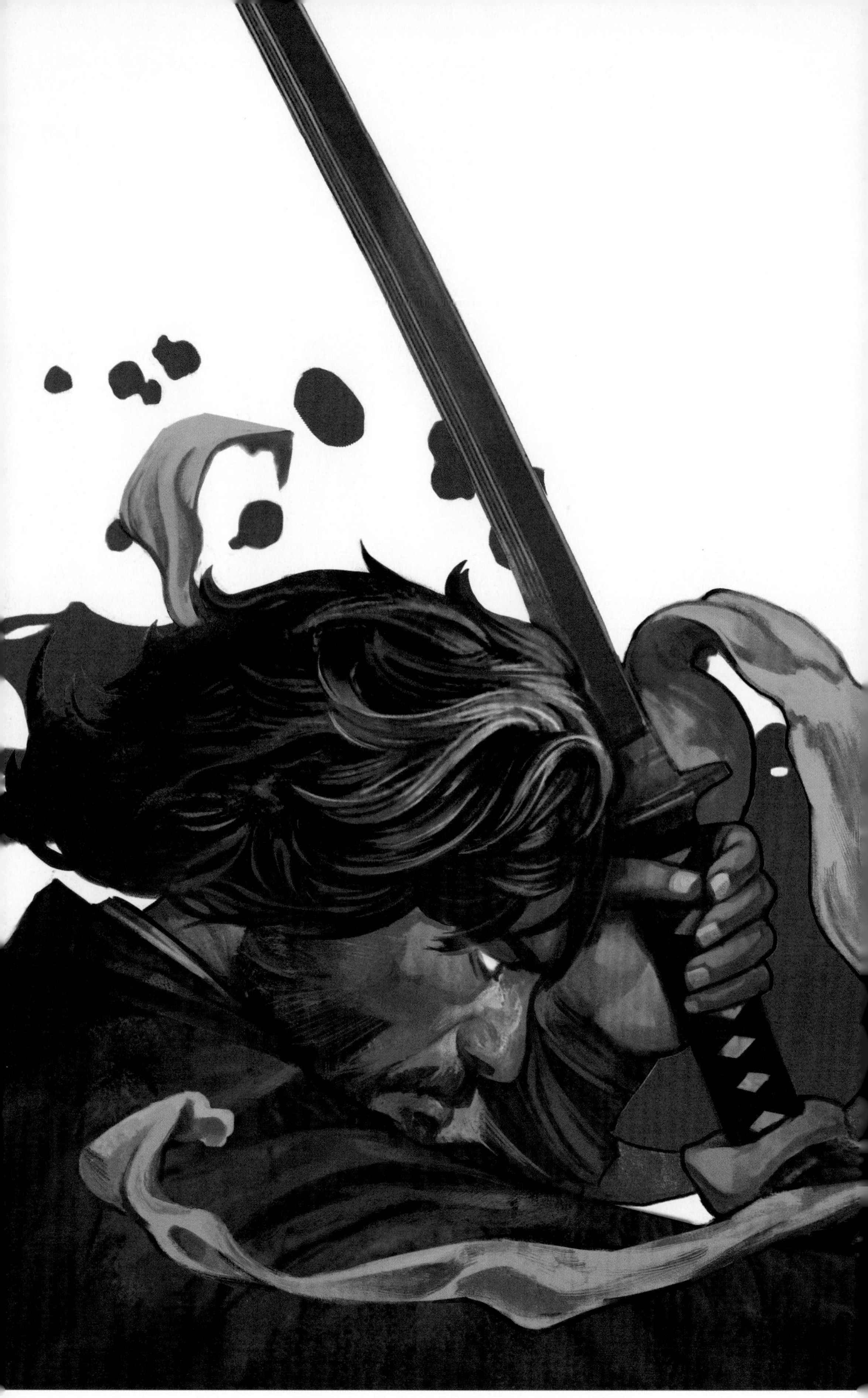

Additional Artwork by **QISTINA KHALIDAH**

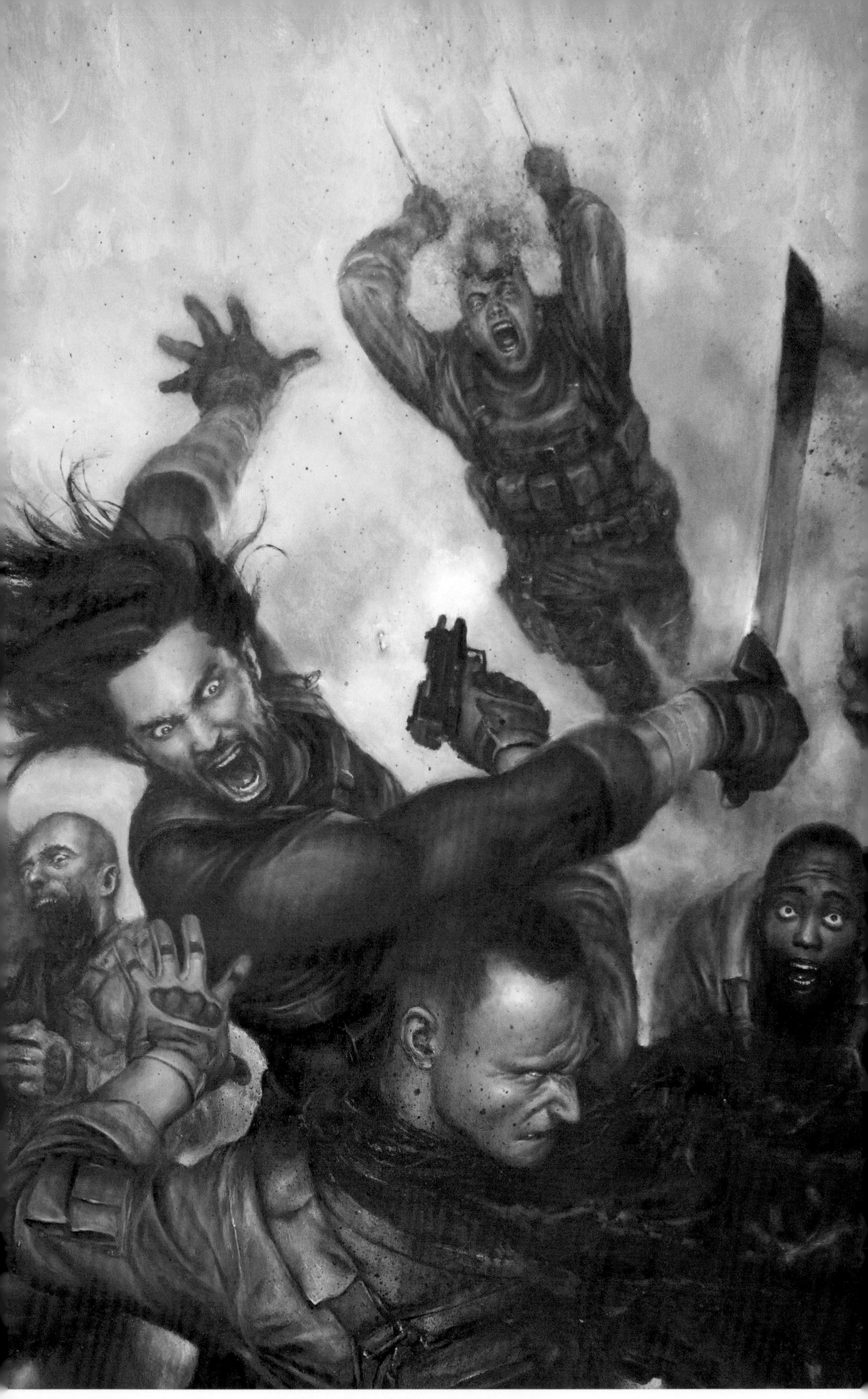

Additional Artwork by **MIKE CHOI**

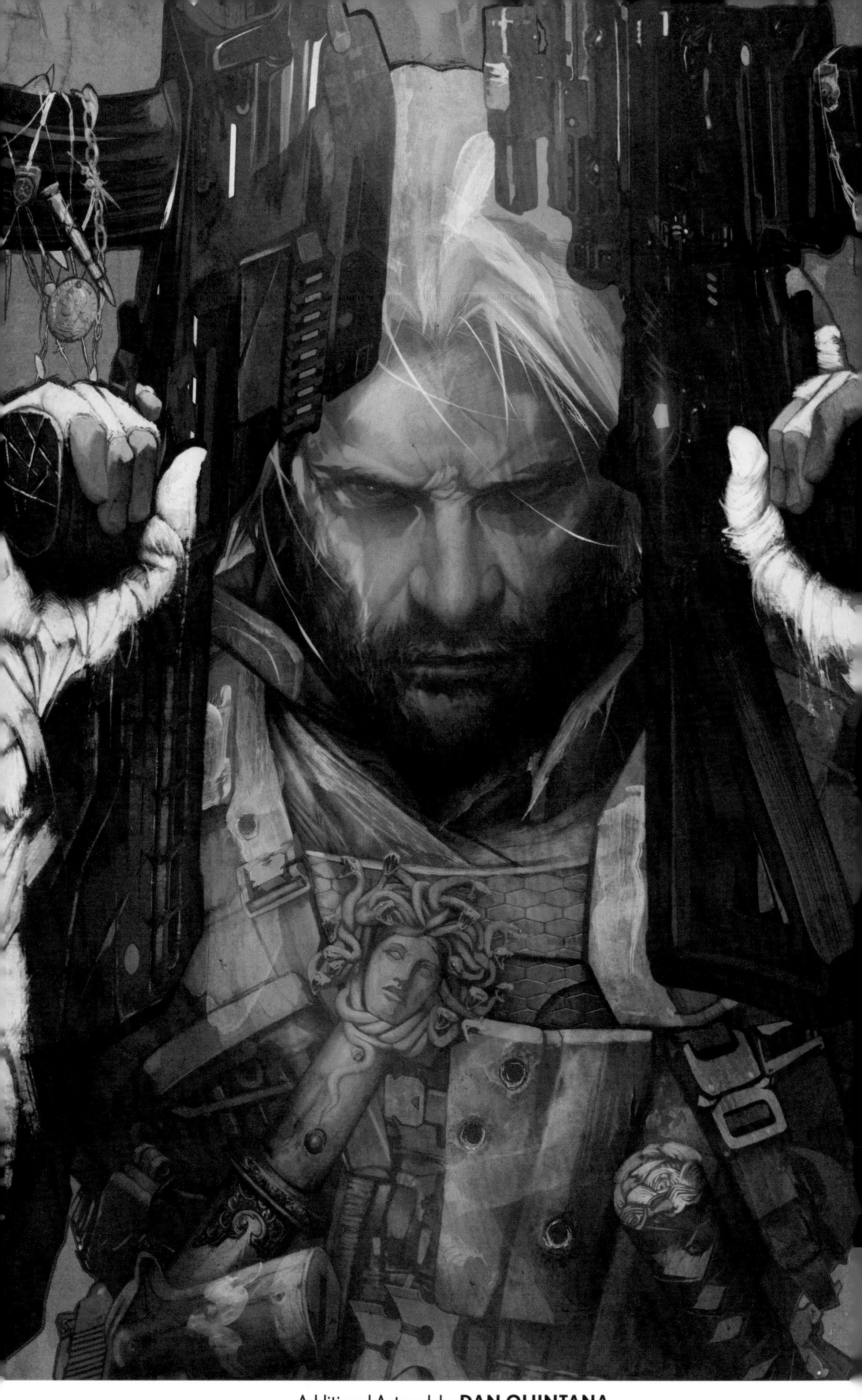

Additional Artwork by **DAN QUINTANA**

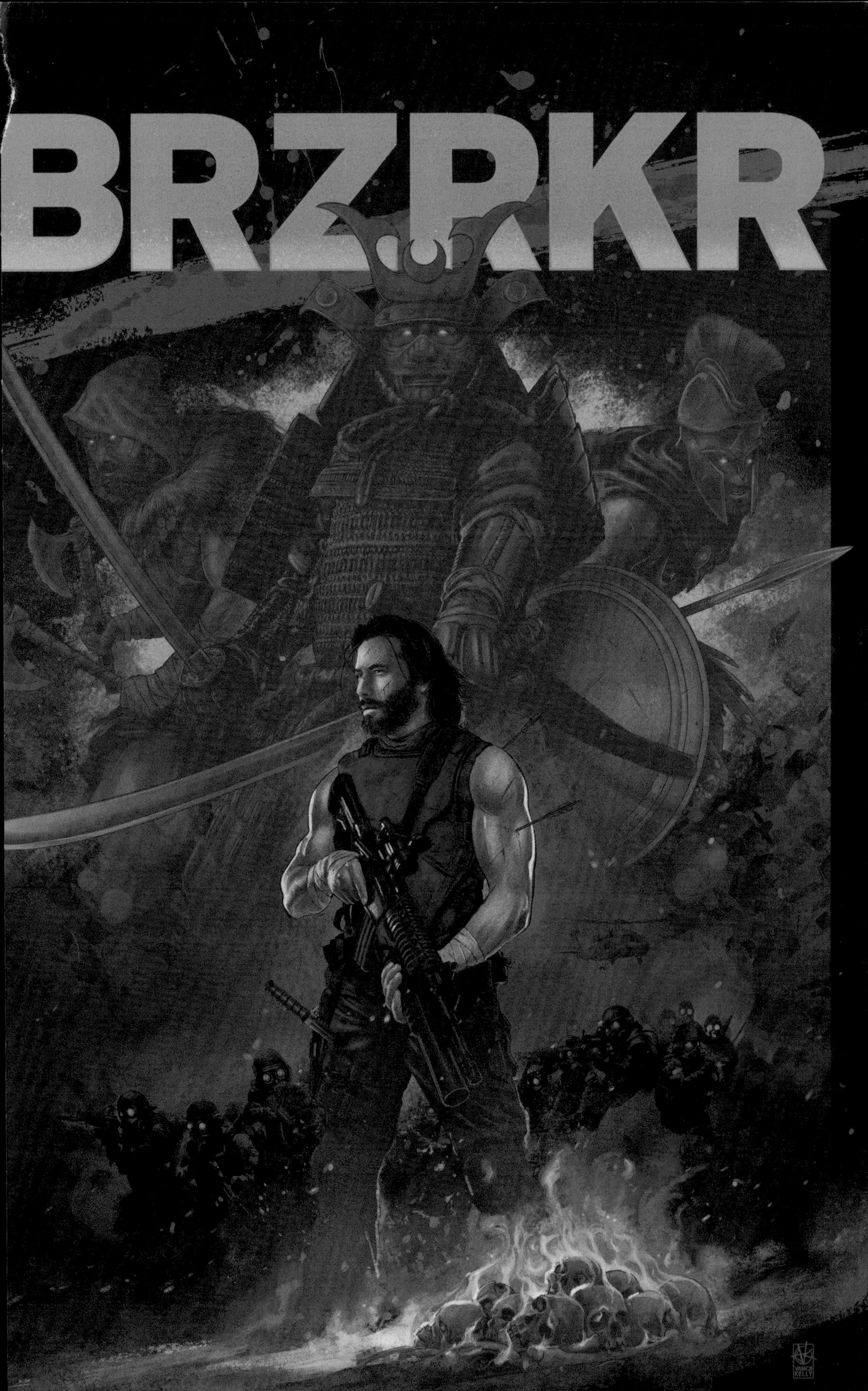
BRZRKR
VANCE KELLY

Additional Artwork by **VANCE KELLY**

KEANU REEVES, the iconic star of feature films such as *John Wick* and *The Matrix*, is the creator and co-writer of *BRZRKR*. Reeves is a celebrated actor whose 35-year film career has garnered enormous success at the box office and received widespread acclaim. *BRZRKR*, his first comic book and graphic novel series, is the highest funded comic book Kickstarter of all time and the highest selling original comic book series debut in over 25 years.

© Jack Guy Photography

MATT KINDT is the *New York Times* bestselling writer and artist of the comics and graphic novels *Dept. H*, *Mind MGMT*, *Revolver*, *3 Story*, *Super Spy*, *2 Sisters*, and *Pistolwhip*, as well as the writer of *Folklords*, *Black Badge*, and the Eisner Award-nominated *Grass Kings* with BOOM! Studios, *Bang!*, *Ether*, *Fear Case*, and *Crimson Flower* with Dark Horse Comics, *Justice League of America* with DC Comics, *Spider-Man* with Marvel Comics, and *Unity*, *Ninjak*, *Rai*, and *Divinity* with Valiant Comics. He has won the PubWest book design award, been nominated for six Eisner Awards and six Harvey Awards (and won once). His work has been published in French, Spanish, Italian, German, and Korean.

Over the course of his 30-year career, **RON GARNEY** has built a large fan following, illustrating some of the industry's greatest characters including Spider-Man, Hulk, Wolverine, Thor, X-Force, Captain America, Ghost Rider, Moon Knight, Silver Surfer, G.I. Joe, and the Justice League of America, along with original series like *Men of Wrath* with Jason Aaron. He recently completed acclaimed runs on *Daredevil* and *Savage Sword of Conan* at Marvel Entertainment. A perennial "Top Ten" artist during his career, Garney has been nominated twice for the industry's coveted Eisner Awards, for Best Artist and Best Serialized Story (*Captain America* with Mark Waid), and has worked in Hollywood on major projects, notably as a costume illustrator for *I Am Legend* (starring Will Smith) and providing illustrations for Marvel's *Daredevil* on Netflix.

BILL CRABTREE has been coloring comics since 2003. His work has been nominated for Harvey and Eisner Awards. Career credits include colors on *Invincible*, *The Sixth Gun*, *The Damned*, *Bang!*, *Crimson Flower* and *BRZRKR*. He lives in Portland, Oregon with his partner, their daughter, two cats, and a dog.

CLEM ROBINS has worked in comics since 1977, and has been all over the place. Projects include *Hellboy*, *X-Men*, *Spider-Man*, *Superman*, *Batman*, *Green Lantern*, *The Fantastic Four*, *Wolverine*, *Teen Titans*, *Preacher*, *Y: The Last Man*, *Deadman*, and many others. His work on *100 Bullets* was nominated for a Harvey Award. He is currently lettering Tom Taylor and Andy Kubert's series *Batman: The Detective*. His 2002 book *The Art of Figure Drawing* was published by North Light Books, and was translated into Spanish, French, Italian, German, and Chinese. His paintings and drawings are in the Eisele Gallery of Fine Art in Cincinnati, and in the permanent collection of the Cincinnati Art Museum. You can see them on his website: www.clemrobins.com.